Samuel
Johnson

Samuel Johnson:

A Critical Study

J. P. Hardy

Routledge & Kegan Paul
London, Boston and Henley

First published in 1979
by Routledge & Kegan Paul Ltd
39 Store Street, London WC1E 7DD,
Broadway House, Newtown Road,
Henley-on-Thames, Oxon RG9 1EN and
9 Park Street, Boston, Mass. 02108, USA
Photoset in 11 on 12 Garamond by
Kelly and Wright, Bradford-on-Avon, Wiltshire
and printed in Great Britain by
Redwood Burn Ltd
Trowbridge and Esher
© J. P. Hardy, 1979
No part of this book may be reproduced in
any form without permission from the
publisher, except for the quotation of brief
passages in criticism

British Library Cataloguing in Publication Data

Hardy, John Philips

Samuel Johnson
1. Johnson, Samuel – Criticism and interpretation
828′.6′09 PR3534 79–40038

ISBN 0 7100 0291 2

HERTFORDSHIRE
LIBRARY SERVICE
828/JOH
9333777

For Adelaide

Contents

Acknowledgments

Sources for Johnson's life are so well indexed that notes have been kept to a minimum. Besides *Boswell's Life of Johnson* (ed. G. B. Hill, rev. L. F. Powell) and *Johnsonian Miscellanies* (ed. G. B. Hill), I have made most use of *Thraliana* (ed. K. C. Balderston) and *The Letters of Samuel Johnson* (ed. R. W. Chapman). Quotations from Johnson's works have, where possible, been taken from the Yale Edition of the Works of Samuel Johnson.

For a year's study leave, which made it possible for me to write this book, I wish to thank the Council of the Australian National University. And for making me so welcome in the Humanities Research Centre during this period, I am grateful to its Director, Professor C. I. E. Donaldson.

I also wish to thank Dr J. D. Fleeman, who kindly read my completed typescript and made some helpful suggestions.

1 Johnson and His Age

I

Samuel Johnson was born during the reign of Queen Anne, and died within five years of the French Revolution. The eighteenth century, before it ended, was to show a dramatic shift in social and political consciousness; nevertheless, despite the wars in Europe and America, and sporadic social unrest at home, Johnson's lifetime spanned what was, on the whole, a fairly settled period. The earlier Revolution settlement had done much to contribute to this, and under the parliamentary system that evolved from it, many Englishmen enjoyed a greater freedom than people elsewhere. Yet it is also true that the make-up of society in the eighteenth century gave little cause for complacency. Opportunity remained largely in the hands of the wealthy and privileged, and early in the century, when mobility generally was more restricted, the distinctions between the social classes tended to be even more marked. Labourers, paupers and vagrants collectively made up a large proportion of the population, and in failing seasons many people found it hard, if not impossible, to survive. In the capital, where the population was more than ten times that of the next largest centre, the extremes of wealth and poverty were plainly visible. The line in Johnson's early poem *London*, 'Slow rises worth, by poverty depress'd', reflected a general truth.

Those who accept the usual stereotype of him as the arch-conservative tend to forget that he could write such a line. Conservative he often was, and in general he supported the status quo where any change was likely to involve a large measure of upheaval or human suffering. Yet though not a social reformer, he became indignant at all forms of human exploitation, and could not only propose a toast to 'the next insurrection of the negroes in the West Indies', but, nearer home, lament the 'unnatural state' of Ireland, where the Catholic 'majority' was so harshly persecuted by the Protestant 'minority'. Personally he had a hankering for what he called 'the old feudal notions', and found it easy to represent to himself the 'good order, virtue and piety' which 'a well-regulated great family' might bring to its 'neighbourhood'. At the same time he realized that one which was 'disorderly and vicious' might be 'very pernicious to a neighbourhood'. He welcomed the system when it worked, yet he was also conscious of its possible abuses. And he was honest enough to acknowledge how largely one-sided was the feeling of well-being that a country gentleman enjoyed by virtue of his superiority 'over the people upon his estate', for, as he said, 'it must be agreeable to have a casual superiority over those who are by nature equal with us'. Though he admitted Boswell's claim that 'there must be a high satisfaction in being a feudal lord', he was convinced that the greater number should not be made 'unhappy for the satisfaction of one'. Boswell, of course, did not give up easily, and later, when he and Johnson were at Slains Castle, put forward the view that 'mankind were happier in the ancient feudal state of subordination, than they are in the modern state of independency'. On this occasion Johnson's answer was quite unequivocal:

> To be sure, the *Chief* was: but we must think of the number of individuals. That *they* were less happy, seems plain; for that state from which all escape as soon as they can, and to which none return after they have left it, must be less happy; and this is the case with the state of dependence on a chief or great man.

Johnson realized a long-standing wish when in 1773 he went to the Highlands of Scotland. He had hoped to see a different pattern of society, one peculiarly formed by ties of consanguinity; but he came too long after the bloody battle of Culloden, and the repressive measures that followed in its wake, to see Highland life as it once had been. His record of the trip, published two years afterwards as *A Journey to the Western*

Islands of Scotland, gains much of its power from the tensions he felt at what he saw. The Highlands were in the throes of rapid change and its people were fast losing the life-style that had traditionally been theirs. Johnson notes with regret the breaking of the bonds designed to hold men together: he sees that the introduction of a money economy is turning 'patriarchal rulers' into 'rapacious landlords', and that many of the people are being forced against their will to emigrate. With a fine sarcasm he questions the wisdom of measures aimed at preventing insurrection by driving away the people. He remains, however, aware of the dangers inherent in the kind of absolute authority the lairds once had, and the continual threat to security clans of armed Highlanders had posed. Though the Disarming Act of 1746 had proved especially galling in proscribing the wearing of Highland dress, he notes its obvious advantages in times of peace. Conscious that something important has been lost, he realizes that the clock cannot be turned back. He was, as Boswell reports, even more apprehensive of what the alternative might have been:

> I have heard him declare that if holding up his right hand would have secured victory at Culloden to Prince Charles's army, he was not sure he would have held it up; so little confidence had he in the right claimed by the house of Stuart, and so fearful was he of the consequences of another revolution on the throne of Great Britain.

The face of England was also to change during the eighteenth century. A growing population, and its concentration in the newly developing industrial areas, made improved methods of farming necessary, and land was gradually enclosed to provide larger arable holdings and the means of better livestock production. These enclosures, which went on at an unprecedented rate from the last quarter of the century onwards, meant a greater accumulation of poor people in the cities. Johnson, who must have seen this happening, once estimated that just over a thousand of these died in London each year from hunger and related diseases – only to be told by an official that the number was in fact higher. Because he became such a thorough-going Londoner, it has sometimes been assumed that he never saw beyond the confines of the place. Certainly one of his best known sayings is, 'When a man is tired of London, he is tired of life; for there is in London all that life can afford.' Yet so extensive was Johnson's curiosity, and so great his interest in all forms of human activity, that he made contact with many aspects of eighteenth-century life. He had, after all, come from the country, and while he ridiculed any attempt to see it in a romantic light, he knew the solid virtues of its people, and the contribution they made in working close to the soil. Johnson had an especially keen sense of the importance of primary production. His *Journey* shows his serious concern with much-needed attempts to improve agriculture in the Highlands, while his 'Further Thoughts on Agriculture', a magazine article published in 1756, demonstrates his appreciation of the central importance of farming to the economic life of the nation.

Johnson was also well aware of the importance of trade, which expanded rapidly during this century. In the preface he wrote (1756) for Richard Rolt's *Dictionary of Trade and Commerce* – without having met the man or read his book – he described the commercial activity that was gripping not just England but Europe: 'It may be properly observed that there was never, from the earliest ages, a time in which trade so much engaged the attention of mankind, or commercial gain was sought with such general emulation.' Boswell found in this preface 'such a clear and comprehensive knowledge of the subject as might lead the reader to think that its author had devoted all his life to it'; in its author's own words, he 'knew very well what such a dictionary should be'. Johnson supported the idea of trade, not only because the exchange of different commodities enriched ordinary life, but because it provided man with the opportunity of improving his lot. 'If there were no trade', he once said, 'many who are poor would always remain poor.' According to Fanny Burney, he looked upon an English merchant as 'a new species of gentleman'. When, after the death of his friend Henry Thrale the brewer (who became MP for Southwark), Johnson as one of his executors appeared at the sale of the brewery, he remarked with a characteristic vividness: 'We are not here to sell a parcel of boilers and vats, but the potentiality of growing rich beyond the dreams of avarice.'

Riches of this sort he was never grudging about. He appreciated the risks involved in commercial enterprise, and thought its rewards were therefore deserved. He recognized, too, the need to have a middleman between the manufacturer and the consumer, putting the point most forcibly in his *Journey* in defending the role of the tacksman (a kind of middleman between the owner of the land and the tenant). Here the famous industrialist, Sir Ambrose Crowley, who was distantly related to his own family by marriage, provided him, by way of analogy, with a convenient example:

> If Crowley had sold only what he could make, and all his smiths had wrought their own iron with their own hammers, he would have lived on less, and they would have sold their work for more. The salaries of superintendents and clerks would have been partly saved, and partly shared, and nails been sometimes cheaper by a farthing in a hundred. But then if the smith could not have found an immediate purchaser, he must have deserted his anvil; if there had by accident at any time been more sellers than buyers, the workmen must have reduced their profit to nothing, by underselling one another; and as no great stock could have been in any hand, no sudden demand of large quantities could have been answered, and the builder must have stood still till the nailer could supply him.

Johnson's ample curiosity also extended to scientific and industrial processes. He was a member of the Society for the Encouragement of Arts, Manufactures and Commerce, and at one meeting, at least, he was heard to speak on a subject related to 'mechanics' with 'a propriety, perspicacity and energy which excited general admiration'. During the tour he took with the Thrales in 1774, he visited while at Birmingham Matthew Boulton's famous iron-works (though he was forced to record in his diary, 'I could not distinctly see his enginery'). After viewing at Holywell the manufacture of copper, brass and iron, he wrote: 'I have enlarged my notions.' While at Derby, the party went to the famous Lombe silk mill on the Derwent, and there he 'remarked a particular manner of propagating motion from a horizontal to a vertical wheel'. Three years later, when he was in the same town, he saw china being manufactured. Boswell once twitted him about the dearth of industry in his native Lichfield, and to this Johnson had a ready answer: 'Sir, we are a city of philosophers; we work with our heads, and make the boobies of Birmingham work for us with their hands.' This remark, it is true, reflects Johnson's sense of priorities, the intense interest he took in ideas and people rather than in things. Yet we should not forget either the interest he took in details and processes of all kinds, and especially in how things worked. Not only was he intensely interested in chemical experiments, but Arkwright claimed that he was 'the only person who, on a first view, understood both the principle and powers of his most complicated pieces of machinery'.

II

The breadth of Johnson's interests is paralleled by a literary output more various than that of any other English author – biographies, essays, pamphlets, sermons, poetry, a play, a prose tale *Rasselas* (perhaps his greatest creative work), a large amount of literary criticism, a dictionary, and an edition of Shakespeare's plays. He also wrote numerous dedications and prefaces (including one for the catalogue of the vast Harleian library, which the bookseller, Thomas Osborne, purchased after the death of the second Earl of Oxford), contributed substantially both to Robert James's *Medicinal Dictionary* and to the Vinerian lectures on English law delivered at Oxford by his friend Robert Chambers, and reviewed works on a wide variety of topics – among them, Joseph Warton's *Essay on the Writings and Genius of Pope*, Jonas Hanway's 'Essay' condemning tea (which Johnson as 'a hardened and shameless tea-drinker' vigorously defended), William Tytler's *Historical and Critical Enquiry*, with its discussion of the famous 'casket letters' attributed to Mary Queen of Scots, and Soame Jenyns's *Free Inquiry into the Nature and Origin of Evil*, the moral complacency of which provoked Johnson to monumental indignation. His was indeed a life of writing and, whatever his subject, he always tried to get down to fundamentals, to bring it into clear and arresting focus, to show its relevance and importance to human life and experience. Aware of how complex, baffling and chaotic this could often be, he used his impressive intelligence in attempting to make coherent sense of it all. Firmly believing that it was a writer's duty to try to make the world better, he pursued this aim with a strong sense of vocational commitment.

Much of Johnson himself went into what he wrote, and this is true even of his political writings, which are now usually condemned unread. They enable us to gauge his reaction to some of the more important events of his time, and also to glimpse some of his most cherished convictions. More numerous than is generally thought, these writings fall into three main groups: the anti-Walpole satires of the late 1730s (discussed in the next chapter); the essays written at the time of the Seven Years' War; and the pamphlets of the 1770s written in support of government policies – *The False Alarm* (1770), *Thoughts on the Late Transactions respecting Falkland's Islands* (1771), *The Patriot* (1774), and *Taxation No Tyranny* (1775). The care with which Johnson revised these for the collected edition of 1776 suggests that he himself regarded them as of some importance.

In the essays of 1756 (published in *The Literary Magazine*, which Johnson seems for a time to have edited), he shows his dislike of war and aggressive imperialist expansion at the same time as he recognizes the need for Britain's security and independence and for measures aimed at checking the ascendancy of France as her natural rival. 'An Introduction to the Political State of Great Britain' reviews current events in the light of British colonial and foreign policy from the reign of Elizabeth. Sensitive to national interests within the larger European scene, Johnson criticizes James I for refusing to take a firmer line with neighbouring powers, and indicts (without naming Walpole) the earlier Whig policy of peace at almost any price. Yet what especially outraged him was, characteristically, the exploitation which the American natives had been subjected to, and in condemning all those who have acted from motives of greed and self-interest, he sternly reminds his audience that 'no people can be great who have ceased to be virtuous'. In another essay, 'Observations on the Present State of Affairs', he returns to this theme. So liberal are his sentiments on behalf of 'the natural lords and original inhabitants' that he bluntly remarks: 'Such is the contest that no honest man can heartily wish success to either party.' Since, however, England was now faced with war, Johnson realized that the French, by their better treatment of the Indians, had given themselves an advantage. He acknowledges the threat they pose to the commercial interests and expansion of the British colonies, and in doing so recognizes what some people at the time seem to have been slow to recognize – the importance of the American theatre of war in Britain's more general struggle with France.

Johnson's John Bullism finds expression in his 'Observations' on the agreements with Hesse-Cassel and Russia to secure by subsidies the use of foreign troops. Though he extensively reports the arguments on both sides, his sympathies are clearly with 'the advocates for the independence of Britain'. Even those who admit that these treaties might allay the fear of a French invasion are said to consider the introduction of mercenaries as 'the desperate remedy of desperate distress'. Obviously he would himself have supported the bill for establishing a national militia which had been defeated in the Lords and was subsequently pushed through by Pitt. The situation was then very different from what it was earlier this century, but the language of Johnson's essay, in its weighty and moving directness, at times reminds us of Churchill's wartime speeches:

> Nature has stationed us in an island inaccessible but by sea, and we are now at war with an enemy, whose naval power is inferior to our own, and from whom therefore we are in no danger of invasion. . . . That we are able to defend our own country, that arms are most safely intrusted to our own hands, and that we have strength, and skill, and courage equal to the best nations of the continent, is the opinion of every Englishman who can think without prejudice, and speak without influence, and therefore it will not be easy to persuade the nation, a nation long renowned for valour, that it can need the help of foreigners to defend it from invasion. . . . Those men are most likely to fight bravely, or at least to fight obstinately, who fight for their own houses and farms, for their own wives and children.

Johnson's reputation as a Tory die-hard stems mainly from two of his later pamphlets, *The False Alarm*, directed against the popular outcry caused by the Wilkes affair, and *Taxation No Tyranny*, written to answer the arguments of the American colonists who objected to being taxed by the British government. The distance that separates these pamphlets from the youthful satires of the 1730s (including *London*) is obvious enough: they are what we would now call distinctly right wing. Yet we can too easily accuse Johnson of inconsistency for later expressing these views. Many of those who opposed Walpole would naturally have supported the King and his ministers against the claims of John Wilkes; and some of these would also have sided with the government against the American colonists. The eighteenth century was on the whole more apprehensive of popular unrest than dedicated to social reform, and the genuine reformers really belonged to a later generation. Jeremy Bentham was nearly forty years Johnson's junior, and Robert Owen was only five years old when the Declaration of Independence was signed. Given the social and political attitudes of his day, Johnson was more representative than he has often seemed in claiming that 'subordination of rank' contributed a great deal to the happiness of society.

By 1770, however, certain tensions were beginning to come to the surface (even though it was to be another two decades before the various radical societies were formed). 1768–9 were years of general distress in London, and Wilkes, a clever and colourful opportunist rather than a committed radical, was supported in the streets by large numbers of the disaffected. Some years earlier he had published the scandalous *Essay on Woman* and, in his periodical *The North Briton*, a seditious libel on George III, and been not only expelled from the Commons but outlawed when he failed to appear to answer the charges against him. In 1768, however, as the professed enemy of law and order, he was, at a disorderly election, returned for Middlesex, and then had himself arrested as an outlaw. From his prison cell he continued his inflammatory attacks on the government, and when one of these was voted libellous by both Houses, he was again expelled from the Commons. The voters of Middlesex promptly re-elected him, but the House resolved that he 'was, and is, incapable of being elected a member to serve in this present parliament', and then (even more dubiously) declared a beaten candidate elected in his stead. Meantime, petitions on his behalf began to circulate throughout the length and breadth of England, while the opposition's anonymous champion, Junius, penned a letter to the King in which he referred to the 'last enormous attack on the vital principles of the constitution', and went on to deplore the transfer of the right of election 'from the collective to the representative body'. Wilkes also had support within the House: some members felt that no precedent justified its action in excluding him once the majority of electors had decided in his favour.

History has taken the same view, and *The False Alarm* has been condemned as reactionary and illiberal, the work of a servile pensioner (for Johnson had, in 1762, accepted a life pension from the government for his services to literature). His claim in offering to the public 'the reflections of a man who cannot favour the opposition, for he thinks it wicked, and cannot fear it, for he thinks it weak' should, however, be taken at face-value. In defending the autonomy of the House, he clearly thought of himself as supporting one of the corner-stones of liberty, for its independence had traditionally been regarded as an essential part of England's peculiarly balanced constitution. The crux of the matter for Johnson, whose desire for order was so genuinely deep seated, was where the real authority must lie. 'All government', he writes, 'supposes subjects, all authority implies obedience.' He was therefore himself convinced that the right of the House, as an instrument of government, to manage its own affairs was infinitely more important than whether or not the wishes of an electorate like Middlesex had been violated.

It must, however, be said that in reaching this view Johnson was influenced both by Wilkes's past conduct and by his own conviction that it was dangerous to allow the uneducated masses a voice in the affairs of parliament. In *The Patriot* he was later to write: 'He is no lover of his country, that unnecessarily disturbs its peace. Few errors, and few faults of government can justify an appeal to the rabble; who ought not to judge of what they cannot understand, and whose opinions are not propagated by reason, but caught by contagion.' When we remember the ugly scenes that occurred during the Gordon Riots only a few years later, Johnson's sentiment becomes at least more understandable; but Wilkes himself had gained such wide-spread sympathy that his supporters could not be classed as 'the rabble'. Johnson seems not to have been convinced of this, and despite his relentless show of logic to prove the House's right to act as it had, he exerts himself most happily in those paragraphs where he sets out to ridicule the means by which so many supposedly genuine signatures had been collected in Wilkes's cause. He imagines the scene as 'an ejected placeman goes down to his county or his borough, tells his friends of his inability to serve them, and his constituents of the corruption of the government'. After the plentiful provision of 'meat and drink' and a speech made by 'the Cicero of the day', 'the petition is read and universally approved'. 'Those', Johnson continues, 'who are sober enough to write, add their names, and the rest would sign it if they could.' The most trenchant humour is, however, reserved for what the events of the day gain (or lose) in the retelling:

> The poor loiterer, whose shop had confined him, or whose wife had locked him up, hears the tale of luxury with envy, and at last enquires what was their petition. Of the petition nothing is remembered by the narrator, but that it spoke much of fears and apprehensions, and something very alarming, and that he is sure it is against the government; the other is convinced that it must be right, and wishes he had been there, for he loves wine and venison, and is resolved as long as he lives to be against the government.

The thrust of Johnson's argument was that the 'alarm' being expressed over the Wilkes affair was 'false' and unfounded. In one sense he found it sufficiently trivial:

> One part of the nation has never before contended with the other, but for some weighty and apparent interest. If the means were violent, the end was great. The civil war was fought for what each army called and believed the best religion, and the best government. The struggle in the reign of Anne, was to exclude or restore an exiled king. We are now disputing, with almost equal animosity, whether Middlesex shall be represented or not by a criminal from a jail.

Despite the tartness of this, there is the interesting admission that civil war can sometimes appear almost justifiable. Johnson was not prepared to deny what Locke had argued for in his influential treatise on civil government – the people's ultimate right of revolution. Just two years later, when Sir Adam Fergusson (afterwards MP for Ayrshire) suggested the importance of keeping up 'a spirit in the people so as to preserve a balance against the crown', Johnson rounded on him:

> Sir, I perceive you are a vile Whig. – Why all this childish jealousy of the power of the crown? The crown has not power enough. When I say that all governments are alike, I consider that in no government power can be abused long. Mankind will not bear it. If a sovereign oppresses his people to a great degree, they will rise and cut off his head. There is a remedy in human nature against tyranny, that will keep us safe under every form of government.

Again he is prepared to admit, at least in theory, the validity of Locke's principle: when past history is sufficiently remote, he can gloss over the dangers of such an extreme form of opposition. But the kind of 'tyranny' that human nature ought to oppose was capable of being interpreted in different ways, and future events were to make this abundantly clear. It was the principle Locke had enunciated which the American colonists were soon to invoke in support of their own cause, and their subsequent Declaration of Independence was, even to its wording, inspired by the ideas that he had made current.

The attempt to raise money in the colonies through direct taxation led, during the years that followed, to a series of incidents and retaliatory measures that only served to deepen the spirit of American resentment. The Rockinghams, while accepting the principle that Britain had a right to tax the colonies, pointed out the inadvisability of insisting upon it; but Johnson was in no doubt that the colonists, as subjects of the Crown, were bound to pay whatever tax was laid upon them by the home government. True, they were not personally represented, but in this their position was no different from that of many other subjects living within the realm. Johnson went even further in attempting to answer a point put forward both in Thomas Jefferson's *Summary View of the Rights of British America* (1774) and in the *Votes and Proceedings* of the Congress at Philadelphia: because the colonists had voluntarily emigrated to America, they had voluntarily forfeited any rights of representation they might otherwise have had. And since Britain assumed responsibility for their defence (the Seven Years' War having been largely fought for this reason), it was in

Johnson's view only fair that they should make a direct contribution to the expense involved. The very title of *Taxation No Tyranny* sums up his attitude to the point at issue. Beyond that, he remained firmly convinced that the colonists must be made to submit to the authority and overriding interests of the mother country.

In his earlier essay 'An Introduction to the Political State of Great Britain', Johnson had accepted it as axiomatic that 'the interest and affection' of the different parts of the same empire must be, 'however distant', always 'the same'; and he found no reason to change his view though the circumstances had meantime materially altered. Throughout his later pamphlet he therefore approaches the Americans with a measure of ambivalence. America is not only compared with 'any other part of the nation' in its claims on the attention of the British parliament, but, because of its opposition to the government's measures, viewed almost as an alien country. Similarly the colonists are regarded not just as Americans, but (by virtue of the original charters) as British subjects, Englishmen, even 'fellow-subjects'. For this reason Johnson's attitude towards them displays, at bottom, a curious kind of hostility. Their opposition brought out in his nature a decidedly authoritarian streak, but, mixed with this, was a measure of fierce regret that British subjects could behave in this way. Mrs Thrale reports that when someone congratulated him on seeing in the Thames a captured ship flying the American flag, he replied: ''Tis a much greater grief, Sir, that any ship or any such colours should *exist*, than exultation that they should be *here*: I turn my eyes from the sight on't.'

Because Johnson considered the Americans as renegade British subjects, he condemned their actions as 'sedition'; and that he could make this charge shows that he apparently had no conception of the groundswell of opinion which was already sweeping them on their own course of history. 'Probably in America', he conjectures, 'as in other places, the chiefs are incendiaries, that hope to rob in the tumults of a conflagration, and toss brands among a rabble passively combustible.' Here again he harps on the causes and dangers of mob violence; like many Englishmen of his time, he seems not to have realized that a new nation was already being born. Had he been prime minister he would certainly have done all he could to abort it: one of his American acquaintances was later to record that Johnson told him he would, in that event, 'have sent a ship of war, and levelled one of our principal cities with the ground'.[1] This remark clearly indicates something that was there in his character – an unwillingness to brook any serious opposition. We should, however, also remember that this was very far from the whole man, and the reason he gives for proposing a massive show of British strength against the Americans is also, in its way, thoroughly characteristic of him:

> I cannot forbear to wish, that this commotion may end without bloodshed, and that the rebels may be subdued by terrour rather than by violence; and therefore recommend such a force as may take away, not only the power, but the hope of resistance, and by conquering without a battle, save many from the sword.

III

What seems so authoritarian in Johnson's attitude towards the American colonists can be paralleled in his approach to religion. 'Permitting men to preach any opinion contrary to the doctrine of the established church tends', he said, 'in a certain degree, to lessen the authority of the church, and, consequently, to lessen the influence of religion.' This subject, so important to him personally, made him at once defensive and aggressive. On one occasion when Boswell introduced the subject of toleration, he replied: 'Every society has a right to preserve public peace and order, and therefore has a good right to prohibit the propagation of opinions which have a dangerous tendency.' When it was objected that man has a right of liberty of conscience, Johnson readily agreed, but refused to extend this right to 'liberty of talking' or 'liberty of preaching', adding:

> No member of a society has a right to *teach* any doctrine contrary to what that society holds to be true. The magistrate . . . may be wrong in what he thinks: but, while he thinks himself right, he may, and ought to enforce what he thinks.

On another occasion, when asked by William Seward (in

Boswell's presence) whether he would restrain the private discussion of religious questions, Johnson replied:

> Why, Sir, it is difficult to say where private conversation begins, and where it ends. If we three should discuss even the great question concerning the existence of a Supreme Being by ourselves, we should not be restrained; for that would be to put an end to all improvement. But if we should discuss it in the presence of ten boarding-school girls and as many boys, I think the magistrate would do well to put us in the stocks, to finish the debate there.

In such matters Johnson's attitude was frankly paternalistic: he repeatedly said that the state had a right to regulate the religion of the people, 'who are the children of the state'. And not only did he claim that 'there must be either a natural or a moral stupidity' in such men as paid no heed to religion, but he viewed with profound concern any instance of a person's giving up the religion in which he had been educated. Boswell thought it unreasonable that a physician who had changed his religion should be deserted by his former patients, but Johnson contradicted him: 'Sir, it is not unreasonable; for when people see a man absurd in what they understand, they may conclude the same of him in what they do not understand.' We can, I think, be sure that he was not on this occasion merely talking for victory (as he so often did), for he tended to view such a change of religion as a form of apostasy. When in 1784 his former close friend Mrs Thrale wrote to him of her forthcoming marriage to the Italian musician Gabriel Piozzi, his reaction to the news was, of course, a complicated one. Yet the violence of his reply (2 July) seems in part to have followed from his assumption that she would therefore be giving up her former religion. One sentence of his letter reads: 'If you have abandoned your children and your religion, God forgive your wickedness.'

Once when Johnson was told of a young friend who had left the Church of England to become a Quaker, he began by referring to her as 'an odious wench', claiming that 'we ought not, without very strong conviction indeed, to desert the religion in which we have been educated'. This, he argued, was the religion in which it might be said that a person had been 'placed' by Providence. So violent did he become on the occasion that, as Boswell tells us, he 'rose again into passion, and attacked the young proselyte in the severest terms of reproach', greatly shocking the two ladies who were present. Johnson's anger went very deep, and was surely not unconnected with his own sense of feeling vulnerable or threatened. As he once pointedly remarked, 'Every man who attacks my belief diminishes in some degree my confidence in it, and therefore makes me uneasy; and I am angry with him who makes me uneasy.'

In an interesting passage of the *Life*, Boswell compares Johnson's mind with the 'vast amphitheatre' of the Roman Colosseum:

> In the centre stood his judgment, which, like a mighty gladiator, combated those apprehensions that, like the wild beasts of the Arena, were all around in cells, ready to be let out upon him. After a conflict he drove them back into their dens; but not killing them, they were still assailing him.

The context that gave rise to this comparison was Johnson's fear of death, and his blunt refusal to have the topic pressed further. 'To my question, whether we might not fortify our minds for the approach of death, he answered, in a passion, "No, Sir, let it alone".' Only a Boswell could have put such a question to him! Even more revealing, however, is the massive effort which, it is suggested, Johnson constantly needed to make in order to try and satisfy his desire for certainty and order. Perhaps the most colourful instance of this was his attempt to answer his young friend's suggestion that it was impossible to refute 'Bishop Berkeley's ingenious sophistry to prove the non-existence of matter'. 'I never shall forget', Boswell writes, 'the alacrity with which Johnson answered, striking his foot with mighty force against a large stone, till he rebounded from it, "I refute it *thus*".' Johnson, here, has recourse to the evidence of his senses when he is being threatened with a notion that he is unwilling to contemplate. Nor could he, conversely, remain unmoved whenever the evidence of his senses contradicted what he wished to believe. As his friend and physician Dr Richard Brocklesby wrote of him, 'His Religion . . . made his extraordinary talents of Mind continually at War with each other.'[2] We often sense such a conflict in his writings, and that we do so is important. In general the fullness and honesty of his response prevents him from becoming neatly schematic. His awareness of contradictions – and even of contradictory impulses within himself – is one of the impressive things about him, and suggests the capacity his mind had to be, as it were, embattled against itself.

Inevitably Johnson took some steps to head off the 'beasts' that seemed to threaten him – like limiting the role of reason in divine matters to that 'of judging, not of things revealed, but of the reality of revelation' ('Life of Cowley'), or replying in this manner when asked how the three persons of the Trinity could be one: 'We cannot tell how, and that is the mystery.' Questions of this kind he always shunned, and he censured Soame Jenyns's *Free Inquiry into the Nature and Origin of Evil* for attempting to solve a difficulty 'which must always continue while we see but in part'. What his dictation to Boswell on the same subject really amounts to is a flat refusal to consider the question further:

> With respect to original sin, the inquiry is not necessary; for whatever is the cause of human corruption, men are evidently and confessedly so corrupt that all the laws of heaven and earth are insufficient to restrain them from crimes.

On another occasion when alone with Boswell, Johnson said: 'There are innumerable questions to which the inquisitive mind can in this state receive no answer: Why do you and I exist? Why was this world created? Since it was to be created, why was it not created sooner?'

Whenever the 'beasts' thrust themselves forward, Johnson had recourse to the reasonableness of revelation, for which there was in his view 'such historical evidence, as, upon any subject not religious, would have left no doubt'. Hogarth once said of him: 'That man is not contented with believing the Bible, but he fairly resolves, I think, to believe nothing *but* the Bible.' So fundamentalist was his approach that he even wrote a concluding paragraph for John Kennedy's curious tome *A Complete System of Astronomical Chronology* (1762), in which he stated that 'the truth of the Mosaical account' has been established 'by evidence which no transcription can corrupt, no negligence can lose, and no interest can pervert.' Faced with 'an anti-mosaical remark' which suggested that the world was rather more than some 5,000 years old, he is reported to have said: 'Shall all the accumulated evidence of the history of the world, shall the authority of what is unquestionably the most ancient writing, be overturned by an uncertain remark such as this.' Whenever he becomes as assertive as this, Johnson is concerned with something that touches him deeply. In his review of the *Philosophical Transactions* for 1755, he first praises the volume for its 'many entertaining and many useful narratives and observations', but then complains that 'the sacrosanctity of religion . . . seems treated with too little reverence when it is represented as hypothetical and controvertible that all mankind proceeded from one original'. What so incensed him was a sentence in a paper on one Edward Lambert, the so-called 'porcupine man', whose skin was described as being like the shorn-off quills of a hedgehog (hence his popular name). Lambert suffered from a severe form of *ichthyosis filaris* or 'fish-skin' disease, and his six children were said to have 'the same rugged covering as their father'. The author of the offending paper therefore concluded that differences of race might be similarly explained – 'if', that is, 'mankind were all produced from one and the same stock'.

On such occasions Johnson seems to the twentieth century a very remote figure. Yet the attitudes and beliefs he inherited could also deepen his engagement with distinctly human concerns, and this remains true even where the modern reader is aware of the latent inconsistencies and attempts at rationalization. Hearing that the young Susannah Thrale had met the astronomer William Herschel, Johnson wrote to her (25 March 1784):

> With Mr Herschil it will certainly be very right to cultivate an acquaintance, for he can show you in the sky what no man before him has ever seen, by some wonderful improvements which he has made in the telescope. What he has to show is indeed a long way off, and perhaps concerns us but little, but all truth is valuable and all knowledge is pleasing in its first effects, and may be subsequently useful. Of whatever we see we always wish to know, and congratulate ourselves when we know that of which we perceive another to be ignorant. Take

> therefore all opportunities of learning that offer themselves, however remote the matter may be from common life or common conversation. Look in Herschil's telescope; go into a chymist's laboratory; if you see a manufacturer at work, remark his operations. By this activity of attention, you will find in every place diversion and improvement.

Though Johnson sees that the motives which drive men on are not unmixed with the desire of conscious superiority, the underlying tension in this passage springs from a deeper source. A question has arisen that presents a challenge to older ways of thinking – in particular, to the Church's condemnation of *curiositas* or improper curiosity. Behind the attempt to resolve it lies the whole tradition of Christian humanism that interpreted Raphael's counsel to Adam as an instructive example of what should have a primary hold on man's affections. The question was one that for Johnson could never be finally resolved (though the portrait of the mad astronomer in *Rasselas* had posed it in a sufficiently extreme form). Characteristic, however, is his attempt to resolve it in terms of the importance of all kinds of knowledge, and of all forms of human endeavour. What emerges, above all, from this affectionate letter to a young girl, is the real pleasure to be derived from the very act of learning. As Imlac had said to Rasselas:

> Without knowing why, we always rejoice when we learn, and grieve when we forget. I am therefore inclined to conclude that, if nothing counteracts the natural consequence of learning, we grow more happy as our minds take a wider range.

IV

Johnson's attitude to learning, which he links here with happiness, invites comparison with the broad aims of the Enlightenment. In *The Rambler* he speaks of the 'hereditary stock' of human knowledge as 'the collective labour of a thousand intellects' (no. 121), and observes that 'the most lofty fabrics of science are formed by the continued accumulation of single propositions' (no. 137). More obvious points of similarity also exist. Robert Shackleton has pointed out, not only that in this same essay (no. 137) Johnson alludes to the 'mechanic' arts 'with an interest and enthusiasm not unworthy of Diderot', but that in other respects too – in surveying the different branches of learning for Robert Dodsley's *Preceptor* (1748), and especially in collecting and disseminating knowledge as a lexicographer – he shows his affinities with what was happening on the other side of the Channel, where the compilation of the *Encyclopédie* was to result in the Enlightenment's most typical and monumental work.[3]

It may at first glance seem surprising to link Johnson with this movement. We have already seen what his political attitudes were; nor could he have any truck with the attack on religion which, though it manifested itself in different ways, was broadly representative of the *philosophes*. His antipathy to Voltaire and Rousseau is almost too well-known to quote: 'It is', he said, 'difficult to settle the proportion of iniquity between them.' He was, moreover, an outspoken opponent of moral determinism, and once roundly attacked the extreme position put forward in D'Holbach's *Système de la Nature* (1770). When pressed on the question Hobbes had started, Johnson, who owned a copy of Bishop Bramhall's works, cited his *Defence of True Liberty from Antecedent and Extrinsical Necessity*.[4] Yet he was clearly uneasy when forced to meet the question head on, and Boswell's attempts to draw him on it produced reactions ranging from the surprisingly concessive, 'All theory is against the freedom of the will; all experience for it', to the sharply dismissive, 'We *know* our will is free, and *there's* an end on't.' Ultimately he was forced to argue from his own experience: 'Sir, as to the doctrine of Necessity, no man believes it. If a man should give me arguments that I do not see, though I could not answer them, should I believe that I do not see?' With a sidelong glance at La Mettrie, he is willing to accept the consequences of man's wickedness rather than have him made unspeakably more abhorrent by being dehumanized: 'With all the evil that there is, there is no man but would rather be a free agent, than a mere machine without the evil.' 'If', he significantly adds, 'a man would rather be the machine, I cannot argue with him. He is a different being from me.'

The gulf that separated Johnson from the more extreme of the *philosophes* should not, however, be allowed to obscure the common ground he shared with the Enlightenment's more moderate spirits. The 'obstinate rationality' he once admitted to describes well enough the constant bias of his mind; and the appeal to reason was a distinguishing feature of the work of the *philosophes*. So, too, was an adherence to Lockian epistemology; and here Johnson regarded Locke (who had such a profound influence abroad) as a seminal thinker. He accepted that experience is the source of all knowledge, and that the soul or mind of man, for all its importunity in seeking out things for its employment, cannot be regarded (as Descartes had regarded it) as necessarily always thinking. 'To every act', he writes, 'a subject is required. He that thinks must think upon something' (*Idler* 24). In the gradual process that leads from infancy to maturity and knowledge, he gives, like Locke and Hobbes before him, a central place to experience: 'We all enter the world in equal ignorance . . . every mind, however vigorous or abstracted, is necessitated in its present state of union to receive its information and execute its purposes by the intervention of the body' (*Rambler* 151). To memory Johnson grants the place Locke had assigned it, calling it 'the primary and fundamental power, without which there could be no other intellectual operation'. 'Judgment and ratiocination', he adds, 'suppose something already known, and draw their decisions only from experience' (*Idler* 44).

The appearance, almost at the same time, of *Rasselas* and Voltaire's *Candide* might on the face of it seem to provide further evidence of Johnson's kinship with the Enlightenment. He himself said that if these two works 'had not been published so closely one after the other that there was not time for imitation, it would have been in vain to deny that the scheme of that which came latest was taken from the other'. (Written during 1758 and published at Geneva and Paris early the following year, *Candide* did not receive notices in the London press until after *Rasselas* had appeared.) Both books attack false optimism, and *Candide*, in particular, the Leibnizian belief that the world as created by God is the best of all possible systems. The obvious point of comparison is chapter 22 of *Rasselas*, in which Johnson satirizes vague metaphysical reasoning by having a 'philosopher' tell his pupils that 'the way to be happy is to live according to nature, in obedience to that universal and unalterable law with which every heart is originally impressed'. When Rasselas asks him to explain what he means by this, the philosopher replies:

> To live according to nature is to act always with due regard to the fitness arising from the relations and qualities of causes and effects; to concur with the great and unchangeable scheme of universal felicity; to cooperate with the general disposition and tendency of the present system of things.

As Mary Lascelles rightly notes, this man would have made a good companion for Dr Pangloss, whereas the prince, like Johnson's reader, soon leaves him behind.[5]

This fact points to an essential difference between the two works. *Candide* is exuberant and sustained polemic: the sparkling wit that ridicules the complacency of the prevailing optimism is evident on almost every page. And in being so irrepressible, its cynicism argues a peculiar kind of confidence. Expelled from a Westphalian Eden, Candide eventually finishes up in his own garden, and the point surely is that man is already in the only possible paradise, and that it is up to him, by cultivating the earth, to make of it what he can.[6] This the Enlightenment set out to do, and the general confidence that it as a movement shared is to this extent reflected in the moral fervour of Voltaire's satire. *Rasselas*, however, deals with the central paradox of human life: it describes how the mind constantly outruns itself in its search for happiness. With a remarkably clear-eyed compassion, and a sly yet affectionate humour, Johnson shows how man, by his very nature, seeks to move beyond or by-pass the limitations and disappointments of the present.

V

Though *Rasselas* is today often linked with Johnson's greatest poem *The Vanity of Human Wishes* (1749), in his own day it was often linked with his periodical *The Rambler* (1750–2). Soon after Boswell had met Johnson in 1763, Sir David Dalrymple (afterwards Lord Hailes) wrote to him:

> It gives me pleasure to think that you have obtained the

> friendship of Mr. Samuel Johnson. He is one of the best moral writers which England has produced. At the same time, I envy you the free and undisguised converse with such a man. May I beg you to present my best respects to him, and to assure him of the veneration which I entertain for the author of the Rambler and of Rasselas?

Numbers of the periodical were soon being reprinted in Edinburgh, as well as in provincial magazines, and even in the first year of its publication *The Rambler* was favourably compared with Addison's famous *Spectator*. Knowledge of the work spread, and with it Johnson's reputation as a moral or philosophic sage. In his own periodical *The Bee* (no. 5), Goldsmith has the driver of his Fame Machine accept it (and not the *Dictionary*) from Johnson in payment of his fare: 'Clio', says the coachman, 'who happens to be a little grave, has been heard to prefer it to the *Spectator*.' Ironically, *The Rambler* is, of all Johnson's major works, perhaps the one least read today. It is, however, interesting to note that Joseph Nollekens' clay bust of him (executed in 1777 and exhibited at the Royal Academy) had as its base a thick volume with 'RAMBLER' carved on its spine.[7]

Quotations from this work have already been given to indicate assumptions Johnson shared with the Enlightenment; yet it also expresses a commitment to religion that is both strenuous and orthodox. It was this, together with his constant engagement with moral questions, that so impressed contemporaries. Through these essays he reached a growing reading public, and spoke to it with a real seriousness. We cannot be sure that the clergyman on Skye who confided to Boswell, 'Dr Johnson is an honour to mankind; and, if the expression may be used, is an honour to religion', had read *The Rambler*, for he would have been only a boy when it first appeared. But we do know that the young Bennet Langton of Lincolnshire was so impressed that he came to London chiefly in the hope of meeting its author; and we have, too, the comparison Joseph Towers made between it and the later political pamphlets in *A Letter to Dr Samuel Johnson* (1775):

> Should I hereafter be disposed to read, as I heretofore have done, the most excellent of all your performances, 'The

> Rambler', the pleasure which I have been accustomed to find in it will be much diminished by the reflection that the writer of so moral, so elegant, and so valuable a work, was capable of prostituting his talents in such productions.

Similar (if isolated) assessments of *The Rambler* also come to us from the nineteenth century. Jane Austen must have been thinking of it when she cited Johnson's prose as among her very favourite moral reading; while Ruskin, introduced to its pages by his father's fondness for the work, 'once and for ever' recognized its author as 'a man entirely sincere and infallibly wise in the view and estimate he gave of the common questions, business, and ways of the world'.[8]

In his own time Johnson became almost a household name – as a moralist, as the great English lexicographer so famous for his learning, as a kind of literary oracle, and as a conversationalist without peer. Even George III expressed a desire to meet him, and on one occasion conversed with him in the library of Buckingham House. Bentham reports that he once 'supped at the Mitre Tavern . . . to hear Johnson's good things'; while many of those who came from abroad, and sought him out while in London, would doubtless have agreed with the Scottish laird who remarked to Boswell: 'He is a great orator, Sir; it is music to hear this man speak.' Boswell provides us with a good opportunity of hearing Johnson speak: the *Life* reveals better than any other single source his full and active participation in the intellectual life of his time. In the eighteenth-century club he found his fitting environment; there he could fold his legs and have his talk out. The most famous of these was the Literary Club (later known as The Club): foundation members besides Johnson included Goldsmith, Edmund Burke and Sir Joshua Reynolds, and many other distinguished contemporaries became members during his lifetime.

Johnson also speaks to us through his writings, a fact which has now become more generally recognized. His contemporaries noted how much the same thing it was to hear or to read him, and this involves much more than a superficial resemblance of style. In whatever forum he found himself, his distinct and constant concern was human nature as it embraced both himself and his fellowmen. To quote his own phrase, he was 'perpetually' a moralist, and the aim he pursued throughout his life, often with the intensity of a religious commitment, was to make people know themselves better. Basic to his thinking was his view of man as a social being, whose conduct towards others must be judged on some surer ground than mere impulse. Resolutely setting his face against the increasing influence of the benevolists (who, following Shaftesbury, claimed that goodness was to be measured purely in terms of feeling), Johnson said: 'We can have no dependence upon that instinctive, that constitutional goodness which is not founded upon principle.'

Robert Voitle has pointed out that while Johnson's concept of reason derives from Locke, 'he tends to apply the faculty much as the moralists of the Renaissance did'.[9] Clearly his moral rationalism reflects a strong sense of man's divine origin; as Imlac tells the princess in *Rasselas*: 'When we act according to our duty, we commit the event to him by whose laws our actions are governed, and who will suffer none to be finally punished for obedience.' For this reason, as he says in *The Rambler*, he thought it necessary for man

> to make the future predominate over the present, to impress upon his mind so strong a sense of the importance of obedience to the divine will, of the value of the reward promised to virtue, and the terrors of the punishment denounced against crimes, as may overbear all the temptations which temporal hope or fear can bring in his way (no. 7).

In his own life Johnson always sought to do this – even to the resolutions he was always making to combat idleness or tidy up his books. As he wrote in his diary (20 April 1764), 'Disorder I have found one great cause of idleness.' Here we have an intimate glimpse of something important – the battle he constantly had to keep his own life in order. Though a man of strong feelings, he had strict standards of moral conduct, and mercilessly measured himself against his own idea of Christian 'perfection' or virtue. He was even haunted by a fear of madness. When Imlac remarks, 'No disease of the imagination is so difficult of cure, as that which is complicated with the dread of guilt', Johnson clearly knows what his character is talking about. Yet he also knew, as Imlac says elsewhere, that 'it is not pronounced madness but when it becomes ungovernable, and apparently influences speech or action'.

Johnson fought his fear of madness in various ways, but never more impressively than in the fulness of his engagement with human concerns, and the depth and intelligence with which he wrote about them. What immediately strikes us about him is his largeness as a human being – his sense of involvement in the human condition, and his ability to write about it with such remarkable understanding and compassion. In this lies his real strength and greatness. To Pope's famous line, 'The proper study of mankind is man', Johnson's bosom returned a resounding echo. So intense was his interest in human nature, in how people think and feel and behave, that he brought to his study of this a new vitality and relevance.

2 Beginnings

I

In an imposing house that still overlooks the market-place at Lichfield, Johnson was born in September 1709 to middle-aged parents.[1] As an infant he contracted a disease of the lymph glands ('scrofula') that affected his eyes, and when he was still only two, his mother, in hopes of a cure, took him to London to be 'touched' by the Queen. From his father he inherited, nevertheless, a robust frame, and grew into a large if ungainly boy.

Michael Johnson, a bookseller, was sheriff of Lichfield at the time of his son's birth. Though subject to bouts of melancholy (as Johnson himself later was) he was genuinely proud of his son, and seems to have taken every opportunity to show him off. This, however, embarrassed the boy, who found it impossible to be close to his father. Nor did Michael have a good business head: long-standing debts meant a lack of ready money in the home, and this proved to be a constant source of irritation between him and his wife. Sarah Johnson, who fancied herself better connected than her husband, was always bringing up the unwelcome subject. The boy was aware of his parents' wrangling, and was later to note, 'My father and mother had not much happiness from each other.' Sarah was, however, a conscientious, even anxious, mother, and scrupulously attended to her son's education. 'I remember', he wrote, 'that being in bed with my mother one morning, I was told by her of the two places to which the inhabitants of this world were received after death; one a fine place filled with happiness called Heaven; the other a *sad* place called Hell.' It was instruction he was to remember too well for his own peace of mind.

From 1717 to 1725 Johnson attended Lichfield Grammar School, which in the eighteenth century produced its share of distinguished men (especially in the law). In 1726 he spent six months at the King Edward VI School at Stourbridge, where for part of the time he seems to have been engaged in helping to teach the younger boys. The curriculum at each school was the conventional one – reading in selected classical authors and doing exercises based on the language, with a far larger dose of Latin than Greek. From Edmund Hector, Johnson's closest friend in and out of school, we learn of his idleness as a schoolboy, and of the veneration even then in which his fellows held him. According to Hector, they flattered his 'uncommon abilities' and gained his 'assistance' by in turn calling on him each morning and carrying him to school. Johnson fairly exulted in his intellectual superiority and once said to Boswell: 'They never thought to raise me by comparing me to anyone; they never said Johnson is as good a scholar as such a one, but such a one is as good a scholar as Johnson; and this was said but of one . . . and I do not think he was as good a scholar.' Clearly he was not a swot. 'I have known him', writes Hector, 'after a long vacation, in which we were rather severely tasked, return to school an hour earlier in the morning and begin one of his exercises, in which he purposely left some faults in order to gain time to finish the rest.'

This is revealing: Johnson always put a thing off until the final deadline, but could then complete it with extraordinary dispatch. He seems to have suffered from periods of abstraction, when he was almost unmindful of what was going on around him. Interestingly, however, his moments of concentration could be correspondingly intense. A vivid illustration of this is the account he gives of doing a school exercise when he was once staying with relatives in Birmingham:

> I perceived the power of continuity of attention, of application not suffered to wander or to pause. I was writing at the kitchen windows, as I thought, alone, and turning my head saw Sally dancing. I went on without notice, and had finished almost without perceiving that any time had

> elapsed. This close attention I have seldom in my whole life obtained.

Johnson was forced to change schools because of an extended stay with one of his cousins. Cornelius Ford was a gifted and sociable man who had been a don at Cambridge and cut a figure in London, where he moved easily in literary and social circles. Having married to pay his debts, he proposed to reform and become a clergyman; but the lure of the capital was to prove too strong, and the life he later gave himself to is depicted in Hogarth's 'Modern Midnight Conversation', where the parson ladling punch to a drunken gathering is said to be a portrait of him. In 1725 Johnson would have found him a fascinating companion, and the time he spent with him must have proved intellectually stimulating and increased his knowledge of the world. Ford also gave him a useful piece of advice: 'Learn', said he, 'the leading precognita of all things – no need perhaps to turn over leaf by leaf, but grasp the trunk hard only and you will shake all the branches.' It was advice Johnson never forgot.

The person at Lichfield who did most to introduce him to a wider world was Gilbert Walmesley, the registrar of the ecclesiastical court. More than fifty years later, in his *Lives of the Poets*, Johnson paid him this heartfelt tribute:

> He was of an advanced age, and I was only not a boy; yet he never received my notions with contempt. He was a Whig, with all the virulence and malevolence of his party; yet difference of opinion did not keep us apart. . . .
>
> His studies had been so various that I am not able to name a man of equal knowledge. His acquaintance with books was great, and what he did not immediately know he could at least tell where to find. Such was his amplitude of learning, and such his capaciousness of communication, that it may be doubted whether a day now passes in which I have not some advantage from his friendship.

Of comfortable means, Walmesley lived in the nearby Cathedral Close and welcomed into his house two other Lichfield boys who were to make their mark in the world, Robert James, who published a voluminous medical dictionary, and David Garrick, who became one of the greatest actors of all time. Besides the active encouragement the young Johnson received from Walmesley, arguing with the older man must have sharpened his wits and forced him to work out his own position more clearly.

The greatest advantage Johnson enjoyed during these Lichfield years was in being the son of a bookseller with a well-stocked shop. He became early a voracious reader and, from his childhood, was able to turn volumes over as chance or inclination directed. He read *Hamlet* at such a tender age that the ghost scene terrified him when he was alone. Looking once for apples high on a shelf, he came upon a large folio Petrarch and immediately sat down to read it (he had somewhere seen Petrarch referred to as the 'restorer of poetry'). From his father he received a copy of Martin Martin's *Description of the Western Islands of Scotland* (1703), the book which first made him curious to see that country. The fare was varied and seemingly endless: classical texts, theological works of all sorts (Lichfield was a cathedral city with a number of resident clergy), scientific treatises, especially medical books, volumes of travels and works of literature, including modern poetry and drama (Michael Johnson traded over a wide area, having stalls in several smaller centres, and numbered country gentlemen among his regular customers). His books became his son's library, and there Johnson laid the foundations of his remarkably wide learning. Boswell describes his 'peculiar facility of seizing at once what was valuable in any book, without submitting to the labour of perusing it from beginning to end'. When Johnson advised young people to carry a small book on them that might be read when there was nothing else to do, he was reflecting his own practice. He once said that he read 'very hard' in his early years, from about twelve to eighteen, and knew at that age 'almost as much' as he ever did. Even if one allows for some exaggeration, the benefit he derived from his father's bookshop was clearly very great.

In other respects, however, Johnson's life started without the advantages of birth or wealth, or even of natural charm; nor could his home be called a happy one. His intellect was, he realized, his one real advantage, and he sought to fight his way with that. It had, after all, gained him the notice of men like Walmesley and Ford. As a young man he could no doubt be just as aggressive as he later sometimes was; yet perhaps this formative period contributed to something more than sensitiveness or pride. From it may date his genuine hatred of complacency, the high value he always attached to friendship, and his general awareness of the unhappiness of human life. Such feelings can be explained as part of the moral tradition within which he wrote and lived, but that he held them with such conviction may well owe something to the experience of these early years. So too may the very real compassion he felt for those less fortunate than himself; and his early years in London, when he saw poverty at such close quarters, only deepened this feeling. Mrs Thrale wrote of him: 'He loved the poor as I never yet saw anyone else do, with an earnest desire to make them happy.' His acts of charity ranged from putting pennies into the hands of poor children asleep in the streets so that they might buy themselves a breakfast, to giving shelter in his house and accepting as part of his household several unfortunate people who, though sometimes quarrelsome, had seemingly nowhere else to live, and might have suffered hardship had they not lived with him.

II

It became possible for Johnson, just nineteen, to go up to Pembroke College, Oxford, on his mother's being left a small inheritance. His tutor was William Jorden whom he warmed to as a person; but he did not get from him, or from Oxford generally, the intellectual stimulation he could have wished. (Significant, perhaps, is the picture given in *Rasselas* of sages, teachers, men of learning, who whether inside or outside the Happy Valley have their shortcomings made very plain.) When his schoolfriend John Taylor was to enter the University, Johnson took pains to discover where the best tutor was to be had. Taylor was enrolled at nearby Christ Church, and Johnson went over each day to hear at second hand what his tutor had said – until, that is, his only pair of shoes became too disgraceful to appear in. No doubt poverty reinforced the sense of urgency he felt, since he would have been unable to take a degree until he had kept the required number of terms. Most often he was to be seen lounging about in the gateway, idling away the time in talking with other students. On hearing later that one of the dons had described him as 'a gay, frolicsome fellow', he exclaimed:

> Ah, Sir, I was rude and violent. It was bitterness which they mistook for frolic. I was miserably poor, and I thought to fight my way by my literature and my wit; so I disregarded all power and all authority.

Something of what must have been his thirst for knowledge and wider horizons is indicated by the words he was heard to utter while at Pembroke:

> I have a mind to see how they go on in other places of learning. I'll go and visit the universities abroad. I'll go to France and Italy. And I'll mind my business. For an Athenian blockhead is the worst of all blockheads.

In later life he could speak of the system of education at Oxford in terms approaching praise; and he came to revisit his old college with obvious delight. But by then Johnson was no longer the battling outsider he had at first been. With his own reputation secure, he could easily transfer his reverence for learning to the institution, without feeling that he himself had been sold short. Thomas Warton, an Oxford friend, noted down his interesting comment on meeting again, in 1754, one of his former contemporaries:

> I used to think Meeke had excellent parts, when we were boys together at the College: but, alas!
> 'Lost in a convent's solitary gloom!'
> I remember, at the classical lecture in the Hall, I could not bear Meeke's superiority, and I tried to sit as far from him as I could, that I might not hear him construe. . . . About the same time of life, Meeke was left behind at Oxford to feed on a Fellowship, and I went to London to get my living: now, Sir, see the difference of our literary characters!

Johnson read a lot of Greek at Oxford, as well as ethics and theology (especially the Church Fathers). What, however, affected him most was reading William Law's *Serious Call to a Devout and Holy Life* (1728). Some years before he had ceased to attend seriously to religion, often talking openly against it.

He therefore took up Law's book expecting to find it dull or absurd. Instead it made a deep and lasting impression: 'I found Law', he said, 'quite an overmatch for me.' The standards of conduct that Law expected from the true Christian, and the emphasis he placed on the individual conscience, communicated themselves to Johnson with a rare intensity. All his life afterwards he remained conscience-stricken about his own failings, including idleness, getting up late, erotic thoughts (phrases like 'purify my thoughts from pollutions', 'repress sinful and corrupt imaginations', can be found in his prayers thirty and forty years later). For Johnson there was, as he later wrote to Boswell (3 July 1778), 'but one solid basis of happiness . . . the reasonable hope of a happy futurity', and this conviction had a great impact on his personal life. In Boswell's own words, 'he habitually endeavoured to refer every transaction of his life to the will of the Supreme Being'. Johnson was always troubled, and deeply troubled, at the thought of final judgment, and during the last year of his life he said to his friend Dr Adams, then Master of Pembroke: 'I am afraid I may be one of those who shall be damned.' When Adams politely remonstrated with him, asking what he meant by 'damned', Johnson burst out with 'Sent to Hell, Sir, and punished everlastingly.'

The habit of looking critically at himself began as early as the Latin diary Johnson kept while at Pembroke. Its first entry (October 1729) bids farewell to 'sloth' or *desidia*, described (as in Horace) as a 'Siren'. Indolence was something he was always reproaching himself with, and his feelings of guilt were also increased by what he thought of as culpable sensuality, which Law himself was so strict as to regard as 'self-murder', as rendering the luckless individual 'incapable of the divine favour either here or hereafter' (*A Serious Call*, chapter 9). Mrs Thrale relates the following anecdote:

> One day when my son was going to school, and dear Dr. Johnson followed as far as the garden gate, praying for his salvation, in a voice which those who listened attentively could hear plain enough, he said to me suddenly, 'Make your boy tell you his dreams: the first corruption that entered into my heart was communicated in a dream.' 'What was it, Sir?'

> said I. '*Do* not ask me', replied he with much violence, and walked away in apparent agitation.

Clearly even erotic dreams troubled Johnson's conscience, and he noted in his diary for 3 January 1766: 'No sleep till morning. Strongly tempted in a dream to M.' The attitude reflected here towards such a dream, or the act of supposed self-abuse it might so easily lead to, may provide a clue both to Johnson's fear of madness (popularly associated with such acts) and to his overwhelming sense of guilt.[2]

At the end of 1729 poverty forced Johnson to leave Oxford, and it proved impossible for him to return and take his degree. Back at Lichfield he suffered from acute depression. It has even been suggested that he contemplated suicide[3] (if he thought he had already defiled through 'sensuality' his rational soul – the image of God within him – he might well have looked upon himself as an outcast). He tried to get a position as a schoolmaster, but the lack of a degree stood in his way. These were bleak years for him, but a brighter prospect opened when in 1732, the year after his father's death, Edmund Hector invited him to Birmingham. Here Johnson met the woman who, when later widowed, was to become his wife. Her daughter Lucy Porter described for Boswell what he looked like the first time her mother met him:

> He was then lean and lank, so that his immense structure of bones was hideously striking to the eye, and the scars of the scrofula were deeply visible. He also wore his hair [i.e. his own hair, not a wig] which was straight and stiff, and separated behind; and he often had, seemingly, convulsive starts and odd gesticulations, which tended to excite at once surprise and ridicule.

Mrs Porter, however, saw beneath these surface disadvantages, saying afterwards to her daughter: 'This is the most sensible man that I ever saw in my life.'

While at Birmingham Johnson was persuaded to produce a version of Joachim Le Grand's translation of the travels of the Portuguese Father Jerome Lobo, who took part in the Jesuit missionary expedition to Abyssinia in the seventeenth century. A copy of the French was duly borrowed from Pembroke but the work proceeded slowly; Johnson was suffering from what Boswell calls his 'constitutional indolence', and Hector had to goad him into completing it by saying that the printer's family was suffering because, until it was cleared, he could accept no further work. Johnson lay in bed with the French propped in front of him and dictated the English to Hector, who saw the book through the press. More than twenty years later he returned to the Abyssinian setting in *Rasselas*; yet this early work is primarily of interest in showing, not only that Johnson's balanced and weighty prose style had already been formed, but that he responded to the Portuguese traveller's sober realism with a thorough-going approval.

In the same year (1735) Johnson married Elizabeth Porter – 'Tetty', as he called her. With the money she brought him he rented a large house at Edial (close to Lichfield) where he set up as a schoolmaster. This venture failed because he attracted only a handful of students. One of them was, however, David Garrick who, when the school closed, went with him to London. It was necessary for Johnson to make this journey since he had come to a dead-end. But it involved, as he must have realized, something of a gamble. Though conscious of his own ability, he knew how difficult it would be to establish himself in the capital. At Edial he had been working on a tragedy that he hoped to finish and have accepted for the stage. Only in this way could he be sure of rising above the denizens of Grub Street.

III

London was the centre of the nation's cultural and intellectual life. Looking towards it from Lichfield, Johnson would have been aware of this, and it was a realization that deepened with the years. London was also a place of great contrasts, where the wealthy few lived in fashionable and elegant surroundings, and the large number of the desperately poor lived amid rags and squalor, solaced by cheap gin. How precarious life there could be must have been immediately obvious to any newcomer without wealth, position, or friends to help him. Nor had Johnson any illusions about the kind of economy he would need to practise: an Irish painter he had known in Birmingham had suggested to him how a man could live cheaply in London 'without being contemptible' – by living in a garret, eating one solid meal a day, paying visits on 'clean-shirt day', and spending a few pence in a coffee-house to be 'for some hours every day in very good company'.

Some months after arriving in London, Johnson wrote to Edward Cave, the editor of the highly successful *Gentleman's Magazine*, a monthly miscellany that catered to a growing reading public. As things turned out, it was the phlegmatic, hard-working Cave rather than the carefully nurtured tragedy that gave him his start during these difficult early years. The two men probably met before he returned to Lichfield to bring Tetty to London, and Cave, a shrewd businessman, must have immediately seen how useful Johnson could be to him. From 1738 he became a regular contributor to the magazine, and from 1739 to 1744 was paid a retainer for the share of the editorial work that fell to his lot. This association with Cave was extremely important to him since it put enough money in his pocket to enable him to live.

When Johnson came to London the political scene was causing a good deal of excitement. Walpole was still in office, but the moves against him were strengthening; actually the real height of his power had been some half-dozen years earlier, about the time of the second Treaty of Vienna (1731). In the years that followed he had been forced by popular outcry to drop his scheme for a general excise; while his settled policy of pursuing peace had led, it was widely felt, to a loss of British influence and prestige abroad. In the War of the Polish Succession Walpole had refused to give to Austria the help promised by the treaty, and England was subsequently outmanoeuvred by France and her wily Cardinal Fleury. For some years, too, British shipping in the West Indies had been subjected to a good deal of harassment by Spanish coast-guards carrying out 'the right of search', and popular feeling was particularly inflamed by the account of Captain Robert Jenkins, who told of the loss of his ear – an incident that precipitated the war with Spain. Taking the lead in the opposition to Walpole was a group that had originally joined with the former Tory Bolingbroke and now enjoyed the patronage of the Prince of Wales. Its ablest speaker in the Commons was William

Pulteney, and among the 'boy patriots' who followed Cobham was the young William Pitt. *The Craftsman*, its main journal, was tellingly partisan, and support came also from most of the leading literary figures, including Swift, Pope and Fielding. Johnson would naturally have been drawn to this side. Nor was it long before he met the plausible, cultivated down-and-out, the poet Richard Savage, who claimed to be the illegitimate son of Lord Rivers and the Countess of Macclesfield. Johnson spent a lot of time in Savage's fascinating company and later told his friend Sir Joshua Reynolds that he and Savage, being unable to pay one night for a lodging, had 'in high spirits and brimful of patriotism' walked round and round St James's Square, 'inveighed against the minister, and "resolved they would *stand by their country*".'

It was against this background of opposition to the ministry that Johnson's early publications were produced. *London* (1738), a poetic 'imitation' of Juvenal's famous satire on Rome, first attracted the notice of the literary world. In showing a copy of the manuscript to Cave as supposedly the work of another, Johnson proposed to alter 'any stroke of satire' that seemed to him too offensive. Nor was he, as the real author, being over cautious: the extent of the poem's political satire only becomes clear once it is recognized that the portrait of 'Orgilio' was intended to represent Walpole. The following year Johnson published two prose pamphlets attacking Walpole, *Marmor Norfolciense* and *A Compleat Vindication of the Licensers of the Stage*. Both are, at times, reminiscent of Swift, whose *Windsor Prophecy* (1711) might well have provided the inspiration for *Marmor*.

So blatant is this pamphlet's criticism of the Hanoverian succession and Walpole that it has been said the government issued a warrant for its author's arrest. It tells of the discovery 'in Norfolk, near the town of Lynn' (Walpole was MP for King's Lynn) of a large stone bearing an inscription in Latin verse, which predicted a time of great national distress whenever the stone should be brought to light. The verse – with its English translation – contains allusions of which the import is plain and unequivocal, and the ironic humour of the piece consists in the attempts of the narrator, in the guise of pedantic commentator, to puzzle these out. The method Johnson uses can be seen from his speaker's comments on the lines describing the dangers of a standing-army (the deep-seated distrust of which remained a legacy from the seventeenth century):

Then thro' thy fields shall scarlet reptiles stray,
And rapine and pollution mark their way.
Their hungry swarms the peaceful vale shall fright
Still fierce to threaten, still afraid to fight.

What, asks the narrator, can these be? He thinks first of 'the multitude of lady-birds seen in Kent', but then reflects that 'these creatures, having both wings and feet, would scarcely have been called serpents'. The ironic potential of the shift between the literal and the figurative is often happily exploited:

> Let me only remark farther, that if the style of this, as of all other predictions, is figurative, the serpent, a wretched animal that crawls upon the earth, is a proper emblem of low views, self-interest, and base submission, as well as of cruelty, mischief, and malevolence.

This prepares the way for the obvious polemic:

> We are therefore to remember whenever the pest here threatned, shall invade us, that submission and tameness will be certain ruin, and that nothing but spirit, vigilance, activity and opposition can preserve us from the most hateful and reproachful misery, that of being plundered, starved, and devoured by vermin and by reptiles.

The narrator considers the authorship of these ancient lines and concludes they must have been written by a 'Briton' rather than a Saxon 'foreigner'. He also discounts the suggestion that they were written by a king or a courtier: 'If he ever saw a court, I would willingly believe, that he did not owe his concern for posterity to his ill reception there, but his ill reception there to his concern for posterity.' In this way Johnson sketches in a framework of reference that had served him more fully in *London*. The government newspaper also comes in for unwitting attack from the bumbling commentator, and his party allegiance is further made clear when he proposes an 'excise' or tax on bread so that a learned academy of lawyers and soldiers (both groups had been criticized for collaborating in the overthrow of English liberty) might be set up and paid to decipher the true meaning of the verses. Johnson's satire, then, aims at something of a Swiftian amplitude, even if it does not often display a comparable verve. Its main thrust, however, is to deplore the state to which Walpole and George II have reduced Britain. Not just the dangerous ascendancy of France is pointed to, but the whole process whereby England has become subordinate to Hanover. A horse, so the prophecy runs, shall suck the blood of a cowardly passive lion; here the narrator's express hope is that an interpretation involving Hanover and England (whose arms featured a horse and a lion respectively) 'can enter into the mind of none but a virulent Republican, or bloody Jacobite'. Then follows a passage in which the ambiguities are so skilfully couched that the subtlety of the satire more truly rivals Swift's:

> There is not one honest man in the nation unconvinced how weak an attempt it would be to confute this insinuation. An insinuation which no party will dare to abet, and of so fatal and destructive a tendency, that it may prove equally dangerous to the author whether true or false.

A Compleat Vindication attacked the Stage Licensing Act of 1737 and the Lord Chamberlain's refusal to pass Henry Brooke's *Gustavus Vasa* for the stage. This play, the first to be banned since the Act, has been described as 'a barefaced allegory of the state of England as portrayed in opposition propaganda'.[4] Walpole was never inclined to put up with criticism, and whatever patronage he gave extended only to those writers who supported his policies. Some of Fielding's burlesques made him smart, and he therefore took the opportunity of bringing in tighter controls. In this pamphlet Johnson writes ironically in a tone of mock reasonableness: its subtitle envisages 'making the office of Licenser more extensive and effectual'. Why, asks the fictional speaker, should not old plays be similarly censored, especially those which inculcate virtue, a habit of mind clearly lacking in self-interest? Why not censor the press? Since, however, this would prompt 'the common people' to rise up in its defence, why not make censorship effective at a single blow by abolishing all schools and allowing only those to be taught to read who have obtained 'a license from the Lord Chamberlain'?

Though the Swiftian vein of this is obvious, Johnson's prose sometimes lacks the sharpness and vigour needed to work it successfully. His speaker describes, for example,

> the unaccountable behaviour of these men [i.e. the Opposition], the enthusiastick resolution with which, after a hundred successive defeats, they still renewed their attacks, the spirit with which they continued to repeat their arguments in the senate, though they found a majority determined to oppose them.

The justification for such persistent opposition arises, of course, from the nature of the 'majority' being opposed, yet it is only in the next part of Johnson's sentence ('and the inflexibility with which they rejected all offers of places and preferments') that the point is made trenchantly enough. The same kind of difficulty occurs elsewhere. Is 'unextinguishable zeal' so great a virtue when it is said to be expressed 'with an air of revenge, and a kind of gloomy triumph'? The observation that 'it is common among men under the influence of any kind of frenzy, to believe that all the world has the same odd notions that disorder their own imaginations' can, in fact, cut both ways and point up the dangers of all forms of extremism. More impressive, however, and ultimately more characteristic, is a sentence such as the following:

> This temper which I have been describing is almost always complicated with ideas of the high prerogatives of human nature, of a sacred unalienable birthright, which no man has conferr'd upon us, and which neither kings can take, nor senates give way, which we may justly assert whenever and by whomsoever it is attacked, and which, if ever it should happen to be lost, we may take the first opportunity to recover.

In his pamphlet Johnson not only upholds the right of opposition, but maintains that those in authority must be publicly accountable for their actions. Though he does not in practical terms define what he means by this, he was to return to the idea several times in the years that followed. In the preface he wrote for Dodsley's *Preceptor*, he describes every Englishman as 'a secondary legislator' who

> gives his consent by his representative to all the laws by which he is bound, and has a right to petition the great council of the nation whenever he thinks they are deliberating upon an act detrimental to the interests of the community.

As Johnson had suggested elsewhere (in his preface to *The Gentleman's Magazine* for 1743, and his introduction to *The Harleian Miscellany*), the political structure in England, where people did not live under a form of arbitrary government, made it incumbent not only on them to exercise this right, but on those 'entrusted with the administration of national affairs to give an account of their conduct to almost every man who demands it'.

IV

The Gentleman's Magazine, along with its main rival *The London Magazine*, had for some years breached parliamentary privilege by supplying readers with unofficial versions of the debates that had taken place in both Houses of Parliament. These were, understandably, a popular feature, and when in 1738 it was resolved in the Commons that publication of them involved 'a notorious breach of the privilege of this House', Cave (perhaps at Johnson's suggestion, certainly with the aid of his pen) printed them in a disguised form as 'Debates in the Senate of Magna Lilliputia'. The first instalment told of the voyage of Gulliver's grandson to Lilliput, in this way preparing readers for a further account of its 'historical and political novelties'. The disguise was thin enough but effective, the names of individual speakers being designated by easily recognizable anagrams (like 'Walelop' for Walpole). To begin with, Johnson was employed in revising the speeches compiled by William Guthrie. Later the whole task became his, and he was, to use Boswell's term, 'sole composer' of the debates which appeared between July 1741 and March 1744, and which dealt with events in parliament between November 1740 and February 1743. Johnson apparently worked from notes gathered by others who were employed to attend every sitting, though sometimes, as he told Boswell, 'he had nothing more communicated to him than the names of the several speakers, and the part which they had taken in the debate'.

Johnson's 'reporting' was, under the circumstances, little short of remarkable. The individual speeches were written faster than anything else he wrote (he sometimes filled as much as three columns of the magazine in an hour). All, too, are polished and fully formed, reflecting the measured stateliness of his own prose style. Surprisingly – perhaps because his authorship was such a well-kept secret – they were widely regarded as authentic. Arthur Murphy reports that during a dinner-party at which Johnson was present, Philip Francis, the translator of Demosthenes, remarked that one of Pitt's speeches was 'the best he had ever read'. When its real author admitted having written it 'in a garret in Exeter Street', Francis said: 'Then, Sir, you have exceeded Demosthenes himself; for to say that you have exceeded Francis's Demosthenes would be saying nothing.' According to Murphy, another of those present went on to praise the 'impartiality' of the debates, adding that 'he dealt out reason and eloquence with an equal hand to both parties'. Johnson's reply to this had its usual edge: 'I saved appearances tolerably well; but I took care that the WHIG DOGS should not have the best of it.' This retort admits no simple explanation. It is true that the sentiments against Walpole and his ministry are often vigorously expressed; for example, in the debate (9 March 1742) on the motion 'for inquiring into the conduct of affairs at home and abroad for the last twenty years', it is claimed that 'foreign and domestic affairs have been managed with equal ignorance, negligence or wickedness'. Yet Walpole's severest critics in each House – Carteret in the Lords and Pulteney in the Commons – were both former Whig ministers. What Johnson's remark suggests is not so much a simple opposition between Whig and Tory as his sympathetic identification with all those who made up 'the country party'. This, as he says, derived its name from its 'opposition to the measures of the Court'.

Not only are reasoned arguments given to both sides, but factionalism is clearly recognized as such. Lord Hervey, for example, is credited with pointing out (1 February 1743) – as he takes more than a sidelong glance at the motives of those who had clamoured to have Walpole removed from office – that they very soon embraced policies similar to those they had formerly denounced. Johnson seems fully to realize the strength of party motives, as he also does the genuine complexity of some of the questions at issue. It was perhaps this rather than a deliberate policy of 'impartiality' or non-alignment which led him to be so even-handed in representing opposing points of view. At the very least, his involvement in the debates arguably caused him to moderate some of his own youthful enthusiasm, and be more suspicious of the rancour of factions.

The bulk of Johnson's work for *The Gentleman's Magazine* was a series of biographies, a literary form that was becoming increasingly popular. He had at first proposed to Cave a new English translation of Father Paul Sarpi's history of the Council of Trent, and though the project came to nothing, it did prompt him to write a short life of Sarpi. Over the next four years there followed accounts of the Dutch physician and scholar Hermann Boerhaave, the intrepid Admiral Blake, Drake (mainly a vivid narrative of the voyage of 1572–3 and the circumnavigation of the world), the French child prodigy in languages Jean-Philippe Baratier ('Barretier'), the French physician and botanist Louis Morin, the Dutch classical scholar Pieter Burmann 'the elder', and the seventeenth-century physician Thomas Sydenham (written originally as a preface to an edition of Sydenham's works). For his material Johnson had to rely on secondary sources (the account of Sarpi, for example, is an abridgement of Le Courayer's earlier memoir); yet these works are interesting as his earliest attempts at a favourite form, one he returned to in his *Life of Savage* (1744), in the various biographies of the 1750s and early 1760s (including those of Roger Ascham, Sir Thomas Browne, and the poet Collins), and in his so-called *Lives of the Poets* (1779–81).

Johnson's fondness for biography ('the biographical part of literature is what I love most') was an intellectual predilection that he found it easy to justify. His most famous essay in *The Rambler* (no. 60) is on this topic, and in it he sets out why he valued biography so highly:

> Those parallel circumstances, and kindred images, to which we readily conform our minds, are, above all other writings, to be found in narratives of the lives of particular persons; and therefore no species of writing seems more worthy of

> cultivation than biography, since none can be more delightful or more useful, none can more certainly enchain the heart by irresistible interest, or more widely diffuse instruction to every diversity of condition.

This kind of writing not only fed his love of learning and his interest in new facts (especially those involving people), but allowed him to satisfy the compulsion he always felt to evaluate things according to their 'usefulness', or the moral illumination they could provide. 'We are', he writes in the same essay, 'all prompted by the same motives, all deceived by the same fallacies, all animated by hope, obstructed by danger, entangled by desire, and seduced by pleasure.' And so he saw it as the biographer's primary function 'often to pass slightly over those performances and incidents which produce vulgar greatness, to lead the thoughts into domestic privacies, and display the minute details of daily life, where exterior appendages are cast aside, and men excel each other only by prudence and virtue.'

In Johnson's early biographies this opportunity was not really open to him, though he was aware of the shortcomings of his material and often wished for more information. He was, too, characteristically sceptical of whatever seemed exaggerated or hyperbolic, and consistently sought to delineate character rather than write panegyric. Wherever possible, he interspersed his narratives with moral reflections, a tendency that anticipates his later work as a moral essayist. Drake was supposed to have been left a small ship by the master to whom he had been apprenticed. This, adds his biographer, is

> a circumstance that deserves to be remembered, not only as it may illustrate the private character of this brave man, but as it may hint, to all those who may hereafter propose his conduct for their imitation, that virtue is the surest foundation both of reputation and fortune, and that the first step to greatness is to be honest.

Again, alluding to the belief that the failure of Drake's last voyage had hastened his death, Johnson expresses the hope, 'for the honour of so great a man, that it is without foundation, and that he whom no series of success could ever betray to vanity or negligence could have supported a change of fortune without impatience or dejection'.

Johnson's sympathies are obviously engaged in his account of Boerhaave, who, as a man of learning notable for his piety, is ardently proposed as an example: 'May those who study his writings imitate his life, and those who endeavour after his knowledge aspire likewise to his piety!' Boerhaave's insistence on the importance of 'experimental knowledge' was readily endorsed by Johnson, who, when he writes of the breadth of his intellectual accomplishments, allows an element of self-identification to creep into his language: 'Yet did he not suffer one branch of science to withdraw his attention from others: anatomy did not withhold him from chemistry, nor chemistry, *enchanting as it is*, from the study of botany' (my italics). What he especially admired Boerhaave for was his unshakeable faith in 'the spiritual and immaterial nature of the soul'. The 'kind of experimental certainty' the Dutchman claimed to have had of this is mentioned with obvious approval, and though the meaning of 'experimental' is here being stretched, his biographer seems unaware of any contradiction (except, perhaps, in so far as this is implicit in the urgency of his writing). Boerhaave's serenity must have seemed enviable to Johnson, who describes the apparent ease with which he could limit his intellectual curiosity: 'He worshipped God as he is in himself, without attempting to inquire into his nature.'

Though he never holds genuine piety up to scrutiny, Johnson shows himself at other times capable of a characteristic scepticism. In his life of Drake, for example, he attacks what he considered to be the faulty logic of the primitivists in supposing man in a state of nature happier than civilized man. The absurdity of this doctrine he was prepared to scoff at, just as he was many years later on finding himself, towards the end of his Scottish jaunt, once again in a comfortable coach: 'We had', writes Boswell, 'a pleasing conviction of the commodiousness of civilization, and heartily laughed at the ravings of those absurd visionaries who have attempted to persuade us of the superior advantages of a *state of nature*.' There is too, in the account of Sydenham, Johnson's sharp comment on Sir Richard Blackmore's story that he had been advised by this eminent physician to read *Don Quixote*:

> The relater is hindered by that self-love which dazzles all mankind from discovering that he might intend a satire very different from a general censure of all the ancient and modern writers on medicine, since he might perhaps mean, either seriously or in jest, to insinuate that Blackmore was not adapted by nature to the study of physic, and that whether he should read Cervantes or Hippocrates he would be equally unqualified for practice, and equally unsuccessful in it.

V

The biography of Savage, incomparably greater than anything Johnson had tried in this kind before, is an acknowledged masterpiece. One of his earliest companions in London and certainly one of the most colourful, Savage exerted something of a spell on the younger man. The struggling Johnson knew what it was to be poor and unrecognized, and this can only have ensured his affection for Savage as a person and respect for his talents as an author. The *Life of Savage* is therefore written with a good deal of inward sympathy – though, perhaps partly for this reason, it also contains a shrewd assessment of his character. Its importance derives from this rather than from any advance it marks in the use of new techniques. It does not, for example, include direct speech, even though Johnson had spent a lot of time avidly listening to Savage; nor is there any real attempt to set the scene or provide a dramatic context for events (the account of Savage's trial for murder is something of an exception). Instead this biography holds our interest because of the figure it sets before us – and not least because of the complexity of Johnson's own response to the character he is describing.

Savage's account of his illegitimacy is accepted unquestioningly, and the unnatural cruelty of his presumed mother in opposing his welfare is represented by Johnson as little short of fiendish cruelty. Her conduct is one reason why he is so prepared to make excuses for his former friend: unfairly deprived of the wealth and station in life that should have been his due, Savage is regarded as more sinned against than sinning. He is said to have been 'exposed' to 'temptations' at an early age, and been led by promises or patronage into a way of life that he lacked the means to sustain. His faults, then, tend to be considered as not really his, or not such as he himself should be blamed for. Johnson does not always draw from his language the conclusions it implies (which is further evidence of the inwardness of the portrait): doubtless he felt some sympathy with the impulse towards escapism he observed in Savage; nowhere else, at any rate, except implicitly in *The Vanity of Human Wishes*, does he make such concessions to the determinist position. Savage had been 'obliged from his first entrance into the world to subsist upon expedients': 'His faults were very often the effects of his misfortunes.' His 'slavery to his passions' is ultimately seen by his biographer as both caused by, and in turn the cause of, his 'irregular and dissipated' life. 'He was not', says Johnson, 'master of his own motions.'

This glossing of his friend's faults sometimes leads to an interpretation of events that is obviously partial. In relating that Sir Richard Steele had banished Savage from his house and favour on hearing he had ridiculed him, Johnson attributes 'malice' to the 'tale-bearer' and mere 'imprudence' to Savage. Such things, he argues, can be expected to happen, especially given Steele's character and Savage's liveliness. His fault, he suggests, was not so much 'ingratitude' as 'negligence'. Other episodes, however, force Johnson to acknowledge that Savage was decidedly capable of 'ungenerous reflections', that his 'esteem was no very certain possession' since 'he would lampoon at one time those whom he had praised at another'. And at this point the tension that has been lurking in the writing comes to the surface. Though Johnson offers what may be alleged in Savage's defence, he is also prepared to judge his conduct according to objective moral standards. Elsewhere, too, he attempts to explain the inconsistency (as he sees it) in Savage's character while making both his own sympathy and disapproval obvious:

> It is certain that he was upon every occasion too easily reconciled to himself, and that he appeared very little to regret those practices which had impaired his reputation. The reigning error of his life was that he mistook the love for the practice of virtue, and was indeed not so much a good man as the friend of goodness.

What Johnson points to appears to have been a chronic tendency, one that we should today call paranoia. Savage blamed everyone and everything for his misfortunes, seeing himself as always in the right.

> Though [says Johnson] he did not lose the opportunity which success gave him of setting a high rate on his abilities, but paid due deference to the suffrages of mankind when they were given in his favour, he did not suffer his esteem of himself to depend upon others, nor found anything sacred in the voice of the people when they were inclined to censure him.

Indeed, he was prone 'to exclude all those from the character of men of judgment who did not applaud him'. Savage's method of living 'at peace with himself' was to consider himself as superior to those around him. And he was quick to cast aside even those who had helped him whenever they sought to oppose his whims. He expected to be given money without in return feeling any gratitude for it, and, as Johnson adds, 'a refusal was resented by him as an affront, or complained of as an injury'. It is not therefore surprising that Savage eventually alienated those who had befriended him, since 'he more frequently reproached his subscribers for not giving him more than thanked them for what he received'. In this he acted like a man who thought the world owed him a living, and was peeved when it did not acknowledge the fact as single-mindedly as he did. Johnson's observations bring out this aspect of Savage's nature and delineate with a remarkable suggestiveness his general mental state.

Perhaps it was for this reason that the *Life of Savage* made such an impact on the youthful Joshua Reynolds. The future portrait-painter, who did not then know Johnson, recalled that he 'began to read it while he was standing with his arm leaning against a chimney-piece', and that 'it seized his attention so strongly, that, not being able to lay down the book till he had finished it, when he attempted to move, he found his arm totally benumbed'. Yet the *Life of Savage*, like *London*, was published anonymously, and though the author of these works could not go unnoticed, Johnson up to this time still had his reputation to make. The wish to be famous probably concerned him less than it concerns most men, yet it was doubtless with an eye to establishing his name and making some money that he proposed an edition of Shakespeare's plays. Given, too, all the semi-hackwork he had been doing, he must have looked forward to the challenge of a task of some magnitude. To test the reaction of the public he published *Miscellaneous Observations on the Tragedy of Macbeth* (1745) as a sample of his abilities as editor and critic. This work was justifiably praised. It shows not only his attention to historical method and his willingness to grapple with the meaning of the text, but his keen interest in characterization and the immediacy of his response to Shakespeare's scenes. For many years, however, he was prevented from proceeding with the larger work. His pamphlet had included a separate sheet headed 'Proposals for Printing a New Edition of the Plays of William Shakespeare', and its appearance caused the bookseller Jacob Tonson to write to Cave, warning him that he and his associates alone controlled the copyright of the plays. Clearly Tonson was willing to resort to legal action if Cave invaded what he claimed to be his rights, and the planned edition had therefore to be shelved.

At the time this must have been a bitter blow to Johnson. Nor would it have cheered him to learn that the disappointment he felt on his own behalf was shared by his friends. Late the following year Walmesley wrote to Garrick: 'When you see Mr Johnson, pray my compliments, and tell him I esteem him as a great genius – quite lost both to himself and the world.' An even larger undertaking was, however, beginning to appear over the horizon. Robert Dodsley, one of the booksellers to be concerned in the venture, suggested the idea of producing an English dictionary. Johnson was still relatively unknown, and why he should have been approached is a matter for conjecture. The connection with Dodsley (who had published *London*) was no doubt important; perhaps, too, the *Miscellaneous Observations* had impressed the booksellers. At least they would have known how he had slogged away for years on *The Gentleman's Magazine*, and how invaluable, too, he had been to Thomas Osborne in cataloguing and describing the Harleian collection. Probably they saw in Johnson – and here the *Life of Savage* might also have contributed something – a thorough-going professional who was, unlike the usual penman, a genius. At any rate, the work itself was to more than vindicate their choice.

When Dodsley suggested that an English dictionary would be well received by the public, Johnson 'seemed at first to catch at the proposition, but, after a pause, said in his abrupt, decisive manner, "I believe I shall not undertake it".' He must, however, have found the suggestion too flattering and challenging, as well as too promising financially, to resist. There were, of course, to be years of labour before his dictionary could be ready for publication; and meantime Johnson was to emerge as a literary figure in his own right. First there appeared *The Vanity of Human Wishes*, with his own name on the title-page; then in the following year he began *The Rambler*. By this time he was no longer young but middle-aged; yet after the years of relative obscurity, recognition, when it did come, came quickly.

3
Poetry

I

When *London* was published anonymously, the poem created enough of a stir for Pope to remark that its author would soon be 'déterré'. It appeared at the same time as the first of his own 'Dialogues' (which came to be known as the 'Epilogue to the Satires'), and its trenchant political satire was doubtless responsible for its quick sale and the call for a second edition just one week later. More than ten years were to elapse before Johnson published his other, more famous long poem *The Vanity of Human Wishes*, an 'imitation' of Juvenal's tenth satire. This poem, which touches human life deeply, was praised even in the nineteenth century. Byron greatly admired it, and Tennyson claimed that the 'high moral tone' of some of its couplets had never been surpassed in English satire.

The habit of looking to classical poets as models of style and subject-matter was fostered in the schools (among Johnson's juvenilia are verse translations from Virgil and Horace). Dryden had translated Juvenal's third satire as a schoolboy, and his published version is a translation that preserves the proper names of the original. Already in the seventeenth century, however, a different practice was growing up of replacing Roman names with English ones. The poet John Denham had stated as early as 1656: 'If Virgil must needs speak English, it were fit he should speak not only as a man of this nation, but as a man of this age.'[1] John Oldham agreed, using English names in his translations (including his version of Juvenal's third satire). Johnson's most immediate predecessor in this kind of poetic imitation was Pope, whose English versions of Horace appeared in the 1730s. Like Pope, he drew attention to his originals, printing the relevant passages from Juvenal below the text of *London*, and adding to that of *The Vanity of Human Wishes* the appropriate line numbers. In his letter to Cave prior to the publication of *London* he insisted on such a lay-out since he regarded the adaptation of Juvenal's 'sentiments' to 'modern facts and persons' as 'part of the beauty of the performance'.

The whole question of translating poetry clearly interested Johnson, and in the *Lives of the Poets* he often dwells on it. More recent English poets, especially Pope, seemed to him to have here made a singular contribution, and he praises Pope's translation of the *Iliad* as 'a performance which no age or nation can pretend to equal'. Thoroughly conversant with the seventeenth-century debate concerning the degree of freedom that the translator ought to allow himself, Johnson, in discussing Pope's 'imitations' of Horace, endorses the practice which had by then become established:

> This mode of imitation, in which the ancients are familiarized by adapting their sentiments to modern topics . . . is a kind of middle composition between translation and original design, which pleases when the thoughts are unexpectedly applicable and the parallels lucky. It seems to have been Pope's favourite amusement, for he has carried it further than any former poet.

Yet Johnson was also aware of the inherent difficulties of poetic imitation:

> Such imitations cannot give pleasure to common readers; the man of learning may be sometimes surprised and delighted by an unexpected parallel, but the comparison requires knowledge of the original, which will likewise often detect strained applications. Between Roman images and English manners there will be an irreconcilable dissimilitude, and the work will be generally uncouth and parti-coloured, neither original nor translated, neither ancient nor modern.

Most critics of Johnson's first imitation of Juvenal seem to have taken their cue from these words. Failing to discern the originality of the poem's 'design', they have tended to regard

London as the work of a young poet slavishly and somewhat ineptly following his Latin original. It can, however, be shown that Johnson transformed his source material, giving to many of his details a new poetic energy and life. His poem, unlike Juvenal's, has the breadth and scope of a political satire. Here, too, the influence of Pope was doubtless important, for Pope had not only published his ironic version of Horace's Epistle to Augustus the year before *London* appeared, but had meantime directed some shafts against the government in imitating the first and sixth Epistles of Horace's first book.

II

As a poem on the evils of city life, *London* exploits a familiar theme. Early mention is made of the fires, falling houses, fell attorneys and female atheists that were to be met with in the eighteenth-century capital. These topical details read somewhat oddly in the lines in which they occur, for the poem's prevailing theme is not established all at once. When it is, however, it becomes clear that *London* is also a topical poem in the sense that it satirizes the measures of the government, and the corruption which the government was thought to have fostered. The composition of the poem coincided, as Boswell says, with 'that ferment against the Court and ministry which some years afterwards ended in the downfall of Sir Robert Walpole'. In the domestic sphere, *London* attacks the excise, the Stage Licensing Act, and political pensions; these last, Johnson feared, would lead to a system of administration that encouraged sycophancy. And Walpole's foreign policy was imagined as having similarly dangerous consequences in adopting a servile attitude towards Britain's traditional rivals, France and Spain. In a way that is exaggerated but at its best effective, the poet links the corruption of the whole city with the current political scene. Such is the government's policy that any more obvious form of invasion seems scarcely necessary. Already 'the dregs of each corrupted state' have become 'the cheated nation's happy fav'rites'. Even the country, the natural antithesis of the city, reflects, as we shall see, the prevailing corruption.

Throughout the poem the reprehensible measures of the administration and the moral and even physical degeneracy of the nation are significantly juxtaposed. Thales, the poet's 'friend', awaits transport to the country at its threshold Greenwich, which, as the birthplace of Elizabeth, reminds him of a former race of monarchs, the defeat of the Armada, and a very different foreign policy towards Spain,

> Ere masquerades debauch'd, excise oppress'd,
> Or English honour grew a standing jest.

This kind of juxtaposing reaches its climax near the end of the poem:

> Scarce can our fields, such crowds at Tyburn die,
> With hemp the gallows and the fleet supply.
> Propose your schemes, ye Senatorian band,
> Whose Ways and Means support the sinking land;
> Lest ropes be wanting in the tempting spring,
> To rig another convoy for the K—g.

Juvenal had feared that all the iron needed for agriculture would be unproductively used as fetters for criminals, but Johnson's satire goes deeper. The allusions to 'fields' and 'rope' are especially daring – 'fields' because it evokes both the countryside and (through the juxtaposition) the field at Tyburn, and 'rope' because it links an overcrowded gallows with George II's frequent visits to his mistress Madame Wallmoden in Hanover.

The lines that follow further the implied contrast with a glorious past:

> A single jail, in Alfred's golden reign,
> Could half the nation's criminals contain.

It is this imagined past, peopled by such monarchs as Alfred and Elizabeth, that the corrupt present shames and threatens to obliterate. Seeing a nation overrun with obsequious foreigners, Thales exclaims:

> Ah! what avails it, that, from slav'ry far,
> I drew the breath of life in English air;
> Was early taught a Briton's right to prize,
> And lisp the tale of Henry's victories;
> If the gull'd conqueror receives the chain,
> And flattery subdues when arms are vain?

Previously he had gone even further back into the past, inviting 'Illustrious Edward' – Edward III, the victor at Crécy as Henry was at Agincourt – to survey once again this former land of saints and heroes. The 'rustic grandeur', the 'surly grace', is no longer to be seen. Not merely enslaved but even emasculated by its traditional enemies, the nation is regarded as presenting a sorry contrast to its past greatness:

Behold the warrior dwindled to a beau;
Sense, freedom, piety, refin'd away,
Of France the mimick, and of Spain the prey.

The poem's contrast between the city and the country serves its political ends. Juvenal's pose had been ironic from the outset: there was no place 'so dismal, so lonely' – not even the desolate little island of Procida – which the poet did not pretend to prefer to one of the principal (though noisiest) streets of Rome. The crowded metropolis, despite its discomforts and dangers, exerted its spell on Juvenal; such was its fascination for him that a life of retirement could not in any real sense be contemplated as an alternative. Johnson, however, condemns the city and praises what the still uncorrupted country ought, ideally, to stand for. For Thales the corrupt capital has become an alien land, and when he resolves to flee it, he is prompted not by a desire for rural retirement (the 'rocks of Scotland' appear, anyway, far from inviting in themselves), but a willingness to associate himself with the spirit of his country's ancient inhabitants. Significantly opposed to London are those strongholds of the ancient Britons – Wales, Scotland and Ireland. Thales, a 'true Briton', cannot brook living in the capital under an administration that has sold out to Britain's traditional rivals. Unwilling to compete in lies and flattery with a 'fasting Monsieur' or 'supple Gaul', he is described as 'injur'd'. Wronged by the loss of that freedom which was his birthright, he addresses the poet in words of bitter indignation:

Here let those reign, whom pensions can incite
To vote a patriot black, a courtier white;
Explain their country's dear-bought rights away,
And plead for pirates in the face of day;
With slavish tenets taint our poison'd youth,
And lend a lye the confidence of truth.

Let such raise palaces, and manors buy,
Collect a tax, or farm a lottery,
With warbling eunuchs fill a licens'd stage,
And lull to servitude a thoughtless age.

The language of these lines – 'palaces' (Walpole's palatial Houghton Hall was in Norfolk), 'manors', 'farm' – suggests that even the country is being made to suffer; and most vivid of all is 'warbling' which, so often applied to birdsong, is here forced into a context altogether debased.

Thales is

Resolved at length, from vice and London far,
To breathe in distant fields a purer air;
And, fix'd on Cambria's solitary shore,
Give to St. David one true Briton more.

At St David's (Wales) he will find the perfect retreat, at least in so far as there his safety (like that of the ancient Briton who 'in poverty defy'd his foes') will be assured. And because of the prevailing corruption that constitutes in itself an insidious form of invasion, he proposes that his friend should likewise seek out some corner of their own neglected country:

Could'st thou resign the park or play content,
For the fair banks of Severn or of Trent;
There might'st thou find some elegant retreat,
Some hireling senator's deserted seat;
And stretch thy prospects o'er the smiling land,
For less than rent the dungeons of the Strand;
There prune thy walks, support thy drooping flow'rs,
Direct thy rivulets, and twine thy bow'rs;
And, while thy grounds a cheap repast afford,
Despise the dainties of a venal lord.

In this, one of the more striking reworkings of the *beatus ille* theme in English literature, Johnson depicts the modern Briton's equivalent of Horace's Sabine farm – though the taint of the 'hireling senator' or 'venal lord' is not easily dispelled. Since the whole land is in need of rejuvenation, these degenerate creatures must be replaced by such men as will prefer a virtuous simplicity to corrupting luxury, cultivate a sturdy independence instead of a sycophantic dependence, and bring to moral ugliness and decay a new vitality and beauty.

Johnson's use of 'Briton' to praise the true patriot can be paralleled in both Swift and Pope. In one of his letters (8 March 1735) Swift bequeathed to Pulteney 'an epitaph for forty years hence, in two words, *Ultimus Britannorum*' ('the last of the Britons'). And the second of Pope's 'Dialogues', published two months after *London*, contained the lines,

> Here, last of Britons! let your names be read;
> Are none, none living? Let me praise the dead.

The country, then, as presented in *London* carries overtones of a romantic past. It points up the contrast between the political toady, the 'hireling senator' or 'venal lord', and modern patriots like the poet and his friend. In describing the city Johnson dwells, of course, on the besetting physical dangers; and here, as elsewhere, the quality of the poetry varies. The 'midnight murd'rer' passage is contrived and macabre by comparison with the description of the 'frolic drunkard' that precedes it. In these earlier lines (224ff.) the imitation of the Latin original has a real vividness (seemingly derived, in part, from Johnson's acquaintance with Oldham's earlier version). What is most relevant, however, is that these passages are placed alongside the earlier *beatus ille* passage. By means of this kind of structural counterpointing, the alternatives facing the still virtuous citizen are made very plain.

III

The full extent of the political satire in *London* only becomes clear once it is realized that the portrait of 'Orgilio' (really the only extended portrait in the poem) is a veiled attack on Walpole. This name first occurs as a substitution for Juvenal's Verres. The first collected edition of *The Craftsman* (1731–7) had contained a motto from Cicero's famous indictment of Verres, the implication being that what could be said of this notoriously wicked governor could be said of Walpole as a second Verres. Readers of poetry were practised in making such substitutions, and the first of Pope's 'Dialogues' strongly hints at the same identification:

Agysthus, Verres, hurt not honest Fleury,
But well may put some statesmen in a fury.

It was customary, too, as in Pope's second 'Dialogue', to link Walpole with Wolsey as a type of the wicked statesman – a fact also relevant for the portrait of Orgilio. *The Craftsman* (no. 8) had satirized both these statesmen for their *superbia* or pride; significantly, Wolsey had been criticized by his contemporaries for his 'high, *orgullous*, and insatiable mind' (my italics).[2] The same paper also suggested that a comparison could be made between Wolsey's use of fortune and power and Walpole's. Wolsey is said to have been 'extravagant and ostentatious to the highest degree': 'He built palaces, and his train outshone his master's so much that when he retired into the country, on a party of pleasure, the Court became desert.' Not surprisingly, Walpole was seen as fulfilling a similar role at Houghton Hall. Not only were his levees (held three times a week) thronged with noble suppliants, but ambassadors appointed by him were ready to gratify with expensive gifts from abroad his passion for paintings and sculpture.[3] Johnson's portrait reflects the wide-spread criticism of such proceedings: the imagined destruction and restoration of Orgilio's 'palace' is an attack on what was considered to be Walpole's own means of amassing wealth at Houghton.

Juvenal describes the destruction by fire of 'the great house of Asturicus', the owner of which has no heir and, being very rich, is shamelessly courted by fortune-hunters. This vice was not the social evil in eighteenth-century London that it had been in imperial Rome, and Johnson was accused of transferring from his original a description that had no relevance to his own times. But the political overtones of his passage are plain enough. The manuscript of his poem contained the lines,

With servile grief dependent nobles sigh
And swell with tears the prostituted eye,

and that this couplet was cancelled from the published version was doubtless dictated by prudence, for such 'nobles' could have been 'dependent' only on Walpole. A weaker couplet took its place:

> The laureate tribe in servile verse relate,
> How virtue wars with persecuting fate.

The lines that follow, however, contain unambiguous reference to Walpole's placemen:

> With well-feign'd gratitude the pension'd band
> Refund the plunder of the beggar'd land.
> See! while he builds, the gaudy vassals come,
> And crowd with sudden wealth the rising dome;
> The price of boroughs and of souls restore,
> And raise his treasures higher than before.

Clearly Johnson never intended these lines on Orgilio to be read without political overtones as a simple substitution for Juvenal's – though he did, even so, wish to draw attention to those he was 'imitating'. The Roman poet's scorn had been directed at that childless society of imperial Rome which, by giving rise to a shameless race of legacy-hunters, had fostered an unpleasant and insidious form of dependence. This is the idea Johnson builds on in accommodating Juvenal's implied satire on dependence to his own distinctive theme. Orgilio–Walpole, by fostering a form of dependence even more dangerously insidious, was thought to be perverting the proper instrumentalities of government. To his own placemen went those offices which should rightly have been the prerogative of merit and the birthright of every 'true Briton'.

London is, then, an original reworking of its Latin model. Its material, though seemingly so diverse, is imaginatively organized, at least in so far as the various antitheses reinforce one another in giving expression to its political theme. The poem is also held together by its *saeva indignatio*, by the 'fierce indignation' that the poet (through the speaker) displays. This is evident in the lines on Orgilio already quoted. And nowhere is it more evident than in those earlier lines ('Here let those reign, whom pensions can incite . . .') which depict what follows from such a corrupt system of political patronage.

Johnson's feeling was, however, moved by more than this, for the poem's most famous line, 'Slow rises worth, by poverty depress'd', has a deeper resonance. In its context it can easily be related to the prevailing political satire; but its tone also anticipates the later Johnson, in whom the earlier, more personal quarrel with life (dating from at least the days of undergraduate poverty) comes to be converted into an acceptance at once more sober and compassionate, of the human condition. Though the theme of the vanity of human wishes crops up again and again (in his greatest poem, in the periodical essays, in *Rasselas*), the bitter or sardonic note tends to disappear with *London*. The later imitation of Juvenal is concerned rather with the threat which, in all its tragic restlessness, comes from within – man's awesome propensity to rush headlong on his fate.

IV

From the outset, *The Vanity of Human Wishes* dwells on the emotions and inner drives that lead men astray:

> Then say how hope and fear, desire and hate,
> O'erspread with snares the clouded maze of fate,
> Where wav'ring man, betray'd by vent'rous pride,
> To tread the dreary paths without a guide,
> As treach'rous phantoms in the mist delude,
> Shuns fancied ills, or chases airy good;
> How rarely reason guides the stubborn choice,
> Rules the bold hand, or prompts the suppliant voice.

The imagery of fire (implicit here in the allusion to the *ignis fatuus*) is found throughout the poem. It suggests the burning energy or blazing ambition that drives men on, and proves in the end to be self-consuming:

> With fatal heat impetuous courage glows,
> With fatal sweetness elocution flows,
> Impeachment stops the speaker's pow'rful breath,
> And restless fire precipitates on death.

What is suggested is something restless and resistless. As the preceding couplet makes clear, not just men's wishes but their talents seemingly co-operate with fate:

> Fate wings with ev'ry wish th' afflictive dart,
> Each gift of nature, and each grace of art.

Juvenal, in remarking that the higher one builds the greater is the fall, sees human wishes as extravagant and ill-judged in that men refuse to choose what is good for them. But Johnson (as his imagery of fire itself suggests) also seems more conscious of some inner compulsion. Through his various examples, he not only suggests that life is precarious and embattled, but divines how man's very nature contributes, almost of necessity, to his fall. Juvenal's Sejanus 'did not know what things were to be desired' ('*quid optandum foret ignorasse*'); but Johnson's Wolsey falls not through ignorance but, as it were, through an ungovernable wish to do so:

For why did Wolsey near the steeps of fate,
On weak foundations raise th' enormous weight?
Why but to sink beneath misfortune's blow,
With louder ruin to the gulphs below?

When Democritus is invoked early in the poem, it is suggested that this sage would have plenty to laugh at in witnessing the antics of 'Britain's modish tribe'. Yet Johnson moves on from there to explore the very real misery that on all sides encompasses human life. The shift in tone and perspective is anticipated in these lines:

Unnumber'd suppliants croud Preferment's gate,
Athirst for wealth, and burning to be great;
Delusive Fortune hears th' incessant call,
They mount, they shine, evaporate, and fall.

The element of the ridiculous is qualified by the deeper intensity or pathos suggested by the language ('unnumbered', 'croud', 'athirst', 'burning to be great'). And a further cause of human misery, one that cuts cruelly deep, is suggested in the lines that follow:

On ev'ry stage the foes of peace attend,
Hate dogs their flight, and insult mocks their end.
Love ends with hope, the sinking statesman's door
Pours in the morning worshiper no more.

Here we are shown not merely the kind of pretended love that 'ends with hope', but how relentless the persecution of fallen greatness can be. Because of this we are not surprised to learn that the third couplet of the poem had originally read:

Then say how fierce desire and raging Hate
O'erspread with snares the clouded maze of Fate.

Certainly this wording points to something unmistakably present in *The Vanity of Human Wishes* – the inveterate hatred or malice that turns man against man. It is there in the lines on Archbishop Laud, which represent the culmination of the portrait of the scholar. It is strikingly and chillingly hinted at in the deft and economical portrait of Wolsey. And it is felt, too, in the portrait of Charles of Sweden, who becomes a prey not just to his own arrogant ambitions, but to something altogether more ignominious, even underhand.

V

When Johnson came to review dispassionately the aims of a man like Charles, he could see no reason why he should be celebrated. In one of his later periodical essays (*Adventurer* 99) he refused to distinguish between those who intended and those who accomplished 'mischief', adding, 'I would wish Caesar and Catiline, Xerxes and Alexander, Charles and Peter (the Great) huddled together in obscurity or detestation.' The lines on Charles, however, are among Johnson's best and, as T. S. Eliot has said, nothing short of sublime. The 'moral' pointed by this 'name' and the 'tale' it adorns cannot be taken as any less suggestive than what the poem gives us. While Juvenal's corresponding passage describes Hannibal in terms grotesque and contemptuous, Johnson's use of language ensures a more complex response. The initial description is of a figure of superhuman energy and endurance:

A frame of adamant, a soul of fire,
No dangers fright him, and no labours tire.

Yet his presumption, too, is godlike:

Peace courts his hand, but spreads her charms in vain;
'Think nothing gain'd, he cries, till nought remain,
On Moscow's walls till Gothic standards fly,
And all be mine beneath the polar sky.'

The dramatic irony is obvious: the 'nothing' that remains will be Charles's to have. What makes him into almost a tragic figure is our sense of a tremendous energy that goes to waste, of undreamt-of aspirations that come to naught, of seemingly real loss on a quite colossal scale.

Early in the portrait the language hints at the revenge that will be taken upon Charles:

> O'er love, o'er fear, extends his wide domain,
> Unconquer'd lord of pleasure and of pain.

The meaning to be given to 'love' is qualified by the proximity of 'fear': when he is no longer feared, he will no longer need to be 'loved'. Though a curtain is drawn across the actual battle, Charles, up to this point indomitable, is able to survive it. He survives, however, on an alien stage as less than a shadow of himself, the prey of meaner men:

> The vanquish'd hero leaves his broken bands,
> And shews his miseries in distant lands;
> Condemn'd a needy supplicant to wait,
> While ladies interpose, and slaves debate.

To state, as Johnson does, that this is an 'error' of 'Chance' seems curiously to deny the implications of his earlier lines. Charles's destiny is determined by his character; and it involves suffering a final ignominy at the hands of the world he had sought to conquer:

> His fall was destin'd to a barren strand,
> A petty fortress, and a dubious hand.

The original draft had read 'nameless hand', but the revision is an improvement. Though the meaning 'of questionable or suspected character' is not recorded for 'dubious' until much later, in its context Johnson's use of the word carries overtones of the dubiousness of the act, almost of the underhand that lies in wait for man.

In the portrait of the scholar it is the world and not the individual which finally stands condemned. Again the portrait opens with a description of all-consuming ambition:

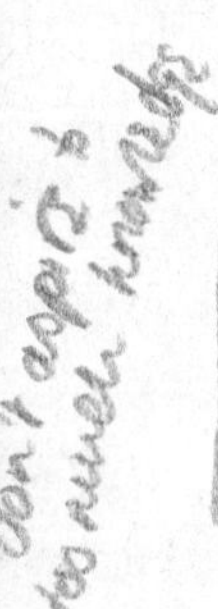

When first the college rolls receive his name,
The young enthusiast quits his ease for fame;
Through all his veins the fever of renown
Burns from the strong contagion of the gown.

Such 'enthusiasm' (a double-edged word in the period) seems both laudable and yet like a disease. Even supposing it were possible to 'indulge the gen'rous heat' of scholarly inquiry until universal knowledge had been gained, to what end? Something approaching admonition is hinted at in the lines,

Deign on the passing world to turn thine eyes,
And pause awhile from letters, to be wise.

Is it, then, that the scholar's 'dreams' persist beyond all reason? The answer comes not only from the way the passage ends, but from the imagery of some of its most evocative lines:

Should Beauty blunt on fops her fatal dart,
Nor claim the triumph of a letter'd heart;
Should no disease thy torpid veins invade,
Nor Melancholy's phantoms haunt thy shade.

In one of his periodical essays Johnson was to write: 'To strive with difficulties and to conquer them, is the highest human felicity; the next is to strive, and deserve to conquer' (*Adventurer* 111). And this is what the dedicated scholar deserves to do, notwithstanding the indifference or envy of the world.

In this portrait's best known couplet, Johnson changed the reading 'garret' to 'patron' after his brush with Lord Chesterfield over the *Dictionary*:

There mark what ills the scholar's life assail,
Toil, envy, want, the patron, and the jail.

He could, too, bring Lydiat and Galileo forward as examples of the world's neglect and persecution, while his royalist and Anglican sympathies allowed him to present Laud as a victim marked out by his learning. What brings about this fall is made explicit, and it is unmistakably sinister:

See when the vulgar 'scape, despis'd or aw'd,
Rebellion's vengeful talons seize on Laud.

From meaner minds, tho' smaller fines content,
The plunder'd palace or sequester'd rent;
Mark'd out by dangerous parts he meets the shock,
And fatal Learning leads him to the block.

Often in Juvenal the threat to wealth or greatness comes from the emperor; but the forces that in *The Vanity of Human Wishes* combine against greatness or insult its fall are, at times, felt to be even more insidious or disturbing. Johnson was to dwell elsewhere, not only on the 'pain' and 'discontent' wide-spread among men, but also on the 'malice'. 'The highest of mankind', he writes in *Adventurer* 120, 'must always be even more exposed, in the same degree as they are elevated above others, to the treachery of dependents, the calumny of defamers, and the violence of opponents'. As an illustration from his poem, nothing surpasses the account of Wolsey's fall:

At length his sov'reign frowns – the train of state
Mark the keen glance, and watch the sign to hate.
Where-e'er he turns he meets a stranger's eye,
His suppliants scorn him, and his followers fly.

These lines gain in intensity by focusing on the reaction of the Court. More than that, they force the reader to see this through, as it were, Wolsey's eyes; and the most searing detail of all is that his former 'suppliants' now *scorn* him.

VI

It is this kind of perception which, together with the unevenness of the last section, raises doubts about the poem's ending. This has, however, been almost universally praised, and what has been stressed is the 'serenity' of the closing lines, or even that they are 'eminently cheerful'.[4] Obviously Johnson intended them to be a fitting conclusion, and he sought to link the ending to the body of his poem by specific verbal parallels. Several passages, including the reference to 'the suppliant voice' and that to Wolsey's 'suppliants', are recalled by the line,

Still raise for good the supplicating voice

(though we may, frankly, wonder whether Wolsey's 'suppliants' would 'raise' their voices for the 'good' suggested here). Probably Johnson changed the early line in his manuscript, 'Then say how fierce desire and raging Hate', to, 'Then say how hope and fear, desire and hate', in order that this line might be echoed by the first line of the poem's concluding section, 'Where then shall Hope and Fear their objects find?' In the context of the poem, however, what sense is to be given to these terms? Both hope and fear are said to form 'snares' for 'wav'ring man', even though it had been traditional to represent hope as necessary or consoling to those in straitened circumstances, and fear as a warning to the fortunate that their happiness would not last. Johnson's poem certainly illustrates the vanity of human hopes, but what space does it give to the antithesis built into the rhetoric (except in so far as fear can mean something in relation to hope, almost as its reverse side)?

When Johnson later put 'hope' and 'fear' together in *The Rambler*, he was concerned to point out that no amount of planning can anticipate the randomness of human life: 'If it be improper to fear events which must happen, it is yet more evidently contrary to right reason to fear those which may never happen, and which, if they should come upon us, we cannot resist' (no. 29). He was not, even so, advocating Stoicism. His onslaught on this in the poem,

> Must dull Suspence corrupt the stagnant mind?
> Must helpless man, in ignorance sedate,
> Roll darkling down the torrent of his fate?

recalls his conviction that man 'must, in opposition to the Stoic precept, teach his desires to fix upon external things' (*Rambler* 89):

> Must no dislike alarm, no wishes rise,
> No cries attempt the mercies of the skies?

Is there not, however, some juggling going on here? 'Must no dislike alarm . . .?' Can the 'hate' and 'insult' presented in the poem be effectively reduced to this? The next couplet compounds the problem (even though it shows clearly the direction in which Johnson is pushing the ending):

> Enquirer, cease, petitions yet remain,
> Which heav'n may hear, nor deem religion vain.

The person being addressed here is ostensibly someone who has surveyed life in the terms of the poem, who has seen man 'tread the dreary paths without a guide', and who is being credited with a concern to find some answer. One perspective of the 'hate' and 'insult' that attend man's path is what the poem has provided, but already another perspective is being imposed on this. The truth that has been revealed about human nature and human life is being countered by an assertion that the real 'truth' lies elsewhere. And in how naked a manner the assertiveness of the writing makes clear.

In the lines that follow, man is exhorted to leave to 'heaven' the determination of his lot – these, in fact, being the very words Johnson was to use in *Adventurer* 111 in quoting approvingly what he took to be Juvenal's advice. Juvenal is perhaps not as simple as this, but the real point for the reader of *The Vanity of Human Wishes* is that the transition Johnson is here seeking to make – especially in the further meaning he implies 'hope' can have – corresponds to the move that he was elsewhere so concerned to make. As we shall see in the next chapter, many of the periodical essays show a degree of insistence that borders on the obsessional. An example is *Rambler* 184, the only essay which has as its motto Juvenal's lines suggesting that man leave it all to the gods, where Johnson counters his sense of the uncertainty of human life with the assertion that nothing is 'governed by chance', that 'the universe is under the perpetual superintendence of him who created it'. A similar insistence is evident in some of the poem's concluding lines:

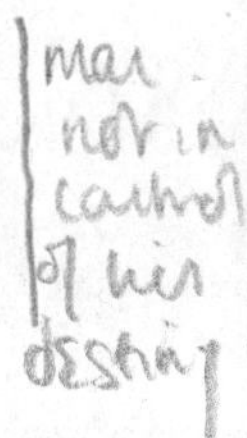

> These goods for man the laws of heaven ordain,
> These goods he grants, who grants the pow'r to gain.

Though the words 'goods' and 'pow'r' are here being asked to do a lot of work, Johnson does not manage to blot out the poem's underlying pessimism. The lines suggest, rather, a desperate clinging to presumed verities; and it is precisely this that makes them so interesting.

As the preceding lines illustrate, these 'goods' are not faith, love and hope, but faith, love and 'patience' – as though Johnson is forced to acknowledge that the only 'hope' a Christian can realistically achieve is something very like patience. Significantly, his awareness of unhappiness and his attempt at reassurance go hand in hand. Yet for all the assertiveness in this last section of the poem, there is, finally, no falseness. A Boswell might have detected in the poet's exhortation his 'celestial' frame of mind, but what remains impressive is surely Johnson's honesty to his own perceptions – that insight conveyed by the closing words which is true to the experience of the poem and the observations on human life it contains:

> With these celestial wisdom calms the mind,
> And makes the happiness *she does not find* (my italics).

An acknowledgment of life's unhappiness is what we are finally left with.

VII

Johnson brought to the Augustan tradition of poetry an individual voice and seriousness. The weight and sonorousness of his best lines (including some lines from the ending of *The Vanity of Human Wishes*) fairly 'sing in the mind';[5] and what makes these lines memorable is the peculiar energy of Johnson's wit that focuses so much of his experience of life. One need not go to his greatest poems to illustrate this; it can be seen, for example, in the epitaph he composed while stirring his tea, 'in a state of meditation', for the poor violinist Claudy Phillips:

> Phillips! whose touch harmonious could remove
> The pangs of guilty pow'r, and hapless love,
> Rest here, distrest by poverty no more,
> Find here that calm thou gav'st so oft before;
> Sleep undisturb'd within this peaceful shrine,
> Till angels wake thee with a note like thine.

The wit of 'touch', as it applies to both the musician's and the healer's skill (Johnson, we remember, had as a child been 'touched' for the King's Evil), extends throughout these verses, and, as Christopher Ricks has said, 'impinges beautifully on the dour fact of Phillips' lowly poverty'.[6] In the last line it brings to him the promise of a serene and fitting awakening.

Johnson's impromptu verse does not always rise to this level of poetry. Yet it is often accomplished. The lines 'To Mrs. Thrale, on her completing her Thirty-fifth Year' she wrote down as Johnson composed them, and they reveal not only his sense of fun but the readiness of his wit. As he himself remarked, it was her fault for coming 'for poetry to a dictionary maker': 'You may observe', he said, 'that the rhymes run in alphabetical order exactly.' While these lines should not be taken any more seriously than that, criticism must also be made of Johnson's more serious verse where it fails to rise above the merely conventional. Sometimes the inherited mode remains tired and lifeless, as in these lines from *London*,

> There ev'ry bush with nature's musick rings,
> There ev'ry breeze bears health upon its wings.

Here Johnson relies on what he assumes will be the reader's response, without sufficiently creating this by a disciplined and evocative use of language.

A number of his occasional poems were addressed to women, and some of these were composed virtually impromptu. 'To a Young Lady on her Birthday', which was probably written as early as 1727 in Edmund Hector's presence, depicts the poet in the conventional pose of lover:

> This tributary verse receive, my fair,
> Warm with an ardent lover's fondest pray'r.

Such poems often display an elaborate gallantry, which can serve as a means of moral suasion ('Those sovereign charms with strictest care employ'), or of paying a graceful compliment. 'To Miss Hickman Playing on the Spinet' – which in imagining the lady as a greater Timotheus shows an obvious debt to Dryden's *Alexander's Feast* – concludes happily enough:

> Had Stella's gentle touches mov'd the lyre,
> Soon had the Monarch felt a nobler fire,
> No more delighted with destructive war,
> Ambitious only now to please the fair,
> Resign'd his thirst of empire to her charms,
> And found a thousand worlds in Stella's arms.

A deeper and more ambiguous note is struck in 'To Miss —— on her playing upon the Harpsichord in a Room Hung with some Flower-Pieces of her own Painting'. What begins as a compliment to the power of Stella's art soon becomes a warning against approaching it too closely:

Ah! think not, in the dang'rous hour,
The nymph fictitious, as the flow'r,
But shun, rash youth, the gay alcove,
Nor tempt the snares of wily love.

Johnson brings together the fictive and the real in order to question the purpose of such artifice:

But on these regions of delight,
Might Truth intrude, with daring flight,
Could Stella, sprightly, fair and young,
One moment hear the moral song,
Instruction with her flow'rs might spring,
And wisdom warble from her string.

This implied admonition becomes a potential compliment as the poet, now addressing the nymph directly, suggests that the ordered harmony of her art can provide a pattern for human behaviour:

Thy pictures shall thy conduct frame,
Consistent still, though not the same;
Thy musick teach the nobler art,
To tune the regulated heart.

It is as though Johnson can now bring himself to approach Stella more closely because 'Truth' has transformed her inherently seductive powers.

Johnson wrote several prologues, and the most celebrated of these was composed for the opening at Drury Lane in 1747. Garrick had newly acquired a joint share in the management of the theatre, and by improving the quality of the entertainment it offered, he hoped to raise the taste of the audience. The prologue opens with Johnson's memorable lines on Shakespeare:

When Learning's triumph o'er her barb'rous foes
First rear'd the stage, immortal Shakespear rose;
Each change of many-colour'd life he drew,
Exhausted worlds, and then imagin'd new:

Existence saw him spurn her bounded reign,
And panting Time toil'd after him in vain:
His pow'rful strokes presiding truth impress'd,
And unresisted passion storm'd the breast.

Shakespeare represents the high point of English dramatic achievement, and there follows a condensed and pointed review of the subsequent history of the stage:

The wits of Charles found easier ways to fame,
Nor wished for Johnson's art, or Shakespear's flame;
Themselves they studied, as they felt, they writ,
Intrigue was plot, obscenity was wit.

In recording such changes of taste, and especially in deploring the shows and farces of the present, Johnson lays an injunction on the audience and brings home to it its ultimate responsibility for improved cultural and moral standards:

Then prompt no more the follies you decry,
As tyrants doom their tools of guilt to die;
'Tis yours this night to bid the reign commence
Of rescu'd Nature, and reviving Sense;
To chase the charms of sound, the pomp of show,
For useful mirth, and salutary woe;
Bid scenic virtue form the rising age,
And Truth diffuse her radiance from the stage.

In 1750 Johnson produced a prologue for a performance of *Comus* which he helped organize as a benefit for Milton's granddaughter, who had been discovered living in poverty. His lines, though sometimes forced, contain an eloquent tribute to Milton's greatness, and an appeal (designed to shame 'the mean pensions' of the present) to the 'patriot crouds' to honour by their 'gen'rous zeal' their great poet's lowly descendant. Far different in spirit is the prologue Johnson wrote – probably during a period of depression – for his friend Goldsmith's *The Good-Natured Man* (1768). It begins sombrely, and the imagery, which alludes to the approaching election, is scarcely calculated to mollify the audience:

The busy candidates for power and fame,
Have hopes, and fears, and wishes, just the same;

Disabled both to combat, or to fly,
Must hear all taunts, and hear without reply.
Uncheck'd on both, loud rabbles vent their rage,
As mongrels bay the lion in a cage.

Johnson did not refrain from speaking his mind even in a prologue! Yet he did this with more success when Hugh Kelly's *A Word to the Wise*, which had at its first performance been damned by the author's political opponents, was later revived as a benefit for his widow and children. Without compromising his own literary standards, Johnson makes a weighty and moving appeal for fair play:

Let no resentful petulance invade
Th' oblivious grave's inviolable shade.
Let one great payment every claim appease,
And him who cannot hurt, allow to please;
To please by scenes unconscious of offence,
By harmless merriment, or useful sense.
Where aught of bright, or fair, the piece displays,
Approve it only – 'tis too late to praise.
If want of skill, or want of care appear,
Forbear to hiss – the poet cannot hear.

Two of Johnson's best short poems were written late in life. In 1780 he sent to his friend Mrs Thrale 'A Short Song of Congratulation', on the occasion of her husband's foolish nephew Sir John Lade's coming of age. Lade once called across a room to ask Johnson whether he advised him to marry, only to receive the sharp side of his tongue: 'I would advise no man to marry, Sir, who is not likely to propagate understanding.' This reproof, like Johnson's lines, seems to have been deserved, for Lade went on to fulfil their prediction by squandering a large fortune. The poem begins by ironically giving the kind of advice that the impatient young heir would have welcomed:

Long-expected one and twenty
  Ling'ring year at last is flown,
Pomp and pleasure, pride and plenty
  Great Sir John, are all your own.

Loosen'd from the minor's tether,
  Free to mortgage or to sell,
Wild as wind, and light as feather
  Bid the slaves of thrift farewell.

Call the Bettys, Kates, and Jennys
  Ev'ry name that laughs at care,
Lavish of your grandsire's guineas,
  Show the spirit of an heir.

The rollicking metre exuberantly captures the young man's extravagance. Later the joke is openly turned against the wanton spendthrift:

Wealth, Sir John, was made to wander,
  Let it wander as it will;
See the jocky, see the pander,
  Bid them come, and take their fill.

When the bonny blade carouses,
  Pockets full, and spirits high,
What are acres? What are houses?
  Only dirt, or wet or dry.

If the guardian or the mother
  Tell the woes of wilful waste,
Scorn their counsel and their pother,
  You can hang or drown at last.

In 1782 Johnson wrote 'On the Death of Dr. Robert Levet', in memory of the poor, self-styled physician who had for so many years received shelter in his house and been his daily companion at breakfast. The age's expectation of elegy is realized in the poem for, as a statement of grief, it has a direct and melancholy seriousness. The opening lines set the tone with their characteristic expression of the illusory nature of hope and the travail of human life:

Condemn'd to hope's delusive mine,
  As on we toil from day to day,
By sudden blasts, or slow decline,
  Our social comforts drop away.

Johnson respected Levet, and in moving lines he puts on record the hidden worth of such a man:

Yet still he fills affection's eye,
  Obscurely wise, and coarsely kind;
Nor, letter'd arrogance, deny
  Thy praise to merit unrefin'd.

When fainting nature call'd for aid,
  And hov'ring death prepared the blow,
His vig'rous remedy display'd
  The power of art without the show.

In misery's darkest caverns known,
  His useful care was ever nigh,
Where hopeless anguish pour'd his groan,
  And lonely want retir'd to die.

Levet had constantly administered to the poor, who often had no money to pay him, and Johnson praises the unstinting use to which he had put his limited powers. The wit of his lines is, in fact, grounded in a sober and just appraisal of Levet's virtues (though such lines from such an author, who was always afraid that he might himself be judged an unprofitable servant, also hover somewhere between praise and prayer[7]):

His virtues walk'd their narrow round,
  Nor made a pause, nor left a void;
And sure th' Eternal Master found
  The single talent well employ'd.

Johnson wrote a number of Latin poems. What began as a school exercise (at Oxford he produced a version of Pope's *Messiah*) became in later life a means of giving expression to a wide variety of more personal feelings. The verses he wrote (1772) after completing the revision of his *Dictionary* make poignant mention of his sense of the *taedium vitae* – the feeling of sluggishness and melancholy that so often afflicted him. On Skye the following year he wrote two odes, and in each the rugged and unfamiliar landscape leads to personal reflection. In the first ('*Ponti profundis clausa recessibus*' – 'Enclosed in the deep recesses of the sea') he reflects on how inadequate man is, without God's help, in calming the surges of the breast. In the second, addressed to Mrs Thrale, he invokes her presence in a mood between sweet reminiscence and conscious gallantry. Another engaging Latin poem takes as its subject the stream at Lichfield where his father taught him to swim. '*Christianus Perfectus*', which, it has been suggested, owes something to the influence of William Law (author of *A Practical Treatise upon Christian Perfection*, 1726), stresses 'the importance of renouncing the world and its pleasures, of living in holiness with every thought directed towards God, of subduing all rebellious feelings, and of striving always to imitate Christ'.[8]

VIII

In setting out for London with the young Garrick, Johnson carried three acts of an unfinished tragedy in his pocket. His own hopes on the occasion are reflected in the recommendation his old friend Gilbert Walmesley gave him: 'Johnson is a very good scholar and poet, and I have great hopes will turn out a fine tragedy writer.' It took him, however, some little time to finish his play, which is based on the story of Irene, a beautiful Greek captured at the sack of Constantinople, who became the adored mistress of Mahomet II. Early hopes of having it staged soon faded: Charles Fleetwood, then manager of Drury Lane, though he gave, it seems, some vague promise, made no definite move to bring the play forward. It was not until Garrick became a manager of the theatre that plans to do so were formed. Early in 1749 it was produced as 'Mahomet and Irene', with a strong cast.

Johnson treated the occasion as an important event in his life, ordering for himself a scarlet waistcoat laced with gold and a gold-laced hat. The production, however, was hardly a cause for triumph since the play was greeted with only polite applause. (The original audience shouted 'Murder' on seeing Irene strangled on stage with a Turkish bowstring – a misguided attempt to enliven the action which Garrick subsequently dropped.) That the play ran for nine nights was really a tribute to the lavish costumes, Garrick's versatile acting, and his astuteness in providing additional, lighter entertainment after the last three performances. The run gave its author three third-night benefits, which, together with the £100 paid for the copyright, meant some welcome financial remuneration for the trouble the play had caused him. It was never revived, and Johnson seems to have taken his disappointment philosophically: in his own words, he remained unmoved 'like the Monument'. Many years later he left a room in which *Irene* was being read, and being asked the reason answered, 'Sir, I thought it had been better.' Once he was introduced to a Mr Pot who thought his play 'the finest tragedy of modern times'. To this came the tart reply: 'If Pot says so, Pot lies!'

Though the story of Irene had been the subject of several earlier plays, in Johnson's hands it becomes a vehicle for presenting apostasy as a clear-cut moral issue: Irene is condemned for embracing another religion purely from motives of expediency. Unfortunately the speeches are written as though to be declaimed rather than spoken, and the characters therefore seem detached from whatever situation professedly involves them. The central issue remains merely a subject for Irene's former friend, the virtuous Aspasia, to expatiate on:

The soul once tainted with so foul a crime,
No more shall glow with friendship's hallow'd ardour:
Those holy Beings, whose superiour care
Guides erring mortals to the paths of virtue,
Affrighted at impiety like thine,
Resign their charge to baseness and to ruin.

This speech forms part of the debate between Aspasia and Irene that occurs at the approximate mid-point of the play (III. viii), and the importance of this scene for Johnson is evident from the number of lines in it which appear in his manuscript first-draft (now in the British Museum), and which make up Aspasia's arguments, not Irene's replies. The evidence, then, points to what hardly needs proving – that the question of apostasy was uppermost in the author's mind, and that Aspasia functions as his mouthpiece. Later, Johnson has even Mahomet condemn Irene's apostasy:

Ambition only gave her to my arms,
By reason not convinc'd, nor won by love.
Ambition was her crime, but meaner folly

Dooms me to loath at once, and doat on falshood,
And idolize th' apostate I contemn.

In reflecting on his First Vizier's treachery, Mahomet sees himself as one who, though apparently successful in 'love' and 'war', is really 'wretched in his double triumph;/His fav'rite faithless, and his mistress base'. Cali Bassa's attempt to overthrow Mahomet provides a further element that helps to fill out the plot, and both elements are again brought together when Mustapha announces to Irene that she is condemned by the Sultan:

Mustapha: Hard was the strife of Justice and of Love;
But now 'tis o'er, and Justice has prevail'd.
Know'st thou not Cali? know'st thou not Demetrius?
Irene: Bold slave, I know them both – I know them traytors.
Mustapha: Perfidious! – yes – too well thou know'st them traytors.
Irene: Their treason throws no stain upon Irene.
This day has proved my fondness for the Sultan;
He knew Irene's truth.
Mustapha: The Sultan knows it,
He knows how near apostacy to treason.

Some irony surrounds the use of words like 'perfidy' and 'fidelity' (which have a common stem). The Greek Demetrius, who loves Aspasia, and who, in order to free his country, falls in with Cali's design, defends Leontius as entirely without 'perfidy', and therefore as eminently worthy of being allowed to join the plot against Mahomet. Later Cali avows to a Mahomet already aware of his treachery his complete 'fidelity'. But no complications – at least none worked out in dramatic terms – are allowed to threaten what the Prologue had announced as the play's 'mighty moral'. When the clear-sighted Aspasia expresses to Demetrius her regret that 'mingled guilt' should 'pollute the sacred cause', his reply takes the form of a convenient (though not unfamiliar) rationalization:

Permitted oft, though not inspir'd by Heav'n,
Successful treasons punish impious kings.

Irene, then, reads more like a treatise than a play. The undramatic quality of its speeches shows a lack of dramatic imagination at the level of its very conception. Shakespeare's kind of 'negative capability' (to use Keats's phrase) was entirely beyond Johnson, who anyway found himself unable to be in uncertainties without irritably reaching after fact and reason. But though he failed as a dramatist, he was soon to hit on a more congenial form. In the periodical essays of the next decade, and particularly *The Rambler*, he found an appropriate vehicle for what as a moralist he wanted to say.

4

Periodical Essays

I

In the 1750s Johnson produced the works which made him so famous in his own day – *The Rambler*, the *Dictionary*, and *Rasselas*. Nor was his output confined to these. During 1753–4 he contributed a large number of essays to John Hawkesworth's periodical *The Adventurer*; then he published *Proposals* (1756) for an edition of Shakespeare's plays; and in 1758 began *The Idler*, a series of weekly essays that ran for two years. In some ways, however, these were difficult years for Johnson. Tetty died in 1752, a loss which he felt keenly. Later his mother died (1759), and he regretted that he had never been back to Lichfield to see her. Twice he was arrested for debt, and had to be relieved by friends. He was also, on occasion, deeply depressed, and the loss of reason in the poet Collins, for whom he felt a tender concern, brought once more before him his own fear of madness. A letter (21 December 1754) to his Oxford friend Thomas Warton, in which he alludes to the death of his wife more than two years before, gives a touching picture of his mental state:

> I have ever since seemed to myself broken off from mankind a kind of solitary wanderer in the wild of life, without any certain direction, or fixed point of view. A gloomy gazer on a world to which I have little relation.

Writing provided Johnson with one means of keeping in touch with mankind, but it hardly gave him the direct contact with others he seems so desperately to have needed. He set great store by friendship; for him it was a cordial, truly the wine of life. And these were at least years when he met some of those who became his closest friends. Perhaps most important was Sir Joshua Reynolds, to whom Johnson was to write in 1764 as 'almost the only man I call a friend'; but there were also others who became important to him: the actor Arthur Murphy, who impressed him by the warmth of his regard and wrote an account of him after his death; Thomas Percy, later Bishop of Dromore, who edited the *Reliques*; Charles Burney, the charming and talented scholar of music who so won Johnson's affection; and two younger men, Bennet Langton of Lincolnshire and the lively Topham Beauclerk.

Johnson is reported to have said that *The Rambler* provided him with 'relief' from his work on the *Dictionary*. Boswell notes that contributing to *The Adventurer* 'relieved the drudgery of his Dictionary, and the melancholy of his grief' after his wife's death. And it has been plausibly conjectured that *The Idler* provided a similar diversion from his Shakesperian labours.[1] Yet these works are by no means slight or unimportant – indeed the reverse. In general they gave him the opportunity of expressing what he had thought about longest and considered most important. In his later *Lives of the Poets* Johnson was to allude as follows to Milton's proposed scheme of education:

> The truth is that the knowledge of external nature, and the sciences which that knowledge requires or includes, are not the great or the frequent business of the human mind. Whether we provide for action or conversation, whether we wish to be useful or pleasing, the first requisite is the religious and moral knowledge of right and wrong; the next is an acquaintance with the history of mankind, and with those examples which may be said to embody truth, and prove by events the reasonableness of opinions.

'We are', he added, 'perpetually moralists . . . our intercourse with intellectual nature is necessary.' The truth of this, so far as Johnson himself was concerned, can be clearly demonstrated from his periodical essays. In them (and especially *The Rambler*) he is constantly and seriously engaged with moral questions.

Many readers, however, came to *The Rambler* with their taste formed by Addison's *Spectator*, which, from the time of its first publication, had enjoyed a great vogue. They expected from

Johnson the same whimsical humour, the same intimacy of tone, and similar pictures of contemporary society; but what they got was something very different, and it took some time for them to adjust to his more serious tone and subject-matter. Sales of the original issues were said to have been hardly encouraging, and the novelist Samuel Richardson suggested in the one paper he wrote for Johnson that the Rambler should 'oftener take cognizance of the manners of the better half of the species', and record for the coming generation the 'fashionable follies' of their mothers as the Spectator had done of their grandmothers. Johnson, however, never stooped to this (and arguably would not have had the lightness of touch for it), even though others held similar views. Miss Hester Mulso (afterwards Mrs Chapone), in requesting some personal details of the author, warned him that, unless he concerned himself with 'the manners of the age', not even 'the genius and correctness of an Addison' would save him 'from neglect' (no. 10). Because the essays were generally regarded as too sombre, his friend Elizabeth Carter sent him two papers that aimed at something more consoling (no. 44) or brighter (no. 100) than his usual vein. Yet in doing so she was scarcely being critical, for in her second paper, on 'modish pleasures', she ironically remarks that if the Rambler would confine himself to these, he would promote 'what everyone seems to confess the true purpose of human existence, perpetual dissipation'.

Johnson catches up such complaints with a certain wry humour:

> Some were angry that the Rambler did not, like the Spectator, introduce himself to the acquaintance of the public, by an account of his own birth and studies, an enumeration of his adventures, and a description of his physiognomy. Others soon began to remark that he was a solemn, serious, dictatorial writer, without sprightliness or gaiety, and called out with vehemence for mirth and humour. Another admonished him to have a special eye upon the various clubs of this great city, and informed him that much of the Spectator's vivacity was laid out upon such assemblies (no. 23).

On another occasion he indulges in a spoof on himself. Writing in the guise of a correspondent who has a tale of woe to proffer, Johnson slyly remarks:

> I cannot but imagine the start of attention awakened by this welcome hint; and at this instant see the Rambler snuffing his candle, rubbing his spectacles, stirring his fire, locking out interruption, and settling himself in his easy chair, that he may enjoy a new calamity without disturbance (no. 109).

He seems, however, to have paid some heed to the complaints of his original readers by trying to inject some variety into the form of his essays: increasingly he came to include the kinds of papers for which *The Spectator* had set a precedent – portraits, allegories, narratives set in distant or exotic parts, and papers on literary topics. The portraits (what he called 'the pictures of life') range from the narrative of character and circumstance, sometimes extended over more than one essay, to the brief sketch designed to illustrate some aspect of human nature. Once or twice a portrait broaches a topic that is then taken up in the following paper; and a sprinkling of essays are cast in letter form – sometimes above an appropriate signature – without being in other respects essentially different from what in his final number he called 'the essays professedly serious'.

'The essays professedly serious', he writes, 'if I have been able to execute my own intentions, will be found exactly conformable to the precepts of Christianity, without any accommodation to the licentiousness and levity of the present age.' Doubtless these were the essays to which he was referring when he later singled out this periodical for special praise: 'My other works', he said, 'are wine and water; but my *Rambler* is pure wine.' It is not only his statement in the final number that stands as a defence of his tone and subject-matter. The seriousness with which he approached his task is also evident from the prayer he composed on beginning *The Rambler*: 'Almighty God, the giver of all good things, without whose help all labour is ineffectual, and without whose grace all wisdom is folly, grant, I beseech Thee, that in this my undertaking thy Holy Spirit may not be witheld from me, but that I may promote thy glory, and the Salvation both of myself and others.' The didactic nature of the essays was as seriously grounded as this; to quote Boswell, the Rambler 'writes like a teacher'. Yet he is, to quote Boswell again, 'a majestic teac as we shall see, it is the quality of Johnson's engagement makes his discussion of moral questions so searching, weig and profound.

II

Johnson's aim in *The Rambler* was 'to consider the moral discipline of the mind, and to promote the increase of virtue rather than of learning'. As an aim this was, he thought, both new and necessary:

> This inquiry seems to have been neglected for want of remembering that all action has its origin in the mind, and that therefore to suffer the thoughts to be vitiated, is to poison the fountains of morality. Irregular desires will produce licentious practices; what men allow themselves to wish they will soon believe, and will be at last incited to execute what they please themselves with contriving (no. 8).

Here Johnson links the themes to which he constantly returns. In stressing the need for all to examine closely their inner thoughts and motives, he acknowledges, with almost a felt conviction, how easily one may be seduced from the path of virtue, and how difficult is the recovery of lost ground. And in pointing to the dangers of self-deception (including self-justification), he places within a firm moral context what in *Rasselas* he was later to call 'the dangerous prevalence of imagination'.

The importance Johnson attached to self-knowledge is abundantly clear from his life and writings. Boswell notes that he was 'at all times a curious examiner of the human mind', and Mrs Thrale that he was 'ever on the watch to spy out those stains of original corruption, so easily discovered by a penetrating observer even in the purest minds.' The Rambler is very much an 'observer' of this sort, and his essays take a long, hard look at human behaviour. People, he realizes, have a very human capacity for deceiving themselves. Either they mistake their talents by assuming roles they cannot sustain; or they decide in their own favour, not by objective standards, but by measuring their conduct against that of others. Incidental acts of goodness they reckon as habitual, and frequent failings as merely occasional lapses. Some, Johnson sees (with perhaps his former friend Savage in mind), are only too ready to equate 'the praise of goodness with the practice' (no. 28); and most are insulated from the kind of criticism that would effectively open their eyes – whether through the pressure of business, or by surrounding themselves with those who are unfit, or not sufficiently disinterested, plainly to tell them their faults.

In all of these instances Johnson is dealing not so much with manifest and palpable wickedness, as with 'the numerous stratagems, by which pride endeavours to recommend folly to regard' (no. 20). It is his sense of the insidiousness of these that leads him to suggest ways of exposing them. He calls for periods of self-examination; not only did he keep a 'journal' or diary, but he encouraged in others this means of reviewing past conduct. And in his essay on biography (no. 60), he is, as we have seen, very ready to insist on the 'instruction' that this can provide. If the reader is faced with a character drawn from the life, he will, it is assumed, be forced to glimpse himself in the mirror of another's shifts and stratagems, and consequently to see more clearly into his own heart and confront human motives at firsthand. Yet Johnson is realistic enough to admit all those things that work against self-discovery, and his objection to biography as it was usually practised is that 'more knowledge may be gained of a man's real character, by a short conversation with one of his servants, than from a formal and studied narrative, begun with his pedigree, and ended with his funeral.'

Johnson's insight into human conduct is sufficiently penetrating. He takes, for example, strong exception to the remark which he attributes to Swift (but which was actually Pope's) that men are 'grateful in the same degree as they are resentful' (no. 4). Part of his objection is, characteristically, to the implied determinism that 'supposes man to act from a brute impulse, and pursue a certain degree of inclination, without any choice of the object'. Particularly noteworthy, however, are his comments on pride: 'Pride, which produces quickness of resentment, will obstruct gratitude, by unwillingness to admit that inferiority which obligation implies; and it is very unlikely, that he who cannot think he receives a favour will acknowledge or repay it.' Also noteworthy is his account of envy:

> All envy is proportionate to desire; we are uneasy at the attainments of another, according as we think our own happiness would be advanced by the addition of that which he witholds from us; and, therefore, whatever depresses immoderate wishes, will, at the same time, set the heart free from the corrosion of envy, and exempt us from that vice which is, above most others, tormenting to ourselves, hateful to the world, and productive of mean artifices, and sordid projects (no. 17).

The intelligence of this kind of analysis is matched by the strenuousness with which it is put forward. Surprisingly, Mrs Thrale was the only contemporary to notice a link between Johnson's essays and the book which had so profoundly influenced him, Law's *Serious Call*. The same point has been made more recently. Though Law was by temperament very different from Johnson, his 'conception of the Christian life and the exigency of his standards' is something that carries over into these essays.[2] Their peculiar resonance comes from this: they open up questions that touched Johnson deeply. Whereas his thoughts on these had often to be confined to the pages of his diary, in *The Rambler* he is able to indulge in a different kind of therapy by exploring and dwelling on them publicly and at length.

In these essays we encounter an idea that permeates the whole of Johnson's experience of life:

> So few of the hours of life are filled up with objects adequate to the mind of man, and so frequently are we in want of present pleasure or employment, that we are forced to have recourse every moment to the past and future for supplemental satisfactions, and relieve the vacuities of our being by recollection of former passages, or anticipation of events to come (no. 41).

'The cravings of intellect' (no. 151) find no satisfaction in the present; 'as the intellectual eye takes in a wider prospect, it must be gratified with variety by more rapid flights, and bolder excursions' (no. 150). 'We contrive in minutes what we execute in years' (no. 8). A favourite scheme is entertained until 'it has wholly engrossed the imagination' (no. 17). The mind can be 'corrupted with an inveterate disease of wishing' (no. 73), or given over to fantasizing on forbidden subjects. The emptiness of the present ('the vacuities of our being') has therefore attendant dangers; 'to be idle', writes Johnson, 'is to be vitious' (no. 85). As W. J. Bate has said, he realized 'that the mind is an *activity*, and that if it is not used in one way it will seek satisfaction or at least outlet in other ways'.[3] When not 'busied' in some way, Johnson saw that it would 'embrace anything, however absurd or criminal, rather than be wholly without an object' (no. 85). It was not simply a matter – as he once expressed it to Boswell – of having something to do for the sake of 'driving on the system of life'. 'We are', he wrote, 'in danger of whatever can get possession of our thoughts' (no. 7). For him the 'airy gratifications' of day-dreaming could 'like the poison of opiates . . . invade the soul' (no. 89). And significant is his suggestion that the mind begins, in its lack of other employment, to prey upon itself. One of his eastern tales pictures the rich heir with 'his heart vacant, and his desires, for want of external objects, ravaging himself' (no. 120).

As the intensity of Johnson's language suggests, his concern that the mind should be made to work in a disciplined way went beyond a concern for rational self-control. With the message of Christ's parables present to him as a living truth, he became desperately anxious about putting the present moment to constructive use. His thoroughly traditional belief – that each man would be called to account at the final Judgment – was stated with a peculiar urgency. In drawing attention, with an almost obsessional insistence, to those periods of inaction which must occur even in the busiest life, Johnson regarded life itself as a balance-sheet in which the losses had to be made good. 'The duties of life', he writes, 'are commensurate to its duration, and every day brings its task which, if neglected, is *doubled* on the morrow' (no. 71, my italics).

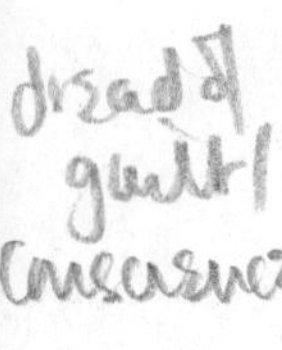

Such passages become more poignant when it is remembered that Johnson so often regarded himself as an unprofitable servant. More than once Boswell refers to his 'constitutional indolence'; it was, indeed, his own admission that 'he always felt an inclination to do nothing'. For this he constantly upbraided himself: again and again in his private meditations he laments his idleness and the time he has mis-spent. And what particularly troubled him was that he had 'neither attempted nor formed any scheme of life' whereby he might 'do good, and please God', that death might 'lay hold' upon him while he was 'yet only designing to live'.[4] The theme of 'the choice of life' was to engage him in *Rasselas* (he had planned his book should have this very title). It was, however, also in his mind when he wrote *The Rambler*, and some of his remarks in the essays make explicit reference to it. 'I have often thought those happy', he writes, 'that have been fixed, from the first dawn of thought, in a determination to some state of life, by the choice of one whose authority may preclude caprice' (no. 19). Always he is concerned to point out that life is short, and that man, though so prone to indulge his hope in plans for the future, has really no time to lose: 'He that steadily endeavours at excellence, in whatever employment, will more benefit mankind than he that hesitates in choosing his part till he is called to the performance' (no. 63).

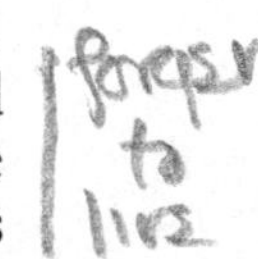

III

Johnson's awareness of how the mind works is no less central to *The Rambler* than to *The Vanity of Human Wishes* and *Rasselas*. In all of these works, and particularly in all three taken together, there is ample evidence of what has been noted before, the capacity his mind had to be embattled against itself. That 'so few of the hours of life are filled up with objects adequate to the mind of man' is a psychological fact that both prompts him to hope and causes him concern. Viewed in one light, it is for him 'a strong proof of the superior and celestial nature of the soul' (no. 41); and notwithstanding this convenient rationalization, Johnson also has a sense of man's capacity, through the workings of imagination, to achieve something and make something of himself and his world. The danger, however, remains that people will either sit down in idleness and complacency, or direct their hopes to impossible and destructive ends. *The Vanity of Human Wishes* gives expression to so grim and tragic a sense of life that it seems to deny the possibility of all hope, resorting instead to an appeal for a Christian kind of 'patience'. In *Rasselas*, on the other hand, the mind's quixotic tendency is explored with sympathetic humour: the importance of hope is a perception there equably, even amiably, entertained. In *The Rambler*, however, Johnson writes more analytically, and the weight of the analysis falls where one would, from his moral and religious preoccupations, expect it to fall.

Realizing that 'the natural flights of the human mind are not from pleasure to pleasure, but from hope to hope', he can see the importance of this as an incentive to achievement: 'There would . . . be few enterprises of great labour or hazard undertaken, if we had not the power of magnifying the advantages which we persuade ourselves to expect from them' (no. 2). At the same time, however, as he recognizes the persistent seductiveness of hope, he appreciates man's understandable reluctance to put it to the test. With a shrewd insight into the motives for procrastinating, he notes that 'the completion of almost every wish is found a disappointment' (no. 71). Yet Johnson could never endorse an approach to life that sought to avoid disappointment by refusing to face up to it. His opposition to the Stoics turns in part on his unwillingness to have the facts of life falsified; and it was also his belief that man must learn to take himself out of himself, by fixing his desires 'upon external things' (no. 89). As he sees it, hope becomes an essential part of man's commitment to life, necessary as a means both of reconciling him to the miseries of the present, and of engaging him in an attempt to make the world itself better and more bearable.

As a moralist Johnson was especially conscious of the responsibility of the individual to society as a whole. 'Men', he writes, 'are designed for the succour and comfort of each other' (no. 24). Aware of their general selfishness and self-absorption, he insists (unlike Shaftesbury and the benevolists) that social virtue can never be a matter of complacency but must be actively striven for. His most devastating attack on complacency occurs outside the pages of *The Rambler*, in his review of *A Free Inquiry into the Nature and Origin of Evil*. Jenyns had assumed that ignorance is 'a cordial, administered by the gracious hand of providence' to enable the poor the better to bear their lot, but such 'happiness' is, writes Johnson, 'like that of a malefactor, who ceases to feel the cords that bind him, when the pincers are tearing his flesh'. What makes one man 'the slave, or tool, or property of another' is, he realizes, 'often felt with very quick sensibility'. One of his more important essays in *The Rambler* discusses 'the necessity of proportioning punishment to crimes' (no. 114). Here Johnson appears as a social critic ahead of his time. He criticizes a judicial system which equates murder with robbery, and remains unimpressed by the claim that unmitigated harshness provides a deterrent. Instead he takes the view that such a system of indiscriminately severe punishments will lead to the suppression of information that might otherwise lead to a conviction – for, as he says, 'the heart of a good man cannot but recoil at the thought of punishing a slight injury with death'. Also characteristic is the way in which he throws the question back, prompting the reader to ask whether he himself is not perhaps just as guilty as 'the criminal dragged to execution':

> On the days when the prisons of this city are emptied into the grave, let every spectator of the dreadful procession put the same question to his own heart. . . . For, who can congratulate himself upon a life passed without some act more mischievous to the peace and prosperity of others, than the theft of a piece of money?

What might, on the face of it, seem to us complacent about the Rambler's own position is his view 'that the universe is under the perpetual superintendence of him who created it' (no. 184); but we have already hinted how necessary this was to Johnson's peace of mind. As he goes on to state and restate the point in this same essay, his insistence borders on the obsessional. He is, of course, forced to be so emphatic because of his realization that life itself is so 'uncertain'. It is this which encourages him to talk in terms of the existence of a future state:

> To contend with the predominance of successive passions, to be endangered first by one affection, and then by another, is the condition upon which we are to pass our time, the time of our preparation for that state which shall put an end to experiment, to disappointment, and to change (no. 151).

What is uncomplacent about this is its conception of the arena of life as a moral testing-ground. And the reason why Johnson was so sceptical about moral writers in general was that they did not sufficiently concern themselves with this. He complains that they content themselves with a secondhand knowledge derived from books 'instead of casting their eyes abroad in the living world' (no. 129). When he himself did this, he saw how inhibiting 'precedent' and the authority associated with it could be (no. 135). Decisions, he realizes, should be a matter of individual judgment and not simply the prerogative of the philosopher; indeed, in one essay (no. 25) he plays on the words *infantes barbati* – that is, 'bearded infants' and 'philosophers (the bearded ones) unable to talk' – in scornfully rejecting the notion that 'every kind of knowledge requires a peculiar genius, or mental constitution'.

Johnson's scepticism, so bracingly astringent when it rubs up against previously accepted notions, is reflected in the structure of many of the essays. His usual strategy is to begin with a general remark and test it against his own observation and experience. Where it stands up to analysis, he reinforces it by argument and example. Often, however, his analysis suggests that important qualifications need to be made, and a 'but' (or reiterated 'but') is a common feature of the essays. An example is *Rambler* 172, which opens with the statement:

> Nothing has been longer observed, than that a change of fortune causes a change of manners; and that it is difficult to conjecture from the conduct of him whom we see in a low condition, how he would act, if wealth and power were put into his hands.

Then follows the observation that 'it is generally agreed, that few men are made better by affluence or exaltation', and another paragraph indicating why this opinion 'is not likely soon to become obsolete': 'The greater part of mankind are corrupt in every condition, and differ in high and in low stations, only as they have more or fewer opportunities of gratifying their desires, or as they are more or less restrained by human censures'.

Johnson, however, continues to probe and question: 'Yet I am willing to believe that the depravation of the mind by external advantages, though certainly not uncommon, yet approaches not so nearly to universality, as some have asserted in the bitterness of resentment, or heat of declamation.' His exploration of the topic, while not losing sight of the 'pride' that so often accompanies advancement, characteristically holds up to scrutiny the motives and behaviour of those who endorse the traditional judgment. 'Riches therefore perhaps do not so often produce crimes as incite accusers'; 'captiousness and jealousy are easily offended'; 'he that can do much good or harm, will not find many whom ambition or cowardice will suffer to be sincere'. As a final antidote to complacency, he concludes that 'few can justly presume that from the same snare they should have been able to escape'. This process of redefinition has the effect of preventing a merely smug acceptance of the original proposition, and even the opening words ('Nothing has been longer observed . . .') come therefore to be shaded with a retrospective irony.

IV

Johnson's portraits or 'pictures of life' in *The Rambler* are, as one would expect, the work of a moralist. The narrative technique is always strictly functional, and the generalizing and moralizing bias (often heralded by a character's very name[5]) precludes those possibilities of psychological development and individualized treatment which are, in the details of some stories, at least potentially there. Reversals of fortune are as inevitable and matter-of-fact as the smallpox that destroys Victoria's beauty, and the reaction of others to such a disaster is as entirely predictable as that of the women who subject her to 'all the strategems of well-bred malignity', and of the men who think her understanding 'impaired' along with her face (nos 130, 133). As this example suggests, Johnson's portraits cannot be easily written off. Often he cuts deep, exposing how empty, vain, hypocritical, selfish and cruel, man and his world can be.

Many of the portraits illustrate the misery of dependence. Zosima, poor and blameless, 'the daughter of a country gentleman', tells of the meanness and insult to which she has been exposed in her attempts to get service in London (no. 12). The cruelty meted out to her is at its nastiest in the reception she gets from Mr Courtly and his lady, where their joking at her expense appears to be a surrogate for sexual gratification. Nor does kinship offer any guarantee of safety since it only makes more likely a direct affront. Hyperdulus, treated as an inferior in his uncle's family, sees his sister exposed to the rude advances of the heir (no. 149). Misella is debauched by the relative who has adopted her, and is finally reduced to the miseries of prostitution (nos 170–1). Though her story is told without any hint of eroticism or semblance of inner motivation, this very lack of dramatic heightening seems calculated to throw into prominence what needs to be taken seriously – the ghastly sufferings of the prostitute who would, in exchange for her present existence, 'exult at the privilege of banishment'.

Time and again the facts of life are administered without any sweetening. An uncle who has absurd ambitions for his nephew is nevertheless unsentimental enough to cut off his large allowance altogether when he becomes overweening. Unable now to mix with his former acquaintances without being treated as an inferior, the young man seeks preferment from any likely quarter, only to find how carelessly indifferent all are (nos 26–7). A rising author is taken up by Aurantius, but kept dangling on a string. When, having lost his other means of support, his circumstances become desperate, he is offered a small measure of security on condition that he marry one of his patron's cast-off mistresses (no. 163). Sometimes misfortunes are self-inflicted, as though by a perverse kind of irony, and the result is both grotesque and sad. Cupidus is led to expect an inheritance for so many years that, by the time his third aunt finally dies, he has lost all his capacity to enjoy it (no. 73). Florentulus, brought up to be an elegant dandy, is at last deserted by the sex whom it has been the business of his life to please (no. 109). Papilius is singled out by the ladies as a wit, but finds it harder and harder, with advancing years, to keep up the flow of merriment (no. 141).

Many of the figures in Johnson's pages remain effectively cut off from the life round them. The philosopher Gelidus preserves (as his name implies) a cold unconcern and death-like abstraction from life (no. 24). Lady Bustle, a country housewife, is obsessed to the exclusion of all else with cooking and preserving (no. 51). Quisquilius is a virtuoso whose only passion is collecting (no. 82). Nugaculus, who sets out to study human nature, pries out so many secrets that he becomes feared and shunned as a gossip (no. 103). Suspirius, the human 'screech-owl' (who inspired the character of Croaker in Goldsmith's *The Good-Natured Man*), sets out to undermine the confidence of others and is avoided as a prophet of doom (no. 59). As Johnson realizes, people are not merely self-seeking and heartless but basically insecure; what most are unwilling to admit to themselves is their own insignificance. The silly and conceited Frolic, who attempts to impose on the credulity of his country audience by pretending what a great figure he cuts in the capital, provokes Ruricola to an admirably homespun reaction:

> If he has swelled among us with empty boasts, and honours conferred only by himself, I shall treat him with rustic sincerity, and drive him as an imposter from this part of the kingdom to some region of more credulity (no. 61).

Yet the people in the country fare no better when they attempt to compensate for their own insignificance. Euphelia, condemned to spend a summer there, discovers her neighbours harbour resentments so deep that they indulge in a kind of scandal more malevolent, even, than that of the town (nos 42, 46).

Johnson's attitude may be described as antiromantic rather than satiric. Melissa, a well-educated woman of large fortune, finds that her opinion is 'the great rule of approbation', and is delighted with the 'universal veneration' that she is afforded. Her life passes 'like a continual triumph amidst acclamations, and envy, and courtship, and caresses' until the failure of a fund reduces her 'to a frugal competency, which allowed little beyond neatness and independence'. Scorning to conceal her loss, she behaves as before, but her 'friends' take delight in openly mourning her misfortune, and her 'endless train of lovers' immediately withdraw, some revenging their former lack of encouragement by openly courting others in Melissa's presence. Her opinion, too, is now disregarded. As Melissa herself comes to learn:

> It is impossible for those that have only known affluence and prosperity, to judge rightly of themselves or others. The rich

> and the powerful live in a perpetual masquerade, in which all about them wear borrowed characters; and we only discover in what estimation we are held, when we can no longer give hopes or fears (no. 75).

If this is the way of the world, one wonders why it should be suffered to the extent that it is – why, for example, Melissa should be bothered to express opinions that will be 'slighted', sentiments that will be 'criticized', and arguments that will be 'opposed' (given that they are 'opposed by those that used to listen . . . without reply, and struggle to be the first in expressing their conviction'). The answer which Johnson seems to imply is that people have a very understandable compulsion to be involved in life and accepted by those round them. He realized that they like and need to feel important; yet he also realized how a basic feeling of insecurity can lead them to be ungenerous, spiteful or cruel to those less fortunate than themselves.

V

Johnson began writing for *The Adventurer* almost a year after he finished *The Rambler*, contributing twenty-nine essays in all. Among the first of these were the four Misargyrus essays (nos 34, 41, 53, 62), a Rake's Progress with a difference. Whereas Hogarth's young man, dissatisfied with himself as he is, undergoes a progressive and disastrous metamorphosis, Misargyrus, whose round of dissipation has led him into the clutches of the money-lenders and from there to prison, describes his experiences in the hope that others might be saved from a similar fate. While his third letter contains a humorous and instructive account of those inmates whose former delusions remain with them (and who, if redeemed from their present state, would unquestionably go on as before), the fourth sets out the history of those whose charity, or sense of obligation, or failure to obtain the expected preferment, have placed them where they are. Far, then, from presenting the ultimate in distress and humiliation, this essay provides an occasion for questioning the whole system of imprisoning for debt. In

Johnson's view the law ought to be changed, and the

comparison to be drawn is with *Rambler* 114. He cannot see why those who have committed no crime, and who have been, at worst, imprudent or rash, should be left languishing in prison. He deplores the practice whereby a man can be required to stand surety for another: 'Nothing is more inequitable than that one man should suffer for the crimes of another, for crimes which he has neither prompted nor permitted, which he could neither foresee nor prevent.' Particularly offended by the 'avarice and brutality' of creditors, he reserves for them his sharpest scorn:

> Surely, that man must be confessedly robbed, who is compelled, by whatever means, to pay the debts which he does not owe; nor can I look with equal hatred on him, who, at the hazard of his life, holds out his pistol and demands my purse, as on him who plunders under shelter of the law, and, by detaining my sons or my friend in prison, extorts from me the price of their liberty.

Johnson is not turning his back on helping others, but opposing a system that undermines the meaning of individual responsibility. This, as well as the dignity and freedom that goes with it, is what he cares about. Indeed, as he develops the point in another essay, we are reminded of his own life and achievement. Against the pleasure of boasting of one's ancestors, he opposes the satisfaction to be derived from 'owing all' to oneself. As well as the joy of accomplishing something through one's own efforts, there is the self-respect that this brings: 'To strive with difficulties, and to conquer them, is the highest human felicity; the next is to strive, and deserve to conquer' (no. 111). These words have behind them the experience of half a lifetime, as well as an unshakeable faith in the dignity of honest endeavour.

Johnson's fascination with the capital stemmed in part from its streets of crowded activity, and he seems never to have lost the newcomer's eye for all its bustling life (no. 67). Yet his love of London was also inspired by its rich intellectual life; as he once said to Boswell, 'There is more learning and science within the circumference of ten miles from where we now sit, than in all the rest of the kingdom.' What the intellect can contribute to life is clearly brought out in *The Adventurer*. With no patience for those who despise learning, or look upon libraries as so much 'useless lumber', Johnson says with a finality that brooks no dissent, 'It will, I believe, be found invariably true, that learning was never decried by any learned man' (no. 85). These words make the debate of an earlier generation seem rather quaint; and even the 'projector' is given unusually generous treatment, since Johnson sees that the work of a man like Boyle must, to a large extent, disarm any criticism of his more speculative interest in alchemy:

> A projector generally unites those qualities which have the fairest claim to veneration, extent of knowledge and greatness of design. . . . That the attempts of such men will often miscarry, we may reasonably expect; yet from such men, and such only, are we to hope for the cultivation of those parts of nature which lie yet waste, and the invention of those arts which are yet wanting to the felicity of life (no. 99).

Testimony to the civilizing influence of the human intelligence comes movingly from Johnson, who not only defended scholarship against the presumption of 'modern critics' (no. 58), but even admitted the claims of numerous other, less distinguished publications on the grounds that they might add something to knowledge, or at least make known truths more accessible to a certain class of readers (no. 137). Though he pictures himself, with amused self-mockery, as spending one day 'in consulting the ancient sages, and another in writing Adventurers', a real seriousness underlies the surface humour. He comes to his task, whether *The Adventurer* or something else, with a sense of the intellectual endeavour that has ennobled man's history.

The value Johnson attached to this did not, however, betray him into an unthinking kind of idealism. Individual effort was necessary because the world would be darker without it (no. 137). The idea of a coterie of geniuses – who, in the words of Swift's letter (20 September 1723) to Pope, 'if they could be united, would drive the world before them' – was one he always resisted. Such a view seemed to him exclusive, uncompromising, even faintly totalitarian, and he thinks it 'happy' for mankind 'that of this union there is no probability' (no. 45). He realized, moreover, as clearly as anyone, what keeps people divided from others:

> We are formed for society, not for combination; we are equally unqualified to live in a close connection with our fellow beings, and in total separation from them: we are attracted towards each other by general sympathy, but kept back from contact by private interests.

Here we are reminded of what he had said of envy in *The Rambler*; as he saw, one of the main causes of discontent is that 'every man, like an author, believes himself to merit more than he obtains' (no. 138).

This reference to authors, whose 'querulousness' was so obviously a fact of life, allows Johnson as author of *The Adventurer* to insinuate his point with a certain sly authority. The world of letters becomes a microcosm where the same petty jealousies are displayed as operate in the world at large. Authors are 'very little disposed to favour one another' because they are 'competitors' (no. 115); yet people, too, are 'competitors' and therefore 'more easily disposed to censure than to admiration' (no. 131), 'more credulous of censure than of praise' (no. 138). What makes them vie with one another is, of course, their feeling of insecurity. Even the most insignificant among them needs to think himself 'important'. And so people busy themselves with trifles (no. 128); or they 'counterfeit happiness' (no. 120), presenting an appearance of 'splendour and elegance' as a sign of 'wealth' (no. 119); or they openly despise what they secretly wish was theirs (no. 131); or they refuse to others the 'regard' that they seek for themselves (no. 126). In such passages Johnson makes explicit what he had implied in some of his portraits in *The Rambler*.

VI

The hundred or so essays that make up *The Idler* appeared first as a front-page feature in *The Universal Chronicle*, a weekly newspaper that otherwise attracted little notice and ceased publication with them. They were, however, eagerly pirated by the proprietors of other newspapers and magazines 'to enrich', as Boswell says, 'their publications'. Some (perhaps most) were hastily written. Langton recorded that when he was once with him in Oxford (July 1759), Johnson asked how long it was till the post went, and on being told half an hour, said: 'Then we shall do very well.' He then sat down and wrote an *Idler* (which had to be in London the next day), 'folded it up, and sent it off'; and when Langton wished to read it, he replied, 'Sir, you shall do no more than I have done myself.' Langton's single contribution was number 67 (28 July), so the number in question was probably 65 (on posthumously published manuscripts) or 66 (on the loss of ancient writings), either of which would illustrate from how full a mind Johnson was writing.[6]

The Idler is more varied in tone and subject-matter than the earlier periodicals. It contains several essays that refer to contemporary events, or subjects of interest at the time. The feat of a lady who won her bet by riding 'a thousand miles in a thousand hours' is treated with obvious irony (no. 6); one essay discusses the use of gesture in acting and public speaking (no. 90); two contain comments that, characteristically enough, denounce slavery (nos 11, 87). Several of the more humorous – where the humour is often sardonic – describe the army and its exploits abroad: number 8 is rather Swiftian in suggesting an ingenious method for training English soldiers 'to look an enemy in the face'; number 20 imagines the differing accounts of the capture of Louisburg that will be given by English and French historians. In the earlier numbers there is an attempt at a more whimsical humour; and the tone of the various portraits is much lighter than in *The Rambler*, more gently mocking, and even, at times, playful. Yet increasingly there is an underlying seriousness that carries us back to Johnson's earlier work in the essay form.

A hint of this is present from the outset. The Idler flatters himself with 'universal patronage' – there being 'no single character under which such numbers are comprised'. He also cannot resist remarking that, in being 'satisfied' with whatever lies most immediately to his hand, he 'sometimes succeeds better than those who despise all that is within their reach, and think everything more valuable as it is harder to be acquired'. His second essay touches on another familiar theme: in soliciting contributions he promises that anyone who has a paper published

> will be promoted to the first rank of writers by those who are weary of the present race of wits, and wish to sink them into obscurity before the lustre of a name not yet known enough to be detested.

Clearly there is an edge to this kind of humour, and the envy or defensiveness it points to originates in the 'importance' that each wishes to attach to himself (no. 12), the desire for 'praise' that is often, in fact, 'petty' (no. 23). An example of this is the practice of publishing marriage-notices in the newspapers of the day, and here Johnson taps an inexhaustible fund of humour. At once exquisite and sad is the rodomontade of Timothy Mushroom's mother-in-law, which obliges the bridegroom 'to tell the town' that 'three days ago' he was married to Miss Polly Mohair, 'a beautiful young lady with a large fortune' (no. 28).

Many of the portraits display, in one form or another, this very human prompting. Will Marvel draws attention to himself by describing in ridiculously hyperbolical language the commonplace things that happen to him (no. 49). Dick Minim, a man of little education or native intelligence, comes into money and is 'resolved to be a man of wit and honour' (nos 60–1). Robin Spritely's account of his companions at Tunbridge Wells (nos. 78, 83) shows the lengths to which some will go in concealing their own unimportance. Though Spritely innocently wonders what pleasure they can derive from belonging to such a circle, he nevertheless remarks: 'Our assembly could boast no such constellation of intellects as Clarendon's band of associates. We had among us no Selden, Falkland, or Waller, but we had men not less important in their own eyes, though less distinguished by the public.' Each hopes to shine in order to boost his ego, or at least to prevent himself from appearing insignificant in the eyes of others. Ned Drugget aspires to a house in the country, and is concerned that 'his most reputable friends' should be 'the first witnesses of his elevation to the highest dignities of a shopkeeper' (no. 16). Jack Whirler's constant busyness (no. 19) and Peter Plenty's wife's ridiculous acquisitiveness (no. 35) seem to derive from a similar source. And the attempt to keep 'good company' described in number

53 is born of a defensiveness designed to hold feelings of inadequacy or inferiority at bay. Molly Quick's mistress even takes 'a mean delight' and 'cruel pleasure' in exploiting her position of 'superiority' (no. 46).

One reason why the point is rarely pressed in this way is Johnson's conviction that 'we do not so often endeavour or wish to impose on others as on ourselves' (no. 27). Dick Linger, like Tim Ranger in his futile attempts to find happiness (nos. 62, 64), is, in a sense, merely bored (no. 21), even though he mentions being 'forced upon a thousand shifts' to enable him 'to endure the tediousness of the day'. He nevertheless seems unconscious of any self-irony in proposing to make a new start, and in the kind of language which Johnson was soon to exploit in *Rasselas*, he says that he would look back in despair on his having for the last 'twenty years . . . resolved a complete amendment', if he were not 'now beginning in earnest to begin a reformation'. That we are so misled by 'the force of our own resolutions' (no. 27) is seen by Johnson as part of the tragicomedy of life; yet idleness was for him also a vice, and he not only laments that life is so often 'lost in idleness or vice' (no. 56) but half-seriously suggests that idleness ought to be considered as dangerous a vice as pride (no. 31). This point is then developed in the account of Sober, Johnson's famous self-portrait. Sober's practice is 'to fill the day with petty business', keeping 'the mind in a state of action, but not of labour'. Whenever he can he indulges in 'conversation', his 'chief pleasure', for while 'he still fancies that he is teaching or learning something', he is 'free for the time from his own reproaches'. But there is 'one time at night when he must go home, that his friends may sleep; and another time in the morning, when all the world agrees to shut out interruption' – times 'of which poor Sober trembles at the thought'. Hence his numerous hobbies (especially elementary chemistry), which keep his mind from turning in on itself and upbraiding him for the time he has wasted. Despite the humorous indulgence of the portrait, this gives way, after a final flourish, to an unmistakable seriousness:

> What will be the effect of this paper I know not; perhaps he will read it and laugh, and light the fire in his furnace; but

> my hope is that he will quit his trifles, and betake himself to rational and useful diligence.

When considered in the light of other passages (whether from *The Rambler*, the *Diaries*, or Boswell's *Life*), the portrait of Sober takes on a darker toning. Johnson acknowledges in a later *Idler* that 'the incursions of troublesome thoughts are often violent and importunate', and depicts, in suggesting a remedy, how he sees the mind as working: 'Employment is the great instrument of intellectual dominion. The mind cannot retire from its enemy into total vacancy, or turn aside from one object but by passing to another' (no. 72). Most graphic, perhaps, is the episode in the *Life* where he insists that it is 'madness' to try to get the better of 'distressing thoughts' during periods of sleeplessness. His advice is that 'a man so afflicted . . . should have a lamp burning in his bed-chamber during the night and, if wakefully disturbed, take a book and read, and compose himself to rest'. When Boswell slyly suggested that a course in chemistry might help, Johnson retorted:

> Let him take a course of chemistry, or a course of rope-dancing, or a course of anything to which he is inclined at the time. Let him contrive as many retreats for his mind as he can, as many things to which it can fly from itself.

This is, however, the bind that Sober finds himself in, and in the very next essay (no. 32) the kind of day-dreaming that might take one out of oneself is condemned as 'a temporary recession from the realities of life to airy fictions; and habitual subjection of reason to fancy'. The 'weight of life' is such that 'all shrink from recollection, and all wish for an art of forgetfulness' (no. 44), otherwise self-recrimination becomes inescapable.

As well as pointing the dilemma that confronts the idler, these essays return to the theme of self-knowledge, and the importance Johnson attached to becoming aware of one's 'powers' and one's 'weakness' (no. 27). In his essay on biography in *The Idler* (no. 84), he suggests the importance of autobiography ('Those relations are therefore commonly of most value in which the writer tells his own story'). Since a man knows himself better than anyone else can, his ability to describe his inner thoughts and motives must obviously be unrivalled. That these will be honestly displayed in private and unpublished memoirs is Johnson's large assumption, and the emphasis with which he maintains this is clearly revealing: 'That which is fully known cannot be falsified but with reluctance of understanding, and alarm of conscience; of understanding, the lover of truth; of conscience, the sentinel of virtue.' Given Johnson's argument, it is interesting to note his later involvement in the celebrated case of William Dodd, a clergyman who forged a bond for a large sum in the name of the fifth Earl of Chesterfield (his former pupil), and was in 1777 sentenced to death. For a variety of reasons, compassion, respect for the cloth, the severity of the punishment, Johnson did all he could to have the unfortunate man spared. Just ten days before the sentence was carried out, he wrote a letter (17 June) to Dodd's friend, the printer Edmund Allen, suggesting that the convicted man might profitably write 'the history of his own depravation' and mark 'the gradual declination from innocence and quiet, to that state in which the law has found him'. Though aware that this was asking a lot of Dodd at such a time, Johnson significantly adds: 'The history of his own mind, if not written by himself, cannot be written, and the instruction that might be derived from it must be lost.'

Other parallels with the earlier essays occur in *The Idler*. Despite the clarity with which Johnson saw how 'private interests' keep people apart, he also realized that no one can live in isolation from his fellows. He was therefore disposed to stress the spirit of co-operation and goodwill in which people must try to live together, and in *Idler* 19 refers to mankind as 'one vast republic, where every individual receives many benefits from the labour of others, which, by labouring in his turn for others, he is obliged to repay'. This puts it, as a moral obligation, in terms blunt and contractual, but what makes the 'obligation' necessary and binding is elsewhere expressed with more warmth, and in words closer to the need Johnson himself felt for the company and friendship of others. 'We were born', he writes, 'for the help of one another' (no. 80); 'every man wants others, and is therefore glad when he is wanted by them' (no. 44).

Not only is there humour in *The Idler*, but there is also,

compared with *The Rambler*, a general softening of tone. True, the moral engagement with life is undiminished, but there is also a more obvious tolerance and compassion. This can be seen, for example, in *Idler* 25, where Johnson takes up the commonplace of life as a stage:

> Let me likewise sollicit candour (kindness) for the young actor on the stage of life. They that enter into the world are too often treated with unreasonable rigour by those that were once as ignorant and heady as themselves, and distinction is not always made between the faults which require speedy and violent eradication, and those that will gradually drop away in the progression of life.

Perhaps a more telling example is his description of the ages of man, where he expresses that larger kind of sympathy which suggests an experience inevitably shared with others:

> In childhood, while our minds are yet unoccupied, religion is impressed upon them, and the first years of almost all who have been well educated are passed in a regular discharge of the duties of piety. But as we advance forward into the crowds of life, innumerable delights sollicit our inclinations, and innumerable cares distract our attention; the time of youth is passed in noisy frolics; manhood is led on from hope to hope, and from project to project; the dissoluteness of pleasure, the inebriation of success, the ardour of expectation, and the vehemence of competition, chain down the mind alike to the present scene, nor is it remembered how soon this mist of trifles must be scattered, and the bubbles that float upon the rivulet of life be lost for ever in the gulph of eternity. To this consideration scarce any man is awakened but by some pressing and resistless evil. The death of those from whom he derived his pleasures, or to whom he destined his possessions, some disease which shows him the vanity of all external acquisitions, or the gloom of age, which intercepts his prospects of long enjoyment, forces him to fix his hopes upon another state, and when he has contended with the tempests of life till his strength fails him, he flies at last to the shelter of religion.

Where Johnson speaks out with some savageness in *The Idler*, his remarks proceed from outraged human instincts. In the original number 22, a paper he excluded from the collected edition as too misanthropic, he imitates Swift (and perhaps, more specifically, develops an idea contained in Rochester's *Satyr against Mankind*, ll. 129–32) in elevating vultures above human beings by having them wonder why men so readily engage in the senseless slaughter of warfare without having any intention of eating their dead victims. Also notorious is his outburst against vivisection, which denounces a race of 'wretches, whose lives are only varied by varieties of cruelty; whose favourite amusement is to nail dogs to tables and open them alive; to try how long life may be continued in various degrees of mutilation, or with the excision or laceration of the vital parts' (no. 17). This may not be quite fair, but it does show Johnson's concern with means as well as ends, and his opposition to whatever tends to 'harden the heart' and 'extinguish those sensations which give man confidence in man'. He wrote in *The Idler* two more essays on imprisonment for debt (nos. 22, 38), the second of which was widely praised and many times reprinted. In them he makes emphatic his earlier criticism of the role of the creditor, and cannot see why he who 'shares the act', often 'in hope of advantage to himself', should be not only regarded as blameless, but able to indulge his 'revenge' by condemning another 'to torture and to ruin'.

Johnson wrote *Idler* 41 after learning of his mother's death. In expressing his grief, and showing his attempt to confront it, this number is like an elegy in prose. So keen at first is the sense of 'desolation' that no possibility of happiness seems any longer to exist:

> The loss of a friend upon whom the heart was fixed, to whom every wish and endeavour tended, is a state of dreary desolation in which the mind looks abroad impatient of itself, and finds nothing but emptiness and horror. . . . Other evils fortitude may repel, or hope may mitigate; but irreparable privation leaves nothing to exercise resolution or flatter expectation. The dead cannot return, and nothing is left here but languishment and grief.

The only consolation, if consolation it can be called, is to take 'refuge' in religion by turning to 'a higher and a greater power' – one that promises, in the words of the Gospel, 'life and immortality'. Yet how confident is the hope which Johnson seeks to hold on to? The feeling we are left with is rather that summed up in the final word 'patience' ('Philosophy may infuse stubbornness, but religion only can give patience'); and this word, in the very week after *Rasselas* was written, takes us not so much forward to that work as back to the ending of *The Vanity of Human Wishes*.

What is, paradoxically, most moving about the way this essay ends is the effort that goes into the attempt at reassurance. Faced with the final, overwhelming predicament that confronts man, Johnson can only respond by directing all his energy to the given solution. He must therefore insist, as he insists in his final number of *The Idler*, that a day will come 'in which every work of the hand and imagination of the heart shall be brought to judgment, and an everlasting futurity shall be determined by the past' (no. 103). In one sense, this final comment can stand as an epigraph both to Johnson's periodical essays, and to his life as he tried – so often unsuccessfully – to live it. Yet we are also aware of the compulsion that makes him write it, his very human energy which can find release and seek for reassurance in no other way.

5

Dictionary

I

When Boswell calls Johnson a 'literary Colossus', we perhaps think most readily of *A Dictionary of the English Language*, published in two large folio volumes in 1755. According to Boswell 'the world contemplated with wonder so stupendous a work achieved by one man, while other countries had thought such undertakings fit only for whole academies.' Johnson's *Dictionary* did for England what had been done on the Continent only after a great deal of collective effort. Though produced virtually single-handed in a comparatively short space of time, it rivalled both the *Vocabolario* of the Accademia della Crusca and the *Dictionnaire* of the French Academy. Its author came to be known as 'Dictionary' Johnson, and was regarded as a national hero. The verses Garrick wrote in praise of him make this abundantly clear: in them Johnson joins those earlier heroes, Shakespeare, Milton, Locke and Newton, whose exploits so clearly surpassed whatever the French could muster. Forty of their academicians had worked for as many years on the *Dictionnaire*, and one way of appreciating the magnitude of Johnson's achievement is to be reminded of this. Garrick himself exultantly alludes to it in his closing lines:

> And Johnson, well armed like a hero of yore,
> Has beat forty French, and will beat forty more!

The year after the *Dictionary* appeared, Reynolds painted his first portrait of Johnson, which shows him 'sitting in his easy chair in deep meditation'.[1] On the small table in front of him are some sheets of paper, on which rest the knuckles of his left hand; and in his right hand, which rests down over the arm of the chair, he holds a quill pen. The expression on his face has been aptly described as 'at once indolent and combative';[2] and Boswell, when he first met Johnson in the back-parlour of Tom Davies' bookshop, found that this portrait had given him 'a very perfect idea of Johnson's figure'. Another impression of Johnson about the time the *Dictionary* appeared comes from Bennet Langton. Having so admired *The Rambler* he had formed an idea of its author, only to find that, when he met Johnson, he had been mistaken in picturing him as he had:

> From perusing his writings he fancied he should see a decent, well-dressed, in short a remarkably decorous philosopher. Instead of which, down from his bed-chamber, about noon, came as newly risen a huge uncouth figure, with a little dark wig which scarcely covered his head, and his clothes hanging loose about him.

Langton, however, found Johnson's conversation so rich and animated that it made up for any defect in his appearance, and he went away from the meeting with a greater admiration than he came.

This meeting took place in the handsome house in Gough Square, off Fleet Street, which today bears Johnson's name. In its spacious and elegantly proportioned upper room – the room he called his 'garret' – the *Dictionary* took shape. In those years he had the room fitted up like an old-style counting-house, with a large desk at which his six hired helpers or amanuenses could work. The method he used in compiling the work is best described by his friend Thomas Percy:

> He began his task (as he expressly described it to me) by devoting his first care to a diligent perusal of all such English writers as were most correct in their language, and under every sentence which he meant to quote he drew a line, and noted in the margin the first letter of the word under which it was to occur. He then delivered these books to his clerks, who transcribed each sentence on a separate slip of paper, and arranged the same under the word referred to. By these means he collected the several words and their different significations; and when the whole arrangement was

> alphabetically formed, he gave the definitions of their meanings, and collected their etymologies from Skinner, Junius, and other writers on the subject.

This account does not allow for the fact that Johnson made use of an interleaved copy of an earlier dictionary (Nathan Bailey's *Dictionarium Britannicum*, probably in the edition of 1736). It is, however, valuable in drawing attention to what was so distinctive about Johnson's undertaking.

The reference to 'such English writers as were most correct in their language' reflects one of the booksellers' aims in proposing the work. Even though numerous English 'dictionaries' already existed, what they seem to have had in mind was a standard and standardizing dictionary. Such a work had, from a variety of motives, long been called for, and Dryden, Swift, Addison and Pope had all supported the idea. Not only was it a matter of national honour to produce a dictionary that would rival those of the Continent, but on pragmatic grounds, too, the need for some standard had long been accepted. The Royal Society had sought to have the language 'improved' (setting up in 1664 a committee for the purpose), and its first historian Thomas Sprat expressed the desire for a 'mathematical plainness' in the use of language, a style that would unfailingly accommodate 'words' to 'things'. Men of letters were also of the opinion that 'propriety' needed to be laid down before 'elegance' could be aimed at. Their fear was that, unless the language could be 'fixed' in some way, more recent literary works would ultimately become as unfamiliar as Chaucer's. In the words of Pope's *Essay on Criticism*,

> Our sons their fathers' failing language see,
> And such as Chaucer is, shall Dryden be.

There was, generally, a wish to have English cleared of impurities, of solecisms and improprieties, and made as unchanging and authoritative as Latin.[3] Johnson, however, soon found, from his 'diligent perusal' of English usage, that the prevailing linguistic ideal could not be realized. He acknowledged this most fully in the Preface to his *Dictionary*, but he also made the same point in the early prospectus he published as *Plan of a Dictionary of the English Language* (1747).

Johnson's method of proceeding was important for another reason as well. Having originated in interlinear glosses, dictionaries had developed from lists of 'hard' words to include all kinds of information. Edward Phillips's *New World of English Words*, published in 1658 and subtitled 'A General English Dictionary', contained 'the interpretations of such hard words as are derived from other languages', 'all those terms that relate to the arts and sciences' (from theology to fishing), large amounts of history and geography (both ancient and modern), as well as numerous 'other subjects that are useful, and appertain to our English language'. Clearly Johnson was justified in stating in his *Plan*: 'The title which I prefix to my work has long conveyed a very miscellaneous idea, and they that take a dictionary into their hands have been accustomed to expect from it a solution to almost every difficulty.' In practice there had been little attempt to distinguish between encyclopedias and dictionaries; Bailey's *Dictionarium Britannicum* had, for example, made extensive use of Ephraim Chambers's *Cyclopedia* (1728). But what Johnson produced was first and foremost a dictionary. Whereas it had been customary for dictionary-makers to borrow wholesale from their predecessors rather than consult more primary material, he set himself the Herculean task of making a first-hand study of earlier usage. And in doing so he rightly recognized what must be the lexicographer's prime duty.

II

To some extent, of course, Johnson borrowed from his predecessors (though not on their wholesale scale). It has been mentioned that he used an interleaved copy of Bailey; and some of his introductory material (the 'History of the Language' and 'Grammar') contains, not surprisingly, what was already traditional. Yet Johnson's word-list shows at a glance that his work was not intended as a catch-all for every kind of esoteric knowledge. He follows *act* with *action*, whereas the revision of Bailey that also appeared in 1755, and became in fact his most serious competitor, separates these words by entries under *actaea, Actaeon, Actian Games, Actian Years* or *Actiac Aera, actifs, acting* and *actinobolism*. Determining on a word-list nevertheless presented him, as one might expect, with a problem, and he openly admits in the *Plan*: 'In the first attempt to methodise my ideas I found a difficulty which extended itself to the whole work. It was not easy to determine by what rule of distinction the words of this dictionary were to be chosen.' His discussion of the question is dictated by common sense in that he seeks to be guided by a criterion of general usefulness. He realizes that users of his dictionary will want to have explained to them the meaning of unfamiliar words they are likely to encounter in their reading or in daily life – not just those foreign words that have been 'incorporated' into the language, but some others not thus 'assimilated' or naturalized, where these were legal, theological or medical terms, or found in literature, histories and travel books.

Common sense also dictated his approach to orthography. In deference to one of the remarks made by Lord Chesterfield, who read an early draft of the *Plan*, Johnson notes the 'uncertainty' of English spelling. Characteristically, however, he proposes no change to current practice 'without a reason to balance the inconvenience of change'. Where there seems to be genuine doubt, he takes his cue from the derivation: he proposes to adopt the spelling 'which preserves the greatest number of radical letters, or seems most to comply with the general custom of our language'. This last phrase might seem a trifle vague, as do those other phrases in the Preface and Grammar which refer to 'the genius of the English language' or 'the genius of our tongue'. Yet they at least indicate that he had some feeling for the fabric of the language and how it had been formed. And in the examples he gives, derivation provides him with a reliable enough guide: he writes '*enchant, enchantment, enchanter* after the French, and *incantation* after the Latin', and chooses '*entire* rather than *intire* because it passed to us not from the Latin *integer* but from the French *entier*'.

It is well known that Johnson compiled his *Dictionary* before etymology had developed as a science. Here he often did no better than many of his contemporaries could have done. All he did (and all he pretended to do) was to make use of whatever material was available to him. At times he was clearly aware of the inadequacy of this: though he cites Dutch *droom* in his entry under *dream*, he adds that Casaubon derived the word 'with more ingenuity than truth' from the Greek phrase meaning 'the comedy (*drama*) of life', 'dreams being, as plays are, a representation of something which does not really happen'. Sometimes he makes a similarly rash conjecture. After citing numerous explanations of the etymology of *spider* – including Skinner's more or less correct guess – he adds: 'May not *spider* be *spy dor*, the insect that watches the *dor*?' (*Dorr* he defines as 'a kind of flying insect, remarkable for flying with a loud noise'.) Yet Johnson's sense of a word's derivation or root-meaning was generally important to him, and often influenced his approach to its meaning and use. In the *Dictionary* he first defines *ardent* as 'heat', even though he can find no example to illustrate this 'literal' meaning. His approach is, however, most clearly spelled out in the sample definition he gives of *arrive* in his *Plan*:

> In explaining the general and popular language, it seems necessary to sort the several senses of each word, and to exhibit first its natural and primitive signification; as
>
> To *arrive*, to reach the shore in a voyage: he *arrived* at a safe harbour.
>
> Then to give its consequential meaning, to *arrive*, to reach any place, whether by land or sea; as, he *arrived* at his country-seat.
>
> Then its metaphorical sense, to obtain anything desired; as, he *arrived* at a peerage.
>
> Then to mention any observation that arises from the comparison of one meaning with another; as, it may be remarked of the word *arrive* that, in consequence of its original and etymological sense, it cannot properly be applied but to words signifying something desirable; thus we say, a man *arrived* at happiness, but cannot say, without a mixture of irony, he *arrived* at misery.

Though in the *Dictionary* Johnson cites French *arriver* as the immediate origin of *arrive*, he seems, in thinking about the word, to be going back to its original Latin elements, *ad* ('to', 'towards') plus *ripa* ('shore'). This kind of insistence on the 'original and etymological sense' had, as we shall later see, far-reaching implications. It not merely influenced his work as a lexicographer, but was also instrumental in shaping his own prose style, and even his critical approach to the language of poetry.

III

At the suggestion of Robert Dodsley, Johnson's earlier *Plan* had been addressed to Lord Chesterfield. Dodsley, a friend of both men, seems to have been keen to enlist Chesterfield, an acknowledged leader of taste and fashion, as the patron of the work. Johnson had apparently waited on the nobleman, receiving from him a gift of £10; but nothing more substantial followed. Chesterfield was at the time a busy secretary of state, and there would have been long queues of people soliciting his favour. Temperamentally he was not the kind of man to go out of his way to accommodate them, though he later claimed in his own defence that he had not known Johnson sat among them, and protested to Dodsley that 'he would have turned off the best servant he ever had, if he had known that he denied him to a man who would have been always more than welcome'. Then, some months before the *Dictionary* was published, Chesterfield wrote two papers puffing the forthcoming work. These were doubtless written at Dodsley's suggestion; with an eye to profits, the bookseller had not given up hope of linking his name with the *Dictionary*. Chesterfield's papers, so ineptly timed, were inept in other ways as well. Adhering to the original concept of a prescriptive dictionary, he proposed that Johnson should assume the role of dictator in linguistic matters:

> I give my vote for Mr. Johnson to fill that great and arduous post. And I hereby declare, that I make a total surrender of all my rights and privileges in the English language, as a free-born British subject, to the said Mr. Johnson, during the term of his dictatorship. Nay more, I will not only obey him, like an old Roman, as my dictator, but, like a modern Roman, I will implicitly believe in him as my Pope, and hold him to be infallible while in the chair.

Given his slender contact with Chesterfield since addressing him in the *Plan*, Johnson had every right to feel affronted. He said to some of his friends, 'I have sailed a long and painful voyage round the world of the English language; and does he now send out two cock-boats to tow me into harbour?' Because the *Plan* had been addressed to Chesterfield, his papers would have been readily interpreted as the act of a generous patron helping on the work. Johnson could not let this inference go unchallenged, and therefore wrote to him (7 February 1755) to set the record straight. Chesterfield allowed the letter to lie 'upon his table, where anybody might see it'. According to Dodsley, he read it to him, said, 'This man has great powers', and went on to point out 'the severest passages, and observed how well they were expressed'. This cool display has been interpreted as a generous retraction, reflecting credit on Chesterfield.[4] Given, however, the terms in which Johnson wrote, it could also reflect a peculiar kind of arrogance or insensibility. As the most famous letter in English literature, it deserves to be quoted at length:

> Seven years, My Lord, have now past since I waited in your outward rooms or was repulsed from your door, during which time I have been pushing on my work through difficulties of which it is useless to complain, and have brought it at last to the verge of publication without one act of assistance, one word of encouragement, or one smile of favour. Such treatment I did not expect, for I never had a patron before.
>
> The shepherd in Virgil grew at last acquainted with Love, and found him a native of the rocks. Is not a patron, My Lord, one who looks with unconcern on a man struggling for life in the water and when he has reached ground encumbers him with help. The notice which you have been pleased to take of my labours, had it been early, had been kind; but it has been delayed till I am indifferent and cannot enjoy it, till I am solitary and cannot impart it, till I am known and do not want it.
>
> I hope it is no very cynical asperity not to confess obligation where no benefit has been received, or to be unwilling that the public should consider me as owing that to a patron which Providence has enabled me to do for myself.

Johnson makes the gulf between Chesterfield and himself as uncomfortable for the nobleman as possible: he underlines his insolent treatment of him ('seven years', 'outward rooms', 'repulsed from your door') at the same time as he testifies to his own ability to survive, even in the face of difficulties. It has been suggested that 'seven years' is a deliberate echo of Horace's *Satires*, 2.vi.40, and that the implied comparison of Chesterfield's indifference as a would-be patron and Maecenas's tactful concern is therefore 'bitterly ironical'.[5] The irony is finely calculated to increase Chesterfield's discomfort, and Johnson's rejection of his 'notice' becomes, then, the more stinging. The prose is rhetorical in the best sense – poised, discriminating, enormously telling. And it flows (though not obviously) from a deep personal source. This letter has rightly been praised for its independence of spirit; yet Johnson's own life is also there in the writing – his humble origins, his struggle to establish himself, his recent bereavement, his ability to work uncomplainingly at a task without making excuses or attracting attention to himself, and his justifiable satisfaction at not having laboured in vain.

IV

In one sense the episode with Chesterfield fulfilled Dodsley's intentions: the contents of Johnson's letter got abroad and it became the talk of the town. Much of what he said there is included in the Preface, of which the concluding paragraph gives a moving account of the difficulties he faced in bringing his work to completion:

> Though no book was ever spared out of tenderness to its author, and the world is little solicitous to know whence proceeded the faults of that which it condemns, yet it may gratify curiosity to inform it, that the English Dictionary was written with little assistance of the learned, and without any patronage of the great; not in the soft obscurities of retirement, or under the shelter of academic bowers, but amidst inconvenience and distraction, in sickness and in sorrow.

Johnson's statement ends by becoming still more poignant:

> I may surely be contented without the praise of perfection, which if I could obtain in this gloom of solitude what would it avail me? I have protracted my work till most of those

> whom I wished to please have sunk into the grave, and success and miscarriage are empty sounds.

Boswell suggested that this concluding paragraph reflects a state of deep depression, and sharply contrasted it with 'the vigorous and splendid thoughts' to be found elsewhere in the Preface. Yet far from representing a break with what has gone before, Johnson's conclusion meshes with his realization that language as the instrument of man is subject, like man, to change and decay. He notes that no perfect lexicon has appeared, even of the 'ancient tongues, now immutably fixed, and comprised in a few volumes', and recalls the criticism that had been levelled at the Italian dictionary, and the fact that the French had been obliged substantially to alter theirs for a second edition. 'It may repress the triumph of malignant criticism to observe, that if our language is not here fully displayed, I have only failed in an attempt which no human powers have hitherto completed.'

Swift had published *A Proposal for correcting, improving and ascertaining the English Tongue* (1712), and had it been possible to 'fix' the language as he proposed, this would have satisfied for Johnson a deep personal need. It would have made the world seem somehow more permanent, and human mutability and fallibility less obvious. Yet even in the *Plan* he was unable to flatter either himself or Chesterfield that the gap between 'words' and 'things' did not exist.

> Thus, My Lord, will our language be laid down, distinct in its minutest subdivisions, and resolved into its elemental principles. And who upon this survey can forbear to wish that these fundamental atoms of our speech might obtain the firmness and immutability of the primogenial and constituent particles of matter, that they might retain their substance while they alter their appearance, and be varied and compounded, yet not destroyed?
>
> But this is a privilege which words are scarcely to expect, for, like their author, when they are not gaining strength they are generally losing it. Though art may sometimes prolong their duration, it will rarely give them perpetuity; and their changes will almost always be informing us that language is the work of man, of a being from whom permanence and stability cannot be derived.

This perception is, if anything, deepened in the Preface:

> When we see men grow old and die at a certain time one after another, from century to century, we laugh at the elixir that promises to prolong life to a thousand years; and with equal justice may the lexicographer be derided who, being able to produce no example of a nation that has preserved their words and phrases from mutability, shall imagine that his dictionary can embalm his language, and secure it from corruption and decay, that it is in his power to change sublunary nature, and clear the world at once from folly, vanity and affectation.

Johnson viewed the English language as a complex and changing system, yet he associated change with 'corruption and decay' rather than with anything more positive like growth and renewal. It was, of course, thoroughly characteristic of him to be so apprehensive about change, but to some extent he was also influenced, in approaching language in this way, by the contemporary view of linguistic history as cyclical – as providing, in a sense, a counterpart to world history, to the rise and fall of particular civilizations. This idea is expressed, not only in the Preface, but in his later *Idler* 63: 'Every language has a time of rudeness antecedent to perfection, as well as of false refinement and declension'; 'Language', he claims, 'proceeds, like everything else, through improvement to degeneracy.' In broad terms, such a view governed the selection of examples used to illustrate the meanings of words in his *Dictionary*. It also influenced, in rather precise terms, his own prose style, as well as many of his remarks on poetic language.

V

When Helfrich Peter Sturz (a German diplomat and writer who had accompanied the King of Denmark to London) met in 1768 the great English lexicographer, the conversation turned to language. Though Johnson defended the acquisition of new words on the grounds that new knowledge and ideas made them necessary, he also defended his own prose style, especially the Latinisms he was often reproached with: 'It is', he said, 'my serious opinion that our living languages must be formed quite slavishly on the model of the classics if our writings are to endure.'[6] One such critic of Johnson's style was Lord Monboddo, who complained of the 'richness' of his language and of his 'frequent use of metaphorical expressions'. This criticism Johnson sought to answer by taking a passage that Monboddo admired, his well-known description of Iona ('We were now treading that illustrious island, which was once the luminary of the Caledonian regions'). Johnson says, in effect, that 'illustrious' prepares the way for the ensuing metaphor, where this word's root-meaning is effectively revitalized. Other examples of the same thing can be culled from his prose almost at random. In *Rambler* 172 he writes:

> It is generally agreed that few men are made better by affluence or exaltation, and that the powers of the mind, when they are unbound and expanded by the sunshine of felicity, more frequently luxuriate into follies, than blossom into goodness.

Here the obvious imagery is reinforced and deepened by a use of 'luxuriate' which draws on both meanings inherited from Latin *luxuria*, namely, luxuriance of growth in vegetation, and 'luxurious' or over-indulgent living. When thus contrasted with 'blossom (into goodness)', 'luxuriate' suggests the possibility of a moral rankness requiring pruning.

This kind of accuracy of expression and imagination was to prove a stumbling-block to Johnson's would-be parodists, even though they themselves seem often to have been unaware of the clumsiness of their attempts to imitate him. Boswell tells us that Hugh Blair, in his lectures on style at Edinburgh, tried to rewrite a passage from *The Spectator* (no. 411) in the supposed style of *The Rambler*, suggesting that Addison's words, 'their very first step out of business is into vice or folly', would have been padded out by Johnson as follows: 'Their very first step out of the regions of business is into the perturbation of vice, or the vacuity of folly.' In fact, the phrase 'the regions of business' is never used in *The Rambler*, whose author refers instead (in a way that underlines the activity and bustle he associated with 'busyness') to 'the tumult of business', or 'the tumultuous hurries of business'. And so with Blair's other examples. Logically enough, Johnson associated 'vacuity' with the privative states of idleness and ignorance, not with 'folly'. Doubtless, too, he would have argued, with a characteristic kind of logic, that the man who could indulge in a crowded round of vicious pleasures (Latin *turba*, 'a crowd') felt no 'perturbation'.

The style of the Preface to the *Dictionary* was also subjected to the same kind of heavy-handed imitation. The elder George Colman tried to poke fun at the sentence in which Johnson expresses his sense of the frequent difficulty, and even impossibility, of displaying the different meanings of a word in some sort of logical sequence: 'When the radical idea branches out into parallel ramifications, how can a consecutive series be formed of senses in their natural collateral?' This was mockingly rewritten as follows: 'In vain may the laborious lexicographer boast of having traced every radical word through a collateral series of parallel ramifications.' Here Colman entirely misses the verbal nicety and logic of meaning that had made the original question seem properly rhetorical. To Johnson a 'consecutive series' of 'collateral' things would have been inconceivable, since it would have required that things could be both intertwined like a chain (Latin *series*, 'a chain', *serere*, 'to interweave'), and 'collateral', placed side by side or parallel.

Johnson's insistence, as critic, on 'the original and etymological sense' can be seen from his later criticism of Gray's *Ode on a Distant Prospect of Eton College*. He refuses to accept that 'gales' can be 'redolent of joy and youth', and says that Dryden's phrase, 'honey redolent of spring', is 'an expression that reaches the utmost limits of our language'. Presumably he could just accept this because he could just imagine honey as having the scent of spring; but he was unable to accord to Gray's image a similar metaphoric life. This shows how literal, and hence circumscribed, his approach to imagery could be; and we shall see in a later chapter how this affected his appreciation of Shakespeare's use of language. His remark also indicates, however briefly, where he thought Gray stood in relation to the refinement which Dryden had brought to the language of English poetry, and which Pope had done so much to continue; from these high points of Augustan style, Gray was (in the 'affectation' of his images and the 'harshness' of his language) thought to be actively encouraging decadence. Another phrase in the *Ode* drew from Johnson this comment: 'His epithet ''buxom health'' is not elegant; he seems not to understand the word.' From the late sixteenth century onwards there had been ample precedent for Gray's use of the word in the sense of 'full of health', 'well-favoured', 'comely', but his critic seems concerned not to concede the fact because this meaning could not be related closely enough to the word's 'original and etymological sense'. The entry for *buxom* in the *Dictionary* supports this conjecture. The meanings there assigned the word are first 'obedient', 'obsequious', then 'gay', 'lively', 'brisk' (with the well-known line from 'L'Allegro' quoted as an example of this meaning), then 'wanton', 'jolly'. Yet in his discussion of the etymology of the word (which originally derives from the Old English word meaning 'to bend'), Johnson makes it clear that he regards these later meanings as something of an aberration:

> It originally signified ''obedient'', as John de Trevisa, a clergyman, tells his patron that he is ''obedient and *buxom* to all his commands''. In an old form of marriage used before the Reformation, the bride promised to be ''obedient and *buxom* in bed and at board''; from which expression, not well understood, its present meaning seems to be derived.

This entry reflects the aim that had ostensibly been in view from the outset. In a sense, of course, the attempt to connect 'words' and 'things' was as unreal as it was misguided; yet it did not seem so to an age that had been encouraged in its attempt by the terms Locke had used in his influential discussion of epistemology. The realization that languages are not nomenclatures, that words as arbitrary signs have a purely relational identity, not just to one another, but to what, at any given moment, they are used to express, belonged to a later age. Even so, Johnson, who could not express himself otherwise than in Lockian terms, was at least aware that the eighteenth-century approach, in theory so prescriptive, could not be made to square with the facts of linguistic history or 'the boundless chaos of a living speech'. As he says in the Preface:

> I am not yet so lost in lexicography as to forget that 'words are the daughters of earth, and that things are the sons of heaven'. Language is only the instrument of science, and

> words are but the signs of ideas; I wish, however, that the instrument might be less apt to decay and that *signs might be permanent, like the things which they denote* (my italics).

This wish, in itself genuine enough, reveals the source of the contemporary misconception about language and the problem Johnson faced. He was properly forced to accept it as his role to 'register the language'; yet his remarks on the derivation of *buxom* (especially in the light of his later criticism of Gray's use of the word) indicate how difficult he sometimes found it to be thoroughly empirical. An important side of Johnson's nature was intensely practical, and he sought to see things as in themselves they really were. His intolerance of cant, the result of his innate scepticism, is one of the impressive things about him, and even as a lexicographer he was therefore obliged to conclude that the attempt to 'fix' the language was an 'expectation which neither reason nor experience' could justify. Again as early as the *Plan* the same attitudes are evident: though he accepts that 'all change is of itself an evil', this does not blunt his realization that 'what is so much in the power of men as language will very often be capriciously conducted'.

It is, nevertheless, somewhat surprising that Johnson could affirm this as an unhappy fact and yet speak so highly of the period of English literature from about 1580 onwards (which saw the rise of Shakespeare): 'From the authors which rose in the time of Elizabeth, a speech might be formed adequate to all the purposes of use and elegance.' This was one of the boundaries he set to his undertaking, and his illustrative quotations are in very large measure drawn from the 150-year period that extends from that date. He regarded the works of the pre-Restoration writers as 'the wells of English undefiled', and in the Preface refers somewhat disparagingly to 'modern' decorations'. In using this phrase, he might well have had in mind the work of a poet like Gray. Yet other prejudices were also arguably at work in the stand he explicitly takes:

> Our language, for almost a century, has, by the concurrence of many causes, been gradually departing from its original Teutonic character, and deviating towards a Gallic structure and phraseology, from which it ought to be our endeavour to recall it by making our ancient volumes the groundwork of

> style, admitting among the additions of later times only such as may supply real deficiencies, such as are readily adopted by the genius of our tongue, and incorporate easily with our native idioms.

Here, perhaps, we come up against, not merely Johnson's antipathy to the French, but his criticism of a writer like Hume, of whom he once said: 'Why, Sir, his style is not English; the structure of his sentences is French.'

VI

What makes the *Dictionary* such a landmark in the history of English lexicography is the use of quotations to illustrate its divided and numbered definitions of meaning. 'It is not sufficient', Johnson writes in the Preface, 'that a word is found, unless it be so combined as that its meaning is apparently determined by the tract and tenor of the sentence.' Words, he saw, 'will be better understood as they are considered in greater variety of structures and relations'. Yet it was not merely because he recognized the importance of context to meaning that Johnson chose his quotations with such care. Indeed, he seems to have thought of his definitions and quotations as together making more accessible and intelligible for his readers the works of the great English writers.

In the beginning, Johnson's intention had been to do infinitely more than compile a dictionary: 'When first I engaged in this work, I resolved to leave neither words nor things unexamined.' Though he soon realized he would be unable to fulfil this aim, he still hoped that his quotations would do something more than merely illustrate the meanings of words: 'I therefore extracted from philosophers principles of science; from historians remarkable facts; from chemists complete processes; from divines striking exhortations; and from poets beautiful descriptions.' As his accumulation of material grew, he saw that it would be impossible to include 'all that was useful or pleasing in English literature'. One stage at which he reduced its bulk is evident from the work itself: the letter 'A' occupies proportionally most space, and this – by comparison with the space given to the same letters in the

OED – is afterwards reduced by approximately one-quarter (though the space given to 'B' is reduced by less than one-fifth). Yet enough of the proposed material remains to make the *Dictionary* a kind of florilegium. The work is eminently readable, as those who have used it will know; nor would it have been so interesting had Johnson not set out to 'intersperse with verdure and flowers the dusty deserts of barren philology'. Quotations abound from Spenser, Shakespeare and Milton, Hooker, Bacon and Boyle; and other favourite names also appear frequently – Browne, Dryden, Addison, Prior, Arbuthnot, Swift, Pope, Tillotson, South, Watts, Locke and Newton (to name but some).[7] Johnson was, however, most sedulous in excluding those writers whom he considered 'infidel' or 'immoral', and two notable omissions from his list of authorities are Hobbes and Shaftesbury. He told Mrs Thrale that he would not expose his readers to any author who 'might taint their virtue, or poison their principles'.

The range of reading represented in the *Dictionary* is so extensive that from its quotations one gains some sense of the history of English culture. William Wimsatt has put the point forcibly in arguing that the work is

> not simply a source or a guide to the sources of Johnson's words and ideas, but is itself an important incident in the history of philosophic words and in that of the interaction between natural philosophy and the rest of literature and life.[8]

As a record, too, of English usage in this period, it was unrivalled until the eventual appearance, over many years, of the monumental *New English Dictionary on Historical Principles* (today corrected and reissued as *The Oxford English Dictionary*). And though it is, as we have seen, first and foremost a dictionary, a fascinating amount of more esoteric knowledge is tucked away in its illustrative quotations. Two examples (from the many possible)are the sentence quoted from Browne under *swaggy* ('The beaver is called animal ventricosum, from his swaggy and prominent belly'), and that quoted from Arbuthnot under *unlock* ('A lixivium of quick-lime unlocks the salts that are entangled in the viscid juices of some scorbutic persons').

To open Johnson's *Dictionary* is to have brought home to us what a remarkable polymath he must have been. Clearly the booksellers chose the right man for the job; and working on the *Dictionary* enabled him to renew and extend his contact with literature in all its branches. Yet it was not without mistakes, and Johnson was well aware that some of these must inevitably occur. 'What is obvious', he admits, 'is not always known, and what is known is not always present', and he therefore imagines how the work will be received by the many inclined to scoff: 'A few wild blunders, and risible absurdities, from which no work of such multiplicity was ever free, may, for a time, furnish folly with laughter and harden ignorance into contempt.' As Boswell notes, *windward* and *leeward* are both defined as 'towards the wind'; and the definition given of *pastern* was 'the knee of a horse'. When a lady once taxed Johnson with this, and asked him how he came to make such a blunder, his reply was refreshingly forthright: 'Ignorance, Madam, pure ignorance.' Though he was not inclined to correct such errors in later editions (including the abridgements) because he would not give his critics the satisfaction of seeming to flatter them, this particular entry was corrected in the folio edition of 1773. One other blunder was also corrected, with a characteristically sly humour, in this revised fourth folio; and it had been John Wilkes who had pounced on it as soon as the first edition appeared. Alluding to the statement, in 'A Grammar of the English Tongue', that H 'seldom, perhaps never, begins any but the first syllable', Wilkes produced many examples to the contrary, remarking: 'The author of this observation must be a man of a quick *appre-hension*, and of a most *compre-hensive* genius.' This point struck home, and in the third folio of 1765 Johnson inserted after 'never' the qualification 'except in compounded words'; and in the fourth edition he omitted the words 'perhaps never except in compounded words' and added the sentence: 'It sometimes begins middle or final syllables in words compounded, as *block-head*, or derived from the Latin, as *compre-hended*.'

Johnson himself expected that his definitions would draw most fire from his critics:

That part of my work on which I expect malignity most

> frequently to fasten is the "explanation"; in which I cannot hope to satisfy those who are, perhaps, not inclined to be pleased, since I have not always been able to satisfy myself.

As he says elsewhere in the Preface, 'All the interpretations of words are not written with the same skill, or the same happiness: things equally easy in themselves are not all equally easy to any single mind.' The definitions best remembered are, of course, that handful (out of some 40,000 entries) which clearly display his personal prejudices. *Excise* he defines as 'a hateful tax levied upon commodities, and adjudged not by the common judges of property, but wretches hired by those to whom excise is paid.' The definition of *pension* ('An allowance made to anyone without an equivalent. In England it is generally understood to mean pay given to a state hireling for treason to his country') was to cause its author some slight qualms before, seven years later, he accepted a pension of £300 a year. Perhaps best known is his definition of *oats* – an entry which displays his combative sense of fun (especially given that five of his six amanuenses were Scots). The word had been defined in Bailey as 'a grain, food for horses', but Johnson cannot resist including a pointed joke: '*Oats*. A grain, which in England is generally given to horses, but in Scotland supports the people.' We can only guess that he would have appreciated the later quip by a Scottish peer: 'Very true, and where will you find such *men* and such *horses*?' Apart, however, from the definition of 'pension' (which detractors soon turned against him), what attracted most criticism were those definitions which included long, unfamiliar, and generally Latinate words. One parodist suggested that a supplement to the work containing a vocabulary of the vulgar tongue might define *tit for tat* as 'adequate retaliation', or *hodge-podge* as 'a culinary mixture of heterogeneous ingredients'. Yet Johnson's definition of *hodge-podge* is apt and succinct enough: 'A medley of ingredients boiled together.'

Most notorious of all is the definition he adopted of *network*: 'Anything reticulated or decussated, at equal distances, with interstices between the intersections.' One wonders why Johnson did not define the word in relation to *net*; this the *OED* does, and his definition of *net* ('A texture woven with large interstices or meshes, used commonly as a snare for animals') does not suffer much by any comparison. Perhaps he was concerned to avoid such definitions as seemed in any way circular. His definition of *north* is: 'The point opposite to the sun in the meridian'; and though this is erroneous, it at least avoids the circularity of the definition in *The Shorter Oxford English Dictionary* (which in size is more comparable with the *Dictionary* than the *OED*): 'That one of the four cardinal points which lies on the left hand of a person facing due east.' The *OED*, on the other hand, tries to emend Johnson's definition: 'Towards, or in the direction of, that part of the earth or heavens which (in the northern hemisphere) is most remote from the midday sun.' Not only is a knowledge of 'northern' assumed in this definition of 'north', but the inhabitants of the northern torrid zone might well wonder, at times, about its accuracy!

Later dictionaries have often made use of Johnson's definitions, which are, on the whole, as John Wain has said, 'masterly'.[9] Especially felicitous, for example, is the definition of *tawdry*: 'meanly showy; splendid without cost; fine without grace; showy without elegance'. And even where a definition is not as happy as this, there is always the attempt to be both exact and comprehensive. Nor should this surprise us, given our knowledge of the way in which Johnson's mind worked. Boswell indeed pays tribute, not only to his 'vast and various learning', but to his penchant for clear exposition and his well-developed sense of relevance:

> His superiority over other learned men consisted chiefly in what may be called the art of thinking, the art of using the mind; a certain continual power of seizing the useful substance of all that he knew, and exhibiting it in a clear and forceful manner; so that knowledge, which we often see to be no better than lumber in men of dull understanding, was, in him, true, evident and actual wisdom.

There are many ways of approaching the *Dictionary* and of summarizing Johnson's achievement. One may compare it with what went before and point to his contribution to English lexicography. One may view it against the background of the prevailing linguistic ideal and note his good sense in deciding that this was just not feasible. One may set its definitions against the dictionaries of today and show how well its author often comes out of the comparison. Or one may suggest, as William Wimsatt has, that it demonstrates why 'any study of Samuel Johnson is a far wider study – of an age and intellectual climate, of the English language and its literature'.[10] More recently a reviewer of the new *Compact Edition of the Oxford English Dictionary* claimed that this useful publication was 'the best, but not the greatest', arguing that this title should still be reserved for Johnson's *Dictionary* as 'the work of one mind', of a mind possessed of 'a unique unity and vigour'.[11]

6
Rasselas

I

Johnson wrote *Rasselas* at a time when he was suffering some personal distress. Hearing from Lichfield that his mother was gravely ill, he set his pen to work to earn some money to send her. In his letter (16 January 1759) to his step-daughter Lucy Porter, he says that he has just sent twelve guineas and hopes to be able to send more 'in a few days'. On the same sheet he wrote to his mother: 'Your weakness afflicts me beyond what I am willing to communicate to you. I do not think you unfit to face death, but I know not how to bear the thought of losing you.' On or about this date he must have begun writing what he was to call his 'little story book'. He once told Reynolds that it had been written 'in the evenings of one week', and his letter of Saturday, 20 January, to the printer William Strahan, reads as follows: 'When I was with you last night I told you of a thing which I was preparing for the press. The title will be "The Choice of Life" or "The History of – – Prince of Abyssinia".' Then, after some discussion of the size and price of the work, his letter continues: 'I shall have occasion for thirty pounds on Monday night when I shall deliver the book which I must entreat you upon such delivery to procure me.' Before he wrote again to Lucy Porter, on Tuesday 23rd, Johnson had heard of his mother's death.

Though it may, on the face of it, seem surprising that he could write *Rasselas* when he did, it is tempting to suggest that the external pressures on him at the time made their own significant contribution to the work. Despite its slimness, the book has something quintessential about it, bringing us close to

Johnson's mind and imagination in a way that none of his other works quite does. Ideas found elsewhere, especially in *The Rambler*, are here assimilated and transformed; *Rasselas* is, at one and the same time, both antiromantic and yet strangely optimistic. Most often quoted is the remark that 'human life is everywhere a state in which much is to be endured and little to be enjoyed'; nevertheless, the book's overall movement is, even so, surprisingly buoyant. The last chapter ('The conclusion, in which nothing is concluded') accommodates both aspects of Johnson's complex vision – that human hopes are so boundless as to be unrealizable and yet, in being so irrepressible, are for that very reason so necessary and important.

Johnson had translated Lobo's voyage to Abyssinia from the French version, and seems to have been generally well read in Abyssinian material. Yet this contributes few details to his story, for its purpose is to describe not Ethiopians and Egyptians but, as William Wimsatt has said, 'general human nature'.[1] It is difficult to suggest the work's literary origins or affinities, though some of these clearly have more to contribute than others. What has least is the so-called 'eastern tale' of adventure in the manner of the already popular *Arabian Nights Entertainments* and *Persian Tales*. Like these, *Rasselas* contains, for example, the formal device of the story-within-a-story; but this potential means of diversifying and enriching the narrative does not lead, in Johnson's hands, to further possibilities of fictional suspense and excitement. Even the tradition that placed the Earthly Paradise in Abyssinia is treated with a similar irony, for the Happy Valley is a place of sheer boredom for the youthful travellers. An educational motif is admittedly present in this eastern Grand Tour, but one cannot more directly relate it to the many texts stressing the importance of the education of princes. Imlac, as tutor, is really in no position to teach the young prince anything; that he (or rather we) should learn something is implicit in the story as a fact of life. What, perhaps, of all its 'sources', contributes most to it is the allegorical treatment in periodical literature of the oriental tale – like Addison's 'Vision of Mirzah' (*Spectator* 159), designed to represent 'the vanity of human life'. Johnson had himself devoted two numbers of *The Rambler* (nos 204–5) to an account of ten days in the life of Seged, 'Lord of Ethiopia', who set out to devote himself entirely to 'happiness' only to find that it always eluded his grasp.

II

The first sentence of *Rasselas* provides the text for what follows:

> Ye who listen with credulity to the whispers of fancy, and pursue with eagerness the phantoms of hope, who expect that age will perform the promises of youth, and that the deficiencies of the present day will be supplied by the morrow; attend to the history of Rasselas, prince of Abyssinia.

This is clearly a warning against hoping with a too youthful exuberance: the future will not bring 'happiness' and present hopes will remain unrealized. But it is also a warning against imagining that happiness can be equated with a state of having nothing further to wish for. Every year, during the visitation of the emperor, the inhabitants of the Happy Valley are 'required to propose whatever might contribute to make seclusion pleasant, to fill up the vacancies of attention, and lessen the tediousness of time', and since all that is desired is 'immediately granted', they are therefore deprived of the opportunity of still hoping for something.

Paradoxically, in this consists their boredom. The Happy Valley is described with studied richness ('every blast shook spices from the rocks, and every month dropped fruits upon the ground'), and its inhabitants are granted all that 'art or nature' can provide. So 'blissful' does their 'captivity' seem that every year those musicians and dancers, brought 'to add novelty to luxury', try to outdo one another in order to have themselves shut up in the place. They come to have their senses glutted by a constant round of 'diversions', for Johnson sees what Pascal too had seen – that man, when bored, craves diversion, and is always bored when he has nothing to divert him. This boredom is not, however, admitted openly; indeed, 'the sons and daughters of Abyssinia' are constantly having it dinned into their ears what a happy place the Happy Valley really is. And, frighteningly enough, it is said that 'these methods were generally successful; few of the princes ever wished to enlarge their bounds.' Rasselas, however, is the exception. Satiated by the plenty within his reach, he remains unsatisfied:

> I can discover within me no power of perception which is not glutted with its proper pleasure, yet I do not feel myself delighted. Man has surely some latent sense for which this place affords no gratification, or he has some desires distinct from sense which must be satisfied before he can be happy.

Certain hints are given that the Happy Valley is not such a happy place beneath the surface: the palace is said to have been built 'as if suspicion herself had dictated the plan'; the 'iron gate' (which shuts the inhabitants in) is not only 'secured by all the power of art', but is 'always watched by successive sentinels'; the would-be aviator proposes to make – but only for Rasselas and himself – the wings that will hopefully carry them 'beyond the malice or pursuit of man'; and Imlac later says to the prince, 'I know not one of all your attendants who does not lament the hour when he entered this retreat.' Imlac ascribes their attempt to lure others to share their lot to 'the natural malignity of hopeless misery': 'They are weary of themselves, and of each other, and expect to find relief in new companions. They envy the liberty which their folly has forfeited, and would gladly see all mankind imprisoned like themselves.'

The 'discontent' Rasselas feels – his inner restlessness and the sense of unfulfilment he experiences – is what enables him to survive as a human being even in the Happy Valley. At first, however, he is rather too satisfied with himself in feeling so different from others, and is only prompted to give his thoughts a new direction by a conversation with his former teacher. It is this old man who unwittingly plants in the prince's mind the desire of seeing beyond the walls of his prison, and it is this wish or desire which then keeps him going and gives his imagination something to feed on. Unable to understand why Rasselas should be unhappy in the Happy Valley, his old teacher asks: 'If you want nothing, how are you unhappy.' The prince points out that this is the very reason why he is unhappy, that he has nothing 'to desire'; and when the old man smugly replies that if he had seen 'the miseries of the world' he would know how lucky he was, Rasselas triumphantly seizes on his remark: 'Now', said the prince, 'you have given me something to desire;

I shall long to see the miseries of the world, since the sight of them is necessary to happiness.'

The chapter in which Rasselas feeds on the idea in his imagination is an important one, not least because of the spirit of tolerance it breathes. This permeates the whole story: Johnson is able to come close to the experience of his characters, almost to write himself into it, and yet preserve the kind of detached perspective so necessary to the book's many ironies. The prince spends 'twenty months' in 'visionary bustle', neglecting all this time to 'consider by what means he should mingle with mankind'. And having 'resolved to escape from his confinement', he then spends another 'four months in resolving to lose no more time in idle resolves'. On each occasion he is pulled up short by coming into contact with the world round him: first by having the circle of mountains interrupt his fantasy as he chases, in imagination, a robber who has wronged an 'orphan virgin', then 'by hearing a maid, who has broken a porcelain cup, remark that what cannot be repaired is not to be regretted'. The sequence of diminishing time (years, months, hours) has its wry climax when the prince is said to have 'for a few hours regretted his regret'.

The humour here is obvious, yet the inner poise of the writing reflects, without making this obtrusive, a real seriousness. As Rasselas comes to realize, 'the mind, hurried by her own ardour to distant views, neglects the truths that lie open before her'. This is a realization that would have concerned the author of *The Rambler*, just as it concerned him so deeply in his own private life. In the meditation he composed on Skye within a week of his sixty-fourth birthday, Johnson reflected on what he felt was his inability to make full use of the present:

> My hope is, for resolution I dare no longer call it, to divide my time regularly, and to keep such a journal of my time as may give me comfort in reviewing it. But when I consider my age, and the broken state of my body, I have great reason to fear lest Death should lay hold upon me while I am yet only designing to live.

The vocabulary of 'resolving' is given in *Rasselas* – as it was in the account of Seged – a richly ironic meaning. It recurs throughout large sections of the book with almost the force of a leitmotif, underlining at significant points the irony of resolving on a course of action that will lead to 'happiness'. In another sense it persists until the book's final sentence ('and resolved, when the inundation should cease, to return to Abyssinia'), but this more limited sense of the word only serves to highlight the irony that so often surrounds its earlier use.

This is evident from Imlac's account of his own youthful experiences: 'my father resolved to initiate me in commerce' (for which the son had no inclination); 'being now resolved to be a poet' (which he is later forced to admit 'is indeed very difficult'); 'I then resolved to sit down in the quiet of domestic life' (by addressing a lady who rejected his suit); 'I resolved to hide myself for ever from the world' (spoken at the moment when he is about to agree to re-enter it). In responding to this tale the prince says: 'I am resolved to judge with my own eyes, and then to make deliberately my "choice of life".' And when, having left the Happy Valley, he is 'resolved to begin his experiments upon life', he is still convinced that 'happiness is somewhere to be found'. In seeking this, Rasselas, his sister Nekayah, and her maid Pekuah, traverse the city and country, mix with philosophers and shepherds, enter the homes of the lowly as well as the courts of the great, and encounter youthful roisterers as well as men of venerable age, piety and learning. In all their searches, however, they nowhere find an example of true happiness, and the prince in disappointment is therefore led to observe: 'What then is to be done? . . . the more we enquire, the less we can resolve.'

Rasselas first hears of the world of men from Imlac, who, having himself begun life with a marked 'thirst of curiosity', is drawn to the prince by the 'curiosity' he so clearly displays: 'The poet pitied his ignorance, and loved his curiosity, and entertained him from day to day with novelty and instruction, so that the prince regretted the necessity of sleep, and longed till the morning should renew his pleasure.' As Imlac's story unfolds, the portrait of the young prince is further filled out by his response to it. When his 'blood boils' at an obvious abuse of power, his ardour is seen as 'the natural effect of virtue animated by youth'. The situation is exploited with a nice economy. Imlac tells an incredulous Rasselas how his first companions gratuitously exposed him to 'the theft of servants, and the exaction of officers' – enabling Johnson to push home some characteristically shrewd comments on human nature (though the prince cannot as yet appreciate their force): 'Pride', says Imlac, 'is seldom delicate, it will please itself with very mean advantages; and envy feels not its own happiness but when it may be compared with the misery of others.'

Imlac's history, which brings to the Happy Valley the tale of man's aspirations in the outside world, is an anticipation of Rasselas's own. As a young man he was inspired by the same eager hope, feeling a similarly fresh excitement at the scene that opened before him:

> When I cast my eye on the expanse of waters my heart bounded like that of a prisoner escaped. I felt an unextinguishable curiosity kindle in my mind, and resolved to snatch this opportunity of seeing the manners of other nations, and of learning sciences unknown in Abyssinia.

Yet the sea, which had at first seemed so inviting, becomes in time, like everything else, commonplace and wearisome. And so Imlac is obliged to look forward to the next stage of his journey with the renewed hope of seeing something more various and interesting. When he is further disillusioned by his contact with others, Imlac 'resolves' to be a poet and reads all the poetry he can lay his hands on. But he soon finds that 'no man was ever great by imitation', and is therefore driven back to observing things at first hand – not merely the world of nature (though that, as Rasselas realizes, is an enormous subject in itself), but also human nature and the world of men. Imlac's discourse is not really intended as an account of what the ideal poet must study – even supposing this were possible – in order to become a complete master of his art. Rather it provides a striking example of just how the imagination flies ahead of reality and, as it were, takes over. Ironically, it is now the youthful Rasselas who has to pull the older man up short: 'Imlac now felt the enthusiastic fit, and was proceeding to aggrandize his own profession, when the prince cried out, "Enough! Thou hast convinced me that no human being can ever be a poet".'

III

Imlac's account of himself illustrates with a peculiar vividness what the whole book is concerned with. There is always the wish to make a 'choice of life' that will lead to happiness and fulfilment, but this very act of wishing is itself an example of the mind's own quixotic tendency. Unable to rest contentedly in the present, it is always escaping to those more seductive vistas forever opening before it. The youthful travellers' dreams are constantly being contradicted by the world around them; for example, the princess celebrates the virtues of pastoral felicity even as she observes a group of shepherds and pronounces them 'envious savages'. Later, on hearing of the astronomer's delusions, all three are forced to admit that they have often given themselves up to private fantasies:

> 'I will no more', said the favourite, 'imagine myself the queen of Abyssinia. I have often spent the hours, which the princess gave to my own disposal, in adjusting ceremonies and regulating the court; I have repressed the pride of the powerful, and granted the petitions of the poor; I have built new palaces in more happy situations, planted groves upon the tops of mountains, and have exulted in the beneficence of royalty till, when the princess entered, I had almost forgotten to bow down before her.'
>
> 'And I', said the princess, 'will not allow myself any more to play the shepherdess in my waking dreams. I have often soothed my thoughts with the quiet and innocence of pastoral employments, till I have in my chamber heard the winds whistle, and the sheep bleat; sometimes freed the lamb entangled in the thicket, and sometimes with my crook encountered the wolf. I have a dress like that of the village maids, which I put on to help my imagination, and a pipe on which I play softly, and suppose myself followed by my flocks.'
>
> 'I will confess', said the prince, 'an indulgence of fantastic delight more dangerous than yours. I have frequently endeavoured to image the possibility of a perfect government, by which all wrong should be restrained, all vice reformed, and all the subjects preserved in tranquillity and innocence. This thought produced innumerable schemes of

reformation, and dictated many useful regulations and salutary edicts. This has been the sport and sometimes the labour of my solitude; and I start when I think with how little anguish I once supposed the death of my father and brothers.'

It has been pointed out that *Rasselas* 'implicity mocks' the concept of a journey of education leading to wisdom and happiness – a concept fostered by two traditional allegories, Prodicus's 'Choice of Hercules' and the 'Picture' of human life that was attributed to Cebes.[2] Both these texts were in the eighteenth century commonly used in schools, and were also widely represented in the literature and painting of the period. In the Preface Johnson wrote for Dodsley's *Preceptor*, he refers to the 'fables' of Cebes and Prodicus as 'of the highest authority in the ancient pagan world'; while his own 'Vision of Theodore, the Hermit of Teneriffe' (which he wrote for Dodsley's work, and which he once said, wrongly, was 'the best thing he ever wrote') is obviously indebted to the allegory of Cebes. Similarly *Rambler* 65, a tale with an oriental setting, is an allegory inspired by the idea of a choice between the two paths of 'pleasure' and 'virtue'. Johnson glances at Prodicus's *exemplum* of the two different roads leading to Vice and Virtue in presenting Rasselas's first two 'experiments upon life'. The prince is soon 'disgusted' on meeting 'young men of spirit and gaiety' whose 'pleasures' are 'gross and sensual'; he then listens to the words of 'a wise and happy man' in the shape of a Stoic philosopher. Despite, however, the philosopher's claim that happiness is 'in everyone's power', Rasselas next meets him a broken man, utterly inconsolable at the death of his only daughter.

Rasselas, then, is not moral allegory in any simple sense. It contains no clear-cut values which the travellers can embrace, no point of rest which they can arrive at, no horizon which they can confidently look forward to as the final goal of their quest. What is stressed is the tentative, unpredictable quality of life, and Emrys Jones is surely right to note Johnson's affinity with Sterne – who was to begin *Tristram Shandy* in the same month as *Rasselas* was written – in having 'a subversive attitude to certain kinds of theory and certain kinds of form'.[3] Far from the book's being, as one early critic complained, 'an ill-contrived, unfinished, unnatural and uninstructive tale',[4] there is a significant connection between its form and meaning. What its episodic quality reflects is that there is no road or path of life that will lead the travellers to 'happiness'. Their journey, in fact, illustrates something important – that 'the natural flights of the human mind are not from pleasure to pleasure, but from hope to hope' (*Rambler* 2). By capturing this inescapable fact in the very fabric of his story, Johnson testifies to a characteristically human response which is at a far remove from mere Stoical indifference.

In pursuing their quest for happiness, the youthful travellers are inevitably led forward to consider one state of life after another. Because the present never lives up to expectations, their hope must always be that the future will provide what in the present they have failed to find. The story of the hermit they meet is in this respect instructive. Though he has retired from the world, he has no wish that others should follow his example. In his solitude he is assailed by keen self-doubt, and because he lacks 'opportunities of relaxation or diversion', his imagination 'riots in scenes of folly'. And so it comes as no surprise (though it is said to surprise the travellers) when he digs up his treasure and accompanies them back to Cairo, on which, as he approaches it, he gazes 'with rapture'. The moral point of his story he makes himself. Asked by Imlac to help Rasselas and Nekayah in making a 'choice of life', the hermit answers: 'To him that lives well every form of life is good; nor can I give any other rule for choice than to remove from all apparent evil.' The irony, however, is that, given the way the mind works (the hermit's as much as anyone else's) his answer provides no real solution. Accordingly, it remains for one who afterwards hears his story, and who thinks it likely that he will 'in a few years go back to his retreat', to comment most relevantly upon it:

> The hope of happiness is so strongly impressed that the longest experience is not able to efface it. Of the present state, whatever it be, we feel, and are forced to confess, the misery, yet, when the same state is again at a distance, imagination paints it as desirable.

The point made here is relevant to the presentation of the

youthful travellers, who, at the end of the book, are still able to talk of the 'various schemes of happiness which each of them had formed'. The dreams they entertain are cherished not so much because of what they have seen but in some ways, and importantly, in despite of it. The princess, notwithstanding her experience of the mad astronomer, is eager to dedicate herself to 'knowledge' and 'raise up for the next age models of prudence, and patterns of piety'. Pekuah, the princess's favourite, wishes to become a prioress at the convent of St Anthony, even though the limitations of a monastic life have been pointed out by Imlac a couple of chapters earlier. Being 'weary of expectation and disgust', she 'would gladly be fixed in some unvariable state'. While we see the irony of this (especially coming from someone as lively as herself), we are also made to recognize how unquenchable the human imagination is. But we do not have to wait until the end to appreciate the relevance of the hermit's story, for this is made plain enough in the conversation between the prince and Nekayah that occurs halfway through the book.

As he becomes increasingly disillusioned with Imlac's sober remarks, Rasselas talks more with his sister, 'who had yet the same hope with himself'. They divide the task between them, the prince confining himself to the courts of the great, while Nekayah enters the houses of ordinary people. What they find is depressing in the extreme: hatred and treachery surround people in high places; members of the same family are so divided against one another by jealousy and self-interest that the family, as itself 'a little kingdom', is 'torn with factions and exposed to revolutions'. Not finding happiness himself, Rasselas with his hope still alive is forced on the defensive. He assumes that happiness can be found where he has not looked for it, and he therefore tells his sister that she has 'surveyed life with prejudice, and supposed misery where she did not find it'. His remarks have an exquisite irony since his defence of the magnanimous ruler against 'the greater number' who 'will be always discontented' is a fine example of 'prejudice' or prejudging on his part – this being the role which his imagination has habitually cast him in.

Their dialogue reaches its climax in the debate on marriage. The prince, having already heard from his sister how unhappy are those who remain single, endorses marriage as 'evidently the dictate of nature' and thus 'one of the means of happiness'. The princess is more cautious: from what she has seen she is tempted to reckon it 'one of the innumerable modes of human misery'. Given, however, what she has said before, that 'marriage has many pains, but celibacy has no pleasures', her brother replies with some asperity that she is contradicting herself, and for a moment the debate itself threatens to become a family squabble. It is the princess who shows dignity and restraint, and keeps her equanimity along with her reason. And when Rasselas, quite logically, as he thinks, proposes that marriage late in life will avoid those difficulties which arise between parents and children, Nekayah realizes that the question is not one which logic and reason can decide:

> From their children, if they have less to fear, they have less also to hope, and they lose, without equivalent, the joys of early love, and the convenience of uniting with manners pliant, and minds susceptible of new impressions.

Still unable to relinquish the idea of a 'choice' that will enable alternatives to be embraced within a single scheme of happiness, the prince suggests that perhaps there is an age midway between the two when the advantages of early and late marriages might both be enjoyed. The princess, however, realizes that no one can enjoy the best of both worlds, and that he who tries to do so is in very real danger of enjoying neither: 'There are goods so opposed that we cannot seize both, but, by too much prudence, may pass between them at too great a distance to reach either.'

'It is impossible', says Johnson in *Rambler* 162, 'but that, as the attention tends strongly towards one thing, it must retire from another.' As the princess recognizes, happiness is never possible in the terms which man proposes to himself. She is coming to realize that the world must be taken as it is, and that, though the mind constantly outruns the present in wishing for something else, reality sets finite limits to the possibility of human choice. 'No man', she says, 'can taste the fruits of autumn while he is delighting his scent with the flowers of spring; no man can, at the same time, fill his cup from the source and from the mouth of the Nile.' She anticipates, in fact, the point which their guide and friend makes so explicitly when he next enters: 'It seems to me', said Imlac, 'that while you are making the choice of life, you neglect to live.'

It is, however, not so much the quest for happiness as the questing itself that is important, and the youthful travellers' energetic searching is therefore an indispensable part of living. Such is the nature of the mind that it needs to be kept fully occupied, and Imlac, in proposing the visit to the Pyramids, notes how we must 'enlarge our comprehension by new ideas'. After the travellers have surveyed 'the great pyramid', he attributes its existence to 'that hunger of imagination which preys incessantly upon life, and must be always appeased by some employment':

> Those who have already all that they can enjoy, must enlarge their desires. He that has built for use, till use is supplied, must begin to build for vanity, and extend his plan to the utmost power of human performance, that he may not be soon reduced to form another wish.

This passage, in emphasizing how insatiable, how incapable of resting contentedly in the present, the human imagination is, reflects a deep psychological truth. When man is afflicted with a sense of present unfulfilment, he seeks to counter this by indulging, whether furtively or otherwise, in some form of wish-fulfilment: he either builds real pyramids or castles in the air. And it is precisely because this very human activity is so continuous and compelling that some form of 'employment' or 'diversion' becomes necessary.

IV

Johnson defines *diversion* in the *Dictionary* as 'something that unbends the mind by turning it off from care'. 'To divert' (in this sense) is 'to please', 'to exhilarate'; and under the definition of *amuse* ('to entertain with tranquillity', 'to fill with thoughts that engage the mind, without distracting it') he adds: 'To *divert* implies something more lively, and to *please* something more important. It is therefore frequently taken in a sense bordering on contempt.' Pekuah admits to having welcomed the opportunity of studying astronomy in the Arab's fortress because she found 'some employment requisite to beguile the tediousness of time'; and when Nekayah asks her why, on finding herself bored, she did not enter into the 'diversions' of the other women, and seek, like them, 'business or amusement', her favourite replies:

> The diversions of the women were only childish play, by which the mind accustomed to stronger operations could not be kept busy. I could do all which they delighted in doing by powers merely sensitive, while my intellectual faculties were flown to Cairo.

Rasselas seems to confirm what this exchange suggests – that 'diversion' is used with a conscious sense of how important diversion (as a means of employing the mind) can be. As we have seen, the hermit in his solitude had lacked 'opportunities of relaxation or diversion', and for this reason found his peace of mind threatened. What he needed was some means of escaping, however temporarily, from such a state. The princess, too, after Pekuah has been carried off by Arab horsemen, is able to keep 'her hope alive' so long as she is 'doing something' aimed at getting her favourite back. As time passes and she withdraws into herself, Rasselas first tries to comfort, and then 'to divert' her. Later, after the episode of the mad astronomer, the prince enters and enquires 'whether they had contrived any new diversion for the next day'. The wish to be 'diverted' tends to replace the earlier pattern of impracticable 'resolving', as though Rasselas, in the very language he uses, is at last learning something. This strand of the book's vocabulary catches up, with a nice irony, the previous allusions to the 'diversions' of the Happy Valley, for man in every state finds life wearisome unless he has something to divert him. One difference, however, between the earlier and later uses of the word is underlined by Pekuah's description of life in the Arab's fortress ('powers merely sensitive'); while the prince, too, seems conscious of some difference when he goes on to remark: 'Variety is so necessary to content that even the Happy Valley disgusted me by the recurrence of its luxuries.'

That which 'diverts' must not only be something outside the self, but something that engages and exhilarates the mind (rather than the senses). The mad astronomer claims that he 'feels' his power of controlling the heavenly bodies, even though he cannot 'prove it by external evidence'; such a use of language shows how the merely hallucinatory draws support from the language of 'feeling' and the senses. Again we are made to recognize the importance of diversion as a means of keeping the mind from turning in upon itself – of keeping it employed, in a non-subjective way, on things other than itself. This is the point which Imlac makes so forcibly in referring to 'the dangerous prevalence of imagination':

> No man will be found in whose mind airy notions do not sometimes tyrannise, and force him to hope or fear beyond the limits of sober probability. All power of fancy over reason is a degree of insanity. . . . He who has nothing external that can divert him, must find pleasure in his own thoughts, and must conceive himself what he is not; for who is pleased with what he is?

This is a fact both laughable and true, and the mixed reaction of the youthful travellers to the astronomer's madness indicates precisely this: 'The prince heard this narration with very serious regard, but the princess smiled, and Pekuah convulsed herself with laughter.'

This episode of the mad astronomer, who believes himself to control the weather and seasons, may be regarded as climactic. Neatly following on Pekuah's account of her studies in the Arab's stronghold, it underlines the dangers of abstracting oneself from reality, whether as a result of the vagaries of hope, a wayward imagination, or misdirected curiosity. Johnson, Boswell notes, was 'too ready' to associate madness with any form of depression or melancholia, and once, in a conversation with Boswell and the Burneys, defined the cause of madness as 'too much indulgence of imagination'. He seems not to have distinguished between this and a potentially psychotic state; at the very least, he seemed to think that one could easily become the other. The Rasselas who indulges his imagination by chasing an imaginary robber in the Happy Valley may therefore be seen as exhibiting the same mental condition as, in a more marked degree, afflicts the astronomer. It is this man's history that Imlac brings forward on hearing the prince declare that he will 'devote himself to science, and pass the rest of his days in literary solitude.' Inevitably we recall the sombre line, 'Nor

Melancholy's phantoms haunt thy shade', from Johnson's portrait of the scholar in *The Vanity of Human Wishes*. Momentarily the great poem and the great prose tale come illuminatingly together.

In *Rasselas*, however, Johnson is able the more firmly to underline his point by confining his example to 'one of the most learned astronomer's in the world' – an example which suggests the traditional distinction between self-knowledge and 'star-knowledge', man's 'proper study' as opposed to his vain pursuit of things remote from use. As we saw in the first chapter, Johnson was particularly exercised by the limits to be set to man's curiosity, even though he was himself so intensely curious in the best intellectual sense. 'Curiosity', he remarks in *Rambler* 150, 'is in great and generous minds the first passion and the last; and perhaps always predominates in proportion to the strength of the contemplative faculties.' Elsewhere in his conversation and writings he makes the same point. And a few months before writing *Rasselas* he sent a letter (1 October 1758) to William Drummond, warning him against opposing his son's wish to attend the University of Edinburgh:

> It is very dangerous to cross [i.e. to obstruct] the stream of curiosity; or by opposition and disappointments, which young men (who have not experienced greater evils) often feel with much sensibility, to repress the ardour of improvement, which, if once extinguished, is seldom kindled a second time.

Yet he was also well aware of the traditional condemnation of *curiositas*, and under the first definition of *curious* in the *Dictionary* he gives these examples:[5]

> Be not *curious* in unnecessary matters; for more things are shown unto thee than men understand. (*Ecclus*. iii. 23)

> Even then to them the spirit of lies suggests,
> That they were blind, because they saw not ill;
> And breathed into their uncorrupted breasts
> A *curious* wish, which did corrupt their will. (Davies:
> *Nosce Teipsum*, 'Of Humane Knowledge')

Johnson had in *The Rambler* stressed the dangers of improper curiosity. In number 118 he describes 'curiosity' as 'a passion, which, though in some degree universally associated to reason, is easily confined, overborne, or diverted from any particular object'. In number 105, a dream vision of 'an universal register' of human schemes and desires, Curiosity is not only recognized by Truth as 'among the most faithful of her followers', but is also clearly associated with the host of 'projectors' who (as the word is defined in the *Dictionary*) 'form wild impracticable schemes'. This, then, allows him to relegate the dangers of misdirected curiosity to a convenient limbo, and thereby largely ignore the problem which curiosity in general raised for him. In *Rambler* 180, however, where Raphael's counsel to Adam is explicitly mentioned, he explores the problem in greater depth. He exhorts his readers not to be misled 'too far from that study' which is above all others necessary – 'the art of moderating the desires, of repressing the appetites, and of conciliating, or retaining the favour of mankind.'

Johnson's remarks in this essay seem particularly relevant to *Rasselas*. In at first opposing the suggested visit to the Pyramids, the prince recognizes what 'the proper study of mankind' should be: 'My curiosity', said Rasselas, 'does not very strongly lead me to survey piles of stones, or mounds of earth; my business is with man.' After the loss of Pekuah, the travellers, in great distress, return to Cairo 'repenting of their curiosity'. Later, in replying to a question on the 'choice of life', the astronomer can offer no advice except that he has chosen wrongly: 'I have passed my time in study without experience; in the attainment of sciences which can, for the most part, be but remotely useful to mankind.' In limiting his active participation in the real world, in abstracting himself from man's proper sphere of virtue, the astronomer suffers melancholy and madness. His recovery does not take place all at once, but it begins, significantly, as he comes into contact with the youthful travellers. It is Pekuah's conversation that first takes 'possession of his heart', and the visits of the young people gradually help to restore him to himself:

> They came again and again, and were every time more welcome than before. The sage endeavoured to amuse them, that they might prolong their visits, for he found his thoughts grow brighter in their company; the clouds of

> solicitude vanished by degrees, as he forced himself to entertain them.

The astronomer is now able to admit that, since his 'thoughts have been diversified by more intercourse with the world', he is disposed to question what he had formerly imagined. Entering more and more into the travellers' busy and friendly round, he confesses to Imlac that his earlier conviction is gradually fading from his mind. Imlac, quick to improve on this opportunity, then says to him:

> Open your heart to the influence of the light which, from time to time, breaks in upon you: when scruples importune you, which you in your lucid moments know to be vain, do not stand to parley, but fly to business or to Pekuah, and keep this thought always prevalent, that you are only one atom of the mass of humanity, and have neither such virtue nor vice as that you should be singled out for supernatural favours or afflictions.

V

Imlac's words stress how crucial the contact with reality – or whatever counters disturbing fantasies – can be. Significantly, his reply to the astronomer begins: 'No disease of the imagination is so difficult of cure, as that which is complicated with the dread of guilt.' When we remember Johnson's own struggle with scruples, and the fact that he once described himself as 'mad all my life, at least not sober', these passages in his book take on a deeper resonance. Yet the remarkable thing about *Rasselas* is that it remains so buoyant – almost as though the pressures on Johnson when he wrote it guaranteed an answering upsurge of energy and a compensating liberation of the spirit. In her comments on the Arab's harem, Pekuah underlines the dreariness of an existence which admits 'neither hope nor fear, neither joy nor sorrow'; to exist in such a state is to be effectively dehumanized. Even the 'old man' of chapter 45, for whom 'the world has lost its novelty', is effectively placed, structurally and thematically, by the continuation of the astronomer's story. This old man is entirely dispiriting, and in viewing human endeavour as so futile, he tries to abstract himself 'from hopes and cares'. Though the youthful travellers are perhaps too ready to discount this voice of age and experience, Johnson is also saying that 'hopes and cares' are necessary to human life – otherwise the alternative is this old man.

This figure functions, I believe, primarily as a warning: whatever the sum of human life is, finding it does not involve following his example. The theme of a choice of life remains prominent throughout the last three chapters, but it undergoes subtle modifications as a result of their inherent juxtapositions and contrasts. The topic of monastic retirement is first introduced, and Imlac acknowledges that the monks of St Anthony (at whose monastery Pekuah had been returned to them) 'are less wretched in their silent convent than the Abyssinian princes in their prison of pleasure': 'Their time is regularly distributed; one duty succeeds another, so that they are not left open to the distraction of unguided choice, nor lost in the shades of listless activity.' They clearly have something to do, and they have removed themselves from worldly temptations; but their 'pious abstraction', however inherently seductive, is also rather negative, as Imlac is forced to conclude: 'He that lives well in the world is better than he that lives well in a monastery.' These words may remind us that Johnson had once thought of 'retiring', only to find, as he himself expressed it, that his 'vocation' was rather 'to active life'. Indeed, he could never be convinced that such retirement was compatible with real virtue, with the demands that the real world made on man as a moral being. The choice of *life* must, he sees, clearly lie elsewhere, and as if subtly to press home the point, the debate on monastic life is followed by a visit to the nearby catacombs.

In this chapter so much space is given to Imlac's discourse on the nature of the soul that the choice of life is raised in a wider context. Rasselas notes that those who lie before them 'were, perhaps, snatched away while they were busy, like us, in the choice of life'. And the princess replies that for her the choice of life has 'become less important': 'I hope hereafter to think only on the choice of eternity.' The message of the book has usually been interpreted as encapsulated in this remark. Boswell said that 'Johnson meant, by showing the unsatisfactory nature of things temporal, to direct the hopes of man to things eternal'; and many recent critics have agreed with Boswell. It has, for example, been suggested that the princess's 'celebrated dismissal of the choice of life' marks the point at which, 'logically and aesthetically', 'the structure of *Rasselas* comes to a quiet climax'.[6]

The visit to the catacombs is not, however, the final chapter, and the point to which the whole book tends is contained in what comes next, 'The conclusion, in which nothing is concluded.' As the travellers stand in the catacombs, Rasselas observes that 'what now acts shall continue its agency, and what now thinks shall think on for ever'. His remark, though it looks beyond mere temporal life, also stresses the continuous process that man finds himself engaged in. Even if one were to allow (as Johnson always strenuously maintained) that the business of life is to live with eternity in view, the 'choice' that is so immediate to this life can never become irrelevant or unimportant. Given the faculties that man possesses, the question is rather how the imagination can accommodate itself to the real world. And this is the question that the book leaves us with, most fittingly and revealingly in the final chapter. We admire the curiosity that makes Rasselas want to escape from the confinement of the Happy Valley, even though his expectations, like the astronomer's, have to be in some sense brought down to earth. And we feel how important it is that the youthful travellers should, despite their experience of the world, continue to have the capacity of planning and hoping. That they still have this can be seen from the 'talk' they engage in while waiting for the Nile to subside: 'They diverted themselves with comparisons of the different forms of life which they had observed, and with various schemes of happiness which each of them had formed.'

The most telling detail occurs, appropriately enough, in the presentation of the prince. Having expressed his desire for 'a little kingdom, in which he might administer justice in his own person, and see all the parts of government with his own eyes', 'he could never fix the limits of his dominion, and was always adding to the number of his subjects'. The irony here is obvious; yet, as Johnson realizes, by reaching out in imagination for something more, the prince is proving that he has a characteristically human resilience. Such an 'indulgence of hope' was in Johnson's view 'necessary to the production of everything great or excellent'; 'There would', he wrote, 'be few enterprises of great labour or hazard undertaken if we had not the power of magnifying the advantages which we persuade ourselves to expect from them' (*Rambler* 2). And so it is surely significant that the youthful travellers do not relinquish their dreams, but instead transfer them to a context in which they can be openly indulged. Though they have had plenty of opportunity to see where unreal hopes must end, they are still themselves able to go on hoping and planning. Without this capacity, Johnson seems to be saying, life itself will become dead and empty, a kind of mausoleum of the human spirit.

If this is what the ending of *Rasselas* confirms, what of Imlac and the astronomer, who 'were contented to be driven along the stream of life without directing their course to any particular port'? Is this to be interpreted as wisdom, or a culpable lack of interest or will-power? The weight of other contexts where a similar vocabulary is used would seem to be against them. *Rambler* 102, a dream-vision of life as a voyage, condemns 'the thoughtlessness' with which man 'floats along the stream of time'; in *Rambler* 70 Johnson claims that 'most minds are the slaves of external circumstances', and 'roll down any torrent of custom in which they happen to be caught'; in *Rambler* 127 he pictures the fate of the man to whom life has denied the expected rewards:

> A man thus cut off from the prospect of that port to which his address and fortitude had been employed to steer him, often abandons himself to chance and to the wind, and glides careless and idle down the current of life, without resolution to make another effort, till he is swallowed up by the gulph of mortality.

The language of such passages seems to echo the fate of 'helpless man' in *The Vanity of Human Wishes*, just as in his more recent *Idler* 30 Johnson reminds us of the poem's previous line in describing those who 'find life stagnate, for want of some desire to keep it in motion'. Imlac and the astronomer are, however, at least in touch with 'the stream of life' and to this extent unlike the earlier old man. It is this figure who, despite entertaining some hope of happiness in the next world, seems in his forced abstraction from life perilously close to that state of 'dull suspense' which, in the unforgettable words of the poem, *corrupts* 'the stagnant mind'. Since he has already provided the contrast with the youthful travellers, Imlac and the astronomer can be dismissed not unkindly. Johnson's gentleness of touch is evident in the language: 'were *contented* to be driven *along* the *stream of life*'. Yet consistent with the irony that, at all times, pervades the book, and prevents us from ever being neatly schematic about it, 'particular port' is also nicely double-edged in undercutting the youthful travellers' dreams.

The image of 'the stream of life' remains, nevertheless, curiously suggestive in setting them apart. From the outset the Nile has subtly accompanied them on their search, functioning at significant points of the story almost as a symbol of human life. Rasselas sets out brimful of curiosity from the river's source, which, so long undiscovered, had traditionally come to be associated with human curiosity. During the long debate between the prince and his sister, Nekayah addresses the Nile: 'Answer', said she, 'great father of waters, thou that rollest thy flood through eighty nations, to the invocations of the daughter of thy native king.' No other passage in the book makes the identification between the river and the youthful travellers so complete, and her realization at this point of what human life is like is significantly summed up in an image drawn from the river: 'No man can, at the same time, fill his cup from the source and from the mouth of the Nile.' The final chapter is set against the background of the Nile in flood, and the river's overflow suggests – as it were subliminally – the welling-up of human hope. Though no one in the voyage of life can ever step into the same river twice, hope is seemingly as boundless as the Nile in flood. For this reason it is also, like the waters of the river, essentially life-giving.

7

Edition of Shakespeare

I

An edition of Shakespeare's plays, by the dramatist Nicholas Rowe, appeared the year Johnson was born, and within the next fifty years Pope, Lewis Theobald, Thomas Hanmer and William Warburton were all to produce editions. While the theatre-going public was familiar with the plays (often in a greatly altered form), the work of these editors served to introduce Shakespeare to a wider audience. Johnson, as we have seen, had begun reading the plays as a boy, and had hoped to edit them in the 1740s. Meantime he had seen his old pupil Garrick rise to unparalleled heights as an actor, and the younger man's success must have intensified Johnson's desire to establish his own claim to Shakespeare. He would not, however, admit that editing the plays involved him in work which was especially congenial. When his friend Sir John Hawkins suggested to him that, now that his *Dictionary* was out of the way, he would work on Shakespeare '*con amore*', Johnson contradicted him, saying, 'No, Sir; nothing excites a man to write but necessity.'

There are, too, signs that before he was through with the edition it had become a somewhat arduous task. When Johnson pulished, in June 1756, *Proposals for Printing, by Subscription, the Dramatic Works of William Shakespeare*, it was his intention to get the volumes out by Christmas of the following year. On 21 June 1757 he wrote to Thomas Warton, 'I am printing my new edition of Shakespeare', and when Christmas came, he was still reckoning on publishing it the following Easter. When that time came, he was still hopeful that his edition would be out 'before summer'. It did not, however, appear until late in 1765, when he no longer remembered the names of his subscribers and had long since spent their money. Not only had he meantime begun *The Idler*, but during the early 1760s he suffered from acute melancholia. In his diary he wrote (Easter Eve, 1761): 'Since the Communion of last Easter I have led a life so dissipated and useless, and my terrors and perplexities have so much increased that I am under great depression and discouragement.'

Doubtless the unfinished task contributed to his despondency. In his *Proposals* Johnson had designed 'to correct what is corrupt, and to explain what is obscure'. The knowledge he had gained in compiling the *Dictionary* obviously helped: 'With regard to obsolete or peculiar diction', he writes, 'the editor may perhaps claim some degree of confidence, having had more motives to consider the whole extent of our language than any other man from its first formation.' Yet Shakespeare made, he realized, other demands on his editor. 'The corruptions of the text', he promises, 'will be corrected by a careful collation of the oldest copies'; it was proposed that the edition would contain 'all the observable varieties of all the copies that can be found'. The commentary was to be even more ambitious: 'The editor will endeavour to read the books which the author read, to trace his knowledge to its source, and compare his copies with their originals.' Johnson was ahead of his time in recognizing what needed to be done. In the Preface to his edition, he was also to insist on the textual authority of the First Folio. Yet his own text was largely based on that of his predecessors Theobald and Warburton; nor was he able to consult anything like a complete list of the old quartos. Besides, his knowledge of the literature of Shakespeare's time was, though extensive, not as extensive as he could have wished. As an editor he had, as he must have realized, promised more than he was going to be able to perform.

What Johnson accomplished was nevertheless considerable. His attempts to analyse the meaning of difficult or complicated passages has often proved illuminating to more recent editors, who have sometimes included his paraphrase in their own notes. More significant is his criticism of Shakespeare, especially his famous Preface, which has been almost universally acclaimed. Time and again it is Johnson's comment that we come back to; so often he seems to make the essential point, or really challenging point, about a particular character, scene or play. Even where our formulation differs from his, we often find it hard to discount what he says. And this fact is the more remarkable given that he inherited the assumptions of his age – not merely those relating to dramatic form which were regarded as 'rules' of criticism, but those arising from a concept of language which Shakespearian usage so often flouted. Though it has been said that Johnson was 'an outright dissenter against the neoclassic rules',[1] these frequently provided him with his starting-point. He found it natural to embrace many of the principles they contained, but in taking his stand on the broadest and most important of these, he was, as we shall see, increasingly led to challenge or disregard others.

II

Johnson praised Shakespeare as 'above all writers, at least above all modern writers, the poet of nature; the poet that holds up to his readers a faithful mirrour of manners and of life'. Though 'nature' had become the eighteenth century's most common critical term, it has here an unmistakable pertinence and force. By using it Johnson pays tribute to the impressive lifelikeness, the unique creativity of the poet whose characters seem 'the genuine progeny of common humanity, such as the world will always supply, and observation will always find'. His language suggests how full-bodied was his response to Shakespeare's scenes – the kind of response that represented an engagement at the deepest levels of experience. While it had been traditional to regard 'instruction' and 'delight' as the ends of poetry (often, in practice, with a duality reminiscent of the Horatian tag, *prodesse aut delectare* – 'to benefit or delight'), Johnson's statement in the Preface that 'the end of poetry is to instruct by pleasing' significantly integrates these as a single criterion. The 'pleasure-instruction' afforded him by Shakespeare's scenes derived from his being brought, as reader, into vital contact with 'common humanity'.

Johnson's terminology has nevertheless caused some confusion: 'In the writings of other poets a character is too often an individual; in those of Shakespeare it is commonly a species.' It has been suggested that we shall be surprised by this because 'we are likely to think it the highest praise of Shakespeare that he carefully individualized his characters'.[2] Other comments in the Preface (as well as many of the notes on particular characters) make it, however, clear that Johnson thought so too. Some light is thrown on his use of 'individual' by what he once said to Boswell about the contemporary dramatist and mimic Samuel Foote, who had once audaciously thought of taking him off: 'It is not comedy, which exhibits the character of a species, as that of a miser gathered from many misers: it is farce, which exhibits individuals.' This distinction is reminiscent of the one Dryden had made between the 'forced humours' of farce and the 'natural' characters of comedy – 'such humours . . . as are to be found and met with in the world'.[3]

Given the broad context in which Johnson uses 'species' in the Preface, we must, I think, resist the suggestion that 'when the learned neoclassicist surveyed mankind from China to Peru, he saw a world of identical men, somewhat transparently diversified by an increment of local and individual differences'.[4] Often the view that character must represent a generic human type seems to have amounted to this; and certainly the insistent moralist in Johnson – and it was a very large part of him – welcomed a formulation that stressed the representative. But representative of what? We all surely know what he is getting at when he writes of Shakespeare: 'His persons act and speak by the influence of those general passions and principles by which all minds are agitated, and the whole system of life is continued in motion.' He was, after all, the critic who, objecting to the 'narrower principles' of a Thomas Rymer, John Dennis, or Voltaire, defended Shakespeare for bringing on the stage a foolish senator and a drunken king. Seemingly he conceived the Shakespearian character as formed by the kind of 'pathetic potion' that Fielding describes in *A Journey from This World to the Next* (1743). In this narrative fantasy, 'the whole method of equipping a spirit for his entrance into the flesh' consists in having him swallow, just before birth, the contents of 'a small phial inscribed "The Pathetic Potion".' This potion is 'a mixture of all the passions, but in no exact proportion', so that from every mixture or combination a different character is formed. In the same way Johnson viewed the Shakespearian character as possessing a broad range of human traits as well as a distinct individuality (or distinctive identity).

The term 'poet of nature' has aesthetic and moral implications. Johnson reports Shakespeare's singular ability to look 'upon mankind with perspicacity in the highest degree curious and attentive', to 'sound the depths of the heart for the motives of action'; and he quotes Dryden's view 'that Shakespeare was the man who, of all modern and perhaps ancient poets, had the largest and most comprehensive soul'. These passages express one of the great commonplaces of the century – that Shakespeare was unrivalled as a moral philosopher because of his capacity to present so intimately, so truly and affectingly, the complex workings of the heart. Shaftesbury had used the image of the 'mirror' (which had such a long tradition) to stress the moral importance of 'a kind of vocal looking-glass', and implied that he found in 'the plain and natural turn' of Shakespeare's characters such 'self-study and inward converse' as he looked for in vain among more recent writers. Critics of the period were generally in agreement about Shakespeare's creative empathy, his 'negative capability' in creating character. William Guthrie (Johnson's early collaborator in the parliamentary debates) described him as the 'genius', rather than mere 'poet', who 'wraps himself up in the person he designs'. Lord Kames stressed his ability to 'imitate' rather than merely 'describe', to express 'a passion like one who is under its power'. To Mrs Montagu he seemed to have the art of the dervish 'who could throw his soul into the body of another man, and be at once possessed of his sentiments, adopt his passions, and rise to all the functions and feelings of his situation'. As a strict moralist, Johnson was wary about pushing character-identification too far; well known is his remark that Garrick 'deserved to be hanged' every time he played the part if he really believed himself to be 'that monster, Richard the Third'. Yet his conviction of what could be learnt from the plays seems close to William Richardson's, who, writing almost ten years later, was a precursor of Romantic criticism. In his introduction Richardson claims that Shakespeare's 'imitations' capture those 'passions and feelings of the heart' which by their very nature are so involuntary, fleeting and hard to scrutinize, and that, because of this, his work is potentially instructive. By being moved to experience the plays, as though at first hand, the reader is able to see into human nature, and therefore to learn something important about himself.[5]

Sometimes Johnson's wording seems designed to underline the possibility of such an inference. His note on *Othello*, for example, in praising the richness of characterization as what the attentive reader cannot miss, may be taken as a further illustration of his view (reported in Boswell's *Life*) that this play 'has more moral than almost any play':

> The Beauties of this play impress themselves so strongly upon the attention of the reader, that they can draw no aid from critical illustration. The fiery openness of Othello, magnanimous, artless, and credulous, boundless in his confidence, ardent in his affection, inflexible in his resolution, and obdurate in his revenge; the cool malignity of Iago, silent in his resentment, subtle in his designs, and studious at once of his interest and his vengeance; the soft simplicity of Desdemona, confident of merit, and conscious of innocence, her artless perseverance in her suit, and her slowness to suspect that she can be suspected, are such proofs of Shakespeare's skill in human nature as, I suppose, it is vain to seek in any modern writer.

At other times, too, Johnson's aesthetic and moral judgments seem to go hand in hand. The note on Bertram in *All's Well* is sufficiently pointed, being clearly a criticism of the whole play:

> I cannot reconcile my heart to Bertram; a man noble without generosity, and young without truth; who marries Helen as a coward, and leaves her as a profligate: when she is dead by his unkindness, sneaks home to a second marriage, is accused by a woman whom he has wronged, defends himself by falsehood, and is dismissed to happiness.

Another interesting note occurs in his commentary on *King John*. When the King, thinking the boy Arthur has been murdered, reproves Hubert for supposedly acting on his suggestion, Johnson comments:

> There are many touches of nature in this conference of John with Hubert. A man engaged in wickedness would keep the

> profit to himself, and transfer the guilt to his accomplice. These reproaches vented against Hubert are not the words of art or policy, but the eruptions of a mind swelling with consciousness of a crime, and desirous of discharging its misery on another.
>
> This account of the timidity of guilt is drawn *ab ipsis recessibus mentis*, from an intimate knowledge of mankind, particularly that line in which he says, that 'to have bid him tell his tale' in 'express' words, would have 'struck him dumb'; nothing is more certain, than that bad men use all the arts of fallacy upon themselves, palliate their actions to their own minds by gentle terms, and hide themselves from their own detection in ambiguities and subterfuges.

Here Johnson's insistent moral concern is sharpened to a fine relevance as he penetrates the mask of that 'smooth-faced gentleman, tickling Commodity' so much in evidence throughout this play.

III

In applauding Shakespeare's ability to convey 'human sentiments in human language', Johnson expresses a firm commitment to his enduring centrality. Not only does he recognize the uniqueness of Shakespeare's achievement, but he reveals something important about himself. Percy tells us that when he stayed with him in the summer of 1764, 'he chose for his regular reading the old Spanish romance of *Felixmarte of Hircania*, in folio, which he read quite through'. Interestingly, Percy adds: 'I have heard him attribute to these extravagant fictions that unsettled turn of mind which prevented his ever fixing in any profession.' However much this was, on Johnson's part, a rationalization, it gives added point to those parts of the Preface where he acknowledges both the 'vulgar' fascination with the old romances and Shakespeare's ability to transcend these puerile fictions by writing plays that could equally excite the imagination at the same time as they offered the mind something more substantial to dwell on. His own imagination was easily captivated by all kinds of fiction, though his moral conscience was ready to condemn any indulgence on that score as the literary equivalent of day-dreaming. Accordingly, in praising Shakespeare's human centrality, he acknowledges how therapeutic a contact with his work can be:

> This therefore is the praise of Shakespeare, that his drama is the mirrour of life; that he who has mazed his imagination, in following the phantoms which other writers raise up before him, may here be cured of his delirious extasies, by reading human sentiments in human language.

When Johnson sets the plays against the old romances, he can easily account for their greatness. A more serious problem (one which he never satisfactorily resolves) confronts him, however, when he considers how some of the plays end. He says at one point, eloquently testifying to the power of Shakespeare's art, that 'the end of the play is the end of expectation': 'As he commands us we laugh or mourn, or sit silent with quiet expectation, in tranquillity, without indifference.' Yet when faced with a play that did not adhere to his strict idea of 'poetical justice', Johnson found it necessary to conclude that Shakespeare 'seems to write without any moral purpose'. What bothered him was the dramatist's seeming 'indifference' to the fate of his characters. With his sense of the line that separated order from chaos, and the importance of the moral sanctions that enabled it to be drawn at all, he expected the poet to write with a clear sense of order. If, however, the end of the play really was for him 'the end of expectation', what force can his objection to Shakespeare's failure to preserve 'poetical justice' possibly have?

This question cannot, of course, be neatly answered. But asking it at least alerts us to the fact that Johnson's response to Shakespeare's world was at times a divided one. It was possible for him, as it is for us, to give himself imaginatively to a work and yet entertain reservations on personal and moral grounds. Nowhere is his response more immediate, or phrased with a greater inwardness, than in his remarks on Shakespeare's greatest comic character: 'Falstaff unimitated, unimitable Falstaff, how shall I describe thee?' Before the end of his note, however, Johnson has slanted his response towards the 'moral' to be drawn from Falstaff's influence on Hal. In *Rambler* 72 he had written of Falstaff with an affection like Hal's, only to remark: 'Good humour is indeed generally degraded by the characters in which it is found.' And he concludes his note on the two parts of *Henry IV* by stating:

> The moral to be drawn from this representation is, that no man is more dangerous than he that with a will to corrupt, hath the power to please; and that neither wit nor honesty ought to think themselves safe with such a companion when they see Henry seduced by Falstaff.

Here Johnson, in feeling compelled to say this, is to some extent backing away from his obvious fascination with Falstaff. We are reminded of what Mrs Piozzi said in noting that his praise 'went spontaneously to such passages as are sure in his own phrase to leave something behind them useful on common occasions, or observant of common manners':

> It was not King Lear cursing his daughters or deprecating the storm that I remember his commendations of, but Iago's ingenious malice and subtle revenge, or Prince Hal's gay compliance with the vices of Falstaff, whom he all along despised.

Johnson's silence on *King Lear* need not surprise us, for it moved him as none of the other plays did. But when he came to reflect on Hal's relationship with Falstaff, he was clearly concerned to make the kind of moral point that allowed him to justify or explain it to himself.

Macbeth, which interested Johnson from an early period, provides a further example of a similar sort of thing. Even his earliest notes on this play communicate the excitement with which he read it: 'He that peruses Shakespeare looks round alarmed, and starts to find himself alone'; 'Shakespeare, on this great occasion which involves the fate of a king, multiplies all the circumstances of horror.' Though Johnson did not think it the most actable of plays, it appears to have been in his mind when he was once asked to explain the time-honoured doctrine of 'catharsis'. 'Ambition', he said, 'is a noble passion; but by seeing upon the stage, that a man who is so excessively ambitious as to raise himself by injustice, is punished, we are terrified at the fatal consequences of such a passion.' Yet he apparently had difficulty, even so, in regarding Macbeth's conduct as the centre of moral interest. While he notes the shrewdness of Lady Macbeth's arguments in goading on her husband to murder Duncan, he claims that Shakespeare's 'plan' made the hero's agreement necessary. In his general note on this play Johnson is even more specific. While admitting it to be 'deservedly celebrated for the propriety of its fictions, and solemnity, grandeur and variety of its action', he complains that there are 'no nice discriminations of character': 'The events are too great to admit the influence of particular dispositions, and the course of the action necessarily determines the conduct of the agents.'

Johnson seems to be saying that the prophecies of the Witches (admittedly so prominent in the action) really determine the dramatic outcome. Certain of his notes – including his attempts to explain their historical relevance, the effect they would have had on a credulous audience of Shakespeare's own time – point in this direction. The lines,

> Which fate, and metaphysical aid doth seem
> To have thee crowned withal,

elicit from him the comment: 'For "seem" the sense evidently directs us to read "seek". The crown to which fate destines thee, and which preternatural agents *endeavour* to bestow upon thee.' He also reproduced notes from earlier editions which interpreted the 'weird sisters' as the Fates, or Goddesses of Destiny. *Macbeth* clearly poses, in an acute form, the question of the autonomy and identity of the self; but to assume that its hero is predestined to act as he does is to remove his actions too easily from the sphere of moral responsibility and scrutiny. Perhaps Johnson was so ready to do this because it enabled him to take, in a sense, an easy way out – to provide himself with an explanation, or rationalization, that did not oblige him to approach the play too closely, in all its terrifying detail. What, however, his comments suggest is that he has recognized the central problem, even though he does not choose to explore it.

Johnson's note on *King Lear*, which ostensibly objects to a lack of 'poetical justice', carries us close to what this play forces us to face. He records the 'shock' he felt at Cordelia's death on first reading it, and expresses a preference for Nahum Tate's version with a happy ending in which Lear remains alive and

Cordelia marries Edgar. In alluding to the debate on 'poetical justice' between Addison and Dennis that had been sparked off by Addison's *Cato* (in which the virtuous hero dies), Johnson says:

> A play in which the wicked prosper, and the virtuous miscarry, may doubtless be good, because it is a just representation of the common events of human life: but since all reasonable beings naturally love justice, I cannot easily be persuaded, that the observation of justice makes a play worse; or, that if other excellencies are equal, the audience will not always rise better pleased from the final triumph of persecuted virtue.

It has been suggested that Johnson's remarks on *Cato* in his 'Life of Addison' amount to a 'recantation' of this earlier position, and that he would not later have found fault with the ending of *King Lear*.[6] After liberally quoting Dennis's objections, he sides to this extent with Addison: 'Whatever pleasure there may be in seeing crimes punished and virtues rewarded, yet since wickedness often prospers in real life, the poet is certainly at liberty to give it prosperity on the stage.' But Cordelia's death, he rightly saw, is worlds away from Cato's: he used to say of Addison's play that 'of all things the most ridiculous would be to see a girl cry at the representation of it'. Nor does he bring himself specifically to condone the punishment of innocence (however this might seem to be implied by his argument); instead he talks of allowing wickedness to prosper. This he could apparently view with more equanimity, whereas the punishment of innocence, on the other hand, would remove the incentive to be virtuous. We know how strenuously he supported the maxim, 'Better that ten guilty should escape than one innocent person suffer': when Boswell once joined in an attempt to controvert it, Johnson answered him 'with great power of reasoning and eloquence'. So we must, I think, infer that his response to Cordelia's death would always have been what it was in 1765.

The arguments of the earlier debate were obviously in Johnson's mind when he wrote his note on the play. Rymer had coined the term 'poetical justice', insisting that the wicked must be seen to get their just deserts: '*Poetical Justice* . . . would require that the satisfaction be compleat and full, e're the *Malefactor* goes off the *Stage*, and nothing left to God Almighty, and another World. Nor will it suffer that the Spectators trust the *Poet* for a *Hell* behind the *Scenes*.' Dennis had willingly enough elaborated the point, interpreting what the poet meted out to his 'creatures' as a 'type' (however 'imperfect') of the Judgment of the Creator towards his. Unless in the drama the good were rewarded and the wicked punished, Providence would appear but as Chance or Fate.[7] Johnson does not pursue this analogy; instead he says with a truth there is no gainsaying that 'all reasonable beings naturally love justice'. While he felt saddened by Ophelia's death, and found the scene of Desdemona's murder 'dreadful' and 'not to be endured', the death of Cordelia was clearly of a different order, as the painfulness of this play's ending is for us too. Perhaps the 'shock' Johnson felt at her death was the greater because there is in this play no hint of the kind of justice in the hereafter which is foreshadowed for Ophelia (by Laertes) and Desdemona (by Othello himself). Such 'justice' is, however, even as an afterthought, entirely irrelevant to *King Lear*, which Johnson anyway read as a pagan play, and in which he found (except at one point he considered anachronistic) no evidence of Christian imagery. With the terms of Dennis's argument hovering somewhere in the background, the possibility nevertheless exists that the apparent fortuitousness of Cordelia's death aroused in the depths of his being the fear of annihilation, an idea that, as Boswell reminds us, he found even more insupportable than the prospect of everlasting punishment.

Whatever the precise resonances that entered into Johnson's response, one way of summarizing this is to say that the play moved him so deeply he wished it had ended otherwise. His sense of 'shock' is registered against a deeply felt human experience ('all reasonable beings naturally love justice'); in this respect his comments suggest a response that was surely not so different from ours. The play defeats all expectation of justice, carrying us to the very edge of the stark and searing. We feel at the end that life provides no answer to Lear's final question,

> Why should a dog, a horse, a rat, have life,
> And thou no breath at all?

– no answer, except that life is as it is, and must be faced as such. Johnson found it difficult, even impossible, to accept life on such terms. Yet he was also without Dennis's easy optimism and lacked utterly his complacency. Confronted with the play Shakespeare wrote, he was forced to transform what had served Dennis as an easy assumption into a last desperate line of defence; and how desperate is clear from his realization of just how compelling this play is: 'So powerful is the current of the poet's imagination, that the mind, which once ventures within it, is hurried irresistibly along.' 'I was', he says, 'many years ago so shocked by Cordelia's death, that I know not whether I ever endured to read again the last scenes of the play till I undertook to revise them as an editor.' Though Johnson records his 'shock' in these terms, suggesting how overwhelming it had seemed to be, there are so many quotations from the last act in his *Dictionary* that it could almost be reconstructed from the pages of that work.[8]

IV

What has already been implied about Johnson's criticism and the quality of its engagement with Shakespeare is also apparent from his discussion of other so-called 'rules'. What he offers is a critical appraisal, based on a first-hand response to the plays rather than on what the 'rules' themselves might be supposed to dictate. Other neoclassical critics, who objected to Shakespeare's characterization, or his failure to observe 'poetical justice', were really on the horns of a dilemma. Though ready to acknowledge his great natural gifts, his unrivalled genius in imitating 'nature', they often criticized him for being deficient in 'art', as though conscious only of an antithesis between these terms. Ben Jonson, however, had stressed Shakespeare's claim to both:

> Yet must I not give nature all: thy art,
> My gentle Shakespeare, must enjoy a part.

And Johnson, in recognizing, as Pope had said, that 'nature' is 'At once the source, and end, and test of art', discounted the strictures of his age in claiming that 'there is always an appeal open from criticism to nature'. This is his forthright comment in the Preface, and the attitude it reflects makes his criticism of

Shakespeare very different from that of his neo-classical predecessors. It was, perhaps, for this reason that Adam Smith acknowledged its vigour and independence, hailing the Preface as 'the most *manly* piece of criticism that was ever published in any country'.

Had Johnson published his *Shakespeare* twenty years earlier, at the time he originally proposed an edition of the plays, it seems likely that his attitude would not have been so flexible and independent as it later was. Though he saw as early as 1751 (in *Rambler* 156) that the example of Shakespeare made a redefinition of the 'rules' necessary, he was still at that time somewhat tentative. While properly seeking to make a distinction between 'essential principles' and 'rules which no literary dictator had authority to enact', he adds: 'I do not however think it safe to judge of works of genius merely by the event.' This essay deals primarily with 'tragicomedy' (though other topics are mentioned as well), and here Shakespeare is praised as 'that transcendent and unbounded genius . . . who, to actuate the affections, needed not the slow gradation of common means, but could fill the heart with instantaneous jollity or sorrow, and vary our disposition as he changed his scenes'. Yet Johnson was also ready to suggest that 'perhaps the effects even of Shakespeare's poetry might have been greater, had he not counteracted himself'. In the later Preface, on the other hand, it is explicitly said: 'This reasoning is so specious, that it is received as true even by those who in daily experience feel it to be false.' Johnson's defence of Shakespeare's 'compositions of a distinct kind' has by 1765 become quite unequivocal. A more important perception now leads him to discount his earlier objection, and he takes his stand on 'nature' as at once the source and end and test of Shakespearian 'tragicomedy'.

The question that, more than any other, bedevilled Shakespearian criticism during the eighteenth century was the importance to be attached to the 'unities' of time and place. This is today an unimportant question, and in one sense hardly worth the energy Johnson expended on it. But it remains more interesting than it at first seems because of what it led him to say about the nature of dramatic illusion. In *Rambler* 156 he had spoken of the unities in these terms: 'Probability requires that the time of action should approach somewhat nearly to that of exhibition, and those plays will always be thought most happily conducted which crowd the greatest variety into the least space. But since it will frequently happen that some delusion must be admitted, I know not where the limits of imagination can be fixed.' In tackling this question in the Preface, however, he immediately seizes on the faulty logic of those who, in seeking to uphold the 'unities', confuse the limits of the real world and the play's imagined world: 'The unities of time and place arise evidently from false assumptions'; 'It is false, that any representation is mistaken for reality, that any dramatic fable in its materiality was ever credible, or, for a single moment, was ever credited.'

In reducing the arguments of his opponents to absurdity, Johnson is forced to insist that 'the spectators are always in their senses':

> If the spectator can be once persuaded, that his old acquaintances are Alexander and Caesar, that a room illuminated with candles is the plain of Pharsalia, or the bank of Granicus, he is in a state of elevation above the reach of reason, or of truth. . . . There is no reason why a mind thus wandering in ecstasy should count the clock, or why an hour should not be a century in that calenture of the brains that can make the stage a field.

Given, however, what Johnson rightly says about *King Lear* ('So powerful is the current of the poet's imagination, that the mind, which once ventures within it, is hurried irresistibly along'), we can see the difficulty he gets himself into in answering his opponents in this way. The tangle arises because of the way in which he uses 'imagine': 'Surely he that imagines this may imagine more.' To the extent that the initial act of imagining or presuming is preposterous (since a walk to the theatre is not a voyage to Alexandria, or wherever the first act is set), there is an obvious difficulty about using 'imagine' in a more positive sense.

Because of the terms in which Johnson has conducted his argument, he is bound to explain in what sense a play is 'credited'; and it is here that he succeeds in drawing attention to an important aesthetic principle:

> It will be asked, how the drama moves, if it is not credited. It is credited with all the credit due to a drama. It is credited, whenever it moves, as a just picture of a real original; as representing to the auditor what he would himself feel, if he were to do or suffer what is there feigned to be suffered or to be done. The reflection that strikes the heart is not, that the evils before us are real evils, but that they are evils to which we ourselves may be exposed.

Johnson focuses on what we feel as members of the audience – that what is happening on stage could, under different circumstances, be what we might be exposed to. What we feel 'for the moment' as a real possibility becomes, then, the important thing. And that we can be so moved by it, and still contemplate it with pleasure or 'delight', proceeds, as he saw, from our being at a certain mental distance from what is being presented: 'The delight of tragedy proceeds from our consciousness of fiction; if we thought murders and treasons real, they would please no more.'

It is interesting to note that those who, like Dennis, complained of Shakespeare's lack of 'poetical art' were often the very people who, in upholding the unities of time and place, based their arguments on a preposterous kind of imagining. In effect they left themselves open to the paradoxical charge of being willing to suffer a 'calenture of the brains' while being so rigidly prescriptive as to be seemingly unmoved by the work before them. But there is little to be gained from dragging them into notice, except in so far as this gives us a better sense of what historically was Johnson's achievement. The conclusion he came to was not that Shakespeare wanted 'poetical art', but that he had so much of it that his audience was virtually unconscious of any artifice: 'The dialogue of this author is often so evidently determined by the incident which produces it, and is pursued with so much ease and simplicity, that it seems scarcely to claim the merit of fiction.'

Throughout the Preface Johnson is engaged in a process of weighing-up, of comparing Shakespeare with other authors in an attempt to reach a just appraisal. What he finds is that Shakespeare's world is so full and vital, so packed with incident and vibrant with life, that the conscious 'art' of other dramatists is proved to be mere artifice by the emptiness of his response to it. Johnson had, of course, realized Shakespeare's greatness many years before he published his edition, but not until it appeared did he account for this in such a way as to demonstrate the irrelevance of some of the more influential of the 'rules'. His view is that a play so constructed as to preserve the unities of time and place ought to be considered 'as an elaborate curiosity, as the product of superfluous and ostentatious art'. His imagination is excited by Shakespeare's 'nobler beauties of variety and instruction', and these are what persuade him to defend Shakespearian 'tragicomedy'. Against the artificial (and thoroughly traditional) definitions of form, he sets that peculiarly inclusive quality which makes the plays themselves so rich and unique. There is, then, an easy and logical transition from his praise of Shakespeare's characterization to his defence of his 'compositions of a distinct kind'. Because these exhibit 'the real state of sublunary nature, which partakes of good and evil, joy and sorrow, mingled with endless variety of proportion and innumerable modes of combination', Johnson concludes that in this respect, too, Shakespeare is genuinely 'the poet of nature', who shows 'the course of the world' as it really is.

V

There were, however, presuppositions Johnson shared with his age which, however quaint they now appear, reflected (at least in theory) what the audience was prepared to accept as credible in the theatre. The introduction of an army on stage was regarded by the anonymous author of *Some Remarks on Hamlet* (1736) as 'quite unnatural and absurd'; and Johnson's own *incredulus odi* (I hate what I cannot believe) was so marked that he was not ahead of his age in formulating a less literal-minded set of conventions. For him 'imperial tragedy' was staged more effectively in the reader's imagination than in the theatre, and he was always openly incredulous whenever the physical limitations of the stage seemed too narrow for the scene. When in the chorus to *Henry V* Shakespeare exhorts the audience to 'make imaginary puissance', Johnson comments: 'This passage shows that Shakespeare was fully sensible of the absurdity of showing battles in the theatre, which indeed is never done but tragedy becomes farce. Nothing can be represented to the eye but by something like it, and "within a wooden O" nothing very like a battle can be exhibited.'

What had perhaps the most far-reaching implications for dramatic criticism was the distinction that was made between the different ways, in poetry, of presenting 'the action' of a work. This had been conveniently summarized by the French critic René Le Bossu in a work that was translated into English and appears to have been influential. In distinguishing between the 'historical' mode of epic and 'the most artificial and active form' (drama), Le Bossu says:

> Whatever regard the *Dramatic* Poet has to his Spectators, yet the Persons he introduces in his Poem, who are the only Actors therein, are not in the least acquainted with those before whom the Poet makes them speak: nay more, they don't know what they shall do themselves, nor what the Issue of their Projects will be; and therefore they cannot either advertise the Spectators thereof, or beg their Attention, or thank them for it. So that this kind of Poem, properly speaking, has no parts exempt from the Action that is represented.[9]

This meant, in effect, a set of conventions which placed a decided restraint on what the audience was prepared to accept as credible dramatic speech. Whether the eighteenth century pointed out the unsuitability of rhymed verse in drama, insisted that soliloquies should arise naturally and (as Johnson says of Posthumus's) 'issue warm from the heart', or argued that highly figurative language was inappropriate in the mouth of a character under great emotional pressure, it did so because of its assumption that a character in a play should act and speak as it might be supposed a person would, if placed in the same situation in real life.

What appears to us a rather crude criterion of verisimilitude seemed to the eighteenth century to have its basis in logic and fact. Nor would the age admit that it was thereby confusing the distinction between art and reality. In a work that Johnson praised, Joseph Spence distinguished between what he called the 'use' of art and the 'appearances' of it, condemned 'the impertinent assistance of Art', and held that 'where the passions are to be touch'd, apparent art is apparent fraud'. Lord Kames was later to make the same point:

> Rooted grief, deep anguish, terror, remorse, despair, and all the severe dispiriting passions, are declared enemies, perhaps not to figurative language in general, but undoubtedly to the pomp and solemnity of comparison. . . . In any severe passion which totally occupies the mind, metaphor is unnatural.

This view had been common since Dryden, who claimed that in drama 'all that is said is supposed to be the effect of sudden thought; which, though it excludes not the quickness of wit in repartees, yet admits not a too curious election of words, too frequent allusions, or use of tropes or, in fine, anything that shows remoteness of thought or labour in the writer.' 'No man', Dryden remarked elsewhere, 'is at leisure to make sentences and similes when his soul is in an agony' – not even, as he frankly admitted, his own hard-pressed Montezuma in a scene from *The Indian Emperor*:

> The image had not been amiss . . . at another time, *sed nunc non erat hisce locus* ['but now was not the place for these things']: he destroyed the concernment which the audience might otherwise have had for him; for they could not think the danger near when he had the leisure to invent a simile.'[10]

Because the eighteenth century sought in this way to limit the role of the poet to whatever seemed credible in the mouth of an individual character, many of Shakespeare's speeches attracted a good deal of comment. Johnson, for example, thought that Macbeth's comparison of Banquo's influence on his 'genius' to Caesar's on Antony's ought to be regarded as some player's 'intrusion of a remote and useless image into a speech bursting from a man wholly possessed with his own present condition, and therefore not at leisure to explain his own allusions to himself'. One of Hotspur's extravagant outbursts,

> By heaven, methinks, it were an easy leap
> To pluck bright honour from the pale-faced moon,

also became a subject of debate. Discounting the view that this should be described as 'a ridiculous rant and absolute madness',

Warburton read the speech as 'allegorical', explaining the meaning of Hotspur's lines in the following terms: 'Though some great and shining character in the most elevated orb was already in possession of her (honour), yet it would, methinks, be easy by greater acts to eclipse his glory and pluck all his honours from him.' Johnson, however, was prepared to argue that the speaker was referring to the actual moon:

> This sally of Hotspur may be, I think, soberly and rationally vindicated as the violent eruption of a mind inflated with ambition and fired with resentment; as the boastful clamour of a man able to do much, and eager to do more; as the hasty motion of turbulent desire; as the dark expression of indetermined thoughts.

As one might expect, such a naturalistic approach to dramatic speech occasionally prompted Johnson to ingenious and even subtle commentary. Alluding to the notably figurative passage in which Macbeth explains how the sight of the murdered Duncan led him to kill the grooms, he observes:

> It is not improbable, that Shakespeare put these forced and unnatural metaphors into the mouth of Macbeth as a mark of artifice and dissimulation, to show the difference between the studied language of hypocrisy, and the natural outcries of sudden passion. This whole speech so considered, is a remarkable instance of judgment, as it consists entirely of antithesis and metaphor.

When Iachimo, in his attempt to convince Posthumus that he has enjoyed Imogen, describes the scene on the tapestry of her bedchamber, where 'Cydnus swelled above the banks, or for/The press of boats or pride', Johnson comments: 'His language is such as a skilful villain would naturally use, a mixture of airy triumph and serious deposition. His gaiety shows his seriousness to be without anxiety, and his seriousness proves his gaiety to be without art.' The virtue of these notes lies in their attempt at inwardness – their readiness to alert the reader to a character's state of mind. Most suggestive, however, is that on the 'willow' scene in *Othello*. Though the First Quarto of the play had lacked some twenty lines, including the song itself, Johnson praises the later version of the scene as an improvement:

> This is perhaps the only insertion made in the latter editions which has improved the play. The rest seem to have been added for the sake of amplification or of ornament. . . . This addition is natural. Desdemona can at first hardly forbear to sing the song; she endeavours to change her train of thoughts, but her imagination at last prevails, and she sings it.

What Dryden had termed 'remoteness of thought' was held to be especially inappropriate in more affecting scenes. When Enobarbus, repenting of his treachery, exclaims,

> Throw my heart
> Against the flint and hardness of my fault,
> Which being dried with grief, will break to powder,
> And finish all foul thoughts,

Johnson comments: 'The pathetick of Shakespeare too often ends in the ridiculous. It is painful to find the gloomy dignity of this noble scene destroyed by the intrusion of a conceit so far-fetched and unaffecting.' When Richard II, having expressed himself to Aumerle in 'the natural language of submissive misery' on hearing of Bolingbroke's return, imagines how his tears will devastate the nation and dig his own grave, Johnson observes: 'Shakespeare is very apt to deviate from the pathetic to the ridiculous.' When the Queen, lamenting Edward IV's death, exclaims,

> Give me no help in lamentation,
> I am not barren to bring forth complaints:
> All springs reduce their currents to mine eyes,
> That I, being governed by the wat'ry moon,
> May send forth plenteous tears to drown the world.
> Ah, for my husband, for my dear Lord Edward,

Johnson states that 'the introduction of the moon is not very natural'. No doubt he found the last line much more moving! Again, when King Philip bids Constance moderate her grief after Arthur's capture, Johnson's note is as follows:

> It was necessary that Constance should be interrupted, because a passion so violent cannot be borne long. I wish the following speeches had been equally happy; but they only serve to show, how difficult it is to maintain the pathetic long.

Constance had wished for madness as a release from her grief, but Johnson was forced to suspect her sincerity when she proceeded to pun on 'bonds' and 'liberty'. He also censured Queen Katherine's allusion to 'cardinal sins' when in the presence of Wolsey: 'The distress of Catharine might have kept her from the quibble to which she is irresistibly tempted by the word "cardinal".'

Examples such as these illustrate Johnson's complaint in the Preface that Shakespeare 'is not long soft and pathetick without some idle conceit, or contemptible equivocation': 'He no sooner begins to move, than he counteracts himself; and terror and pity, as they are rising in the mind, are checked and blasted by sudden frigidity.' For a similar reason he objected to Shakespeare's 'declamations or set speeches', which were, he thought, generally too long for the accompanying dramatic situation. In the interests of probability, of what seemed a credible presentation of characters and events, he would have shortened not only Constance's lament, but Gaunt's farewell to his banished son, and even Lady Macbeth's rebuking of her husband during the banquet scene ('This speech is rather too long for the circumstances in which it is spoken'), as well as Henry's famous speech before the battle of Agincourt ('This speech, like many others of the declamatory kind, is too long'). 'Narration in dramatic poetry is', Johnson writes, 'naturally tedious, as it is unanimated and inactive, and obstructs the progress of the action; it should therefore always be rapid, and enlivened by frequent interruption.' On one level this suggests a curious inability to respond to the creative power of Shakespeare's language, which, as we shall see, was characteristic of much eighteenth-century criticism. Before considering this, however, it is worth noting that the tenor of these remarks in the Preface suggests why Johnson made the distinction that has often seemed so puzzling:

> In tragedy he often writes with great appearance of toil and

study, what is written at last with little felicity; but in his comic scenes, he seems to produce without labour, what no labour can improve. . . . His comedy pleases by the thoughts and the language, and his tragedy for the greater part by incident and action. His tragedy seems to be skill, his comedy to be instinct.

VI

The remark just quoted invites us to consider Johnson's objection, not just to Shakespeare's use of dramatic speech, but to Shakespeare's use of language. One recent critic, with this remark in mind, expresses surprise that the tragedies should have been more heavily annotated than the comedies, and 'the sombre "problem comedy"' *Measure for Measure* most heavily of all.[11] But this is precisely what Johnson's notes on the play would lead us to expect: 'There is', he says, 'perhaps not one of Shakespeare's plays more darkened than this by the peculiarities of its author, and the unskilfulness of its editors, by distortions of phrase, or negligence of transcription.' He complains of the 'labour' of its graver scenes, and we learn from the Preface that, in his view, such 'labour' results in 'tumour, meanness, tediousness, and obscurity'.

The language of the first scene, particularly, of *Measure for Measure* is admittedly difficult; but to claim that its 'obscurity' is the result of corruption or 'tumour' is to miss its very real and complex suggestiveness. The Duke's words,

We have with special soul
Elected him our absence to supply,

which immediately look forward to his subsequent words to Angelo,

your scope is as mine own,
So to enforce or qualify the laws,
As to your soul seems good,

were supposed corrupt by both Warburton and Johnson, who read 'seal' for 'soul' to replace Warburton's proposed emendation 'roll': 'A special "seal" is a very natural metonymy for a "special commission".' This example, if it does not quite speak volumes, at least prompts us to wonder less about Johnson's having remarked to Boswell that 'Shakespeare never has six lines together without a fault'. Must we conclude, however reluctantly, that he would have endorsed the frequent rewriting of Shakespeare during this period which, adding up to a large number of denatured texts, was designed to make the plays more acceptable and intelligible to an eighteenth-century audience? Certainly he would often seem not to have responded to that realizing power of language which so singularly substantiates Shakespeare's work to the imagination.[12]

Johnson noted in his *Proposals* that one of the causes of Shakespeare's 'obscurity' was 'that fulness of idea, which might sometimes load his words with more sentiment than they could conveniently convey, and that rapidity of imagination which might hurry him to a second thought before he had fully explained the first'. This remark, in suggesting why eighteenth-century editors thought explication so necessary, reflects the assumptions about language and imagery that led them to offer it in such wholesale proportions. Admittedly Johnson avoided, and clearly became exasperated with, Warburton's own licence in suggesting emendations: his own notes display, by contrast, a greater commonsense, more extensive knowledge of the language, and keener awareness of what he referred to as the 'licentiousness of Shakespeare's mode of expression'. Yet Warburton's insistence on the 'integrity' of metaphor was not something which he brushed lightly aside. He had suggested that Macbeth's 'way of life' should read 'may of life', there being otherwise no relation between it and 'fallen into the sear'; and when this note was reprinted in 1765, he added: 'The author has "may" in the same sense elsewhere' (examples from *Henry V* and *Much Ado* having meantime been quoted in the *Dictionary*.) Similarly, Edmund's 'an essay or taste of my virtue' prompted the note: 'Though "taste" may stand in this place, yet I believe we should read "assay" or "test" of my virtue: they are both metallurgical terms, and properly joined. So in *Hamlet*, "Bring me to the *test*".'

These notes indicate the kind of metaphorical consistency which the eighteenth century usually looked for. A good deal of Shakespearian annotation is of this sort, even though John

Upton, for example, had as early as 1746 been disposed to remark: 'The poet is to take his share of the faults, and the critic is to keep his hands from the context.'[13] Johnson was by his own account 'not much a friend to conjectural emendation', and looking back in 1773 on earlier editorial practice, including his own, he expressed the wish that 'we all explained more and emended less'. Yet whatever restraint he tried to show (and we have seen that he sometimes tried to support with other examples a proposed change of reading), he could not in practice escape the linguistic assumptions of his age. Often he found it necessary to describe a Shakespearian metaphor as 'harsh', and some account of why he did so will perhaps best throw light on his frequent criticism of the language of the plays.

The term 'harsh' had been used before, most revealingly by Berkeley in 1710: 'It sounds very harsh to say we eat and drink ideas, and are clothed with ideas . . . and it is certain that any expression which varies from the familiar use of language, will seem harsh and ridiculous.' Not only had Dryden advocated 'more proper, more sounding, and more significant' words, but Defoe had spoken of 'a direct Signification of Words, or a *Cadence in Expression*, which we call speaking *Sense* . . . the contrary to which we call *Nonsense*'. Kames was later to make use of the same analogy:

> A figure of speech is precisely similar to concordant sounds in music, which, without contributing to the melody, make it harmonious. . . . The beauty of the figure depends on the intimacy of the relation betwixt the figurative and proper sense of the word. A slight resemblance, in particular, will never make this figure agreeable. The expression, for example, *drink down a secret*, for listening to a secret with attention, is harsh and uncouth, because there is scarce any resemblance betwixt *listening* and *drinking*.[14]

The authority of Locke also stands behind such a passage, not merely in the implied connection between 'words' and 'things', but also in the insistence on 'resemblance', which recalls Locke's influential definition of 'wit' (quoted in the *Dictionary*). Johnson also stated in the *Dictionary* that 'a metaphor is a simile comprised in a word'; and this understanding (or rather misunderstanding) of how metaphor works explains many of his comments on Shakespeare's use of language.

The lines Johnson unreservedly praises seem to be those containing figures that allow his imagination to work in a straightforward way, as though a clear one-to-one relationship is involved in the 'resemblance'. For example, he describes as 'exquisitely beautiful' the words Canterbury uses of Henry V: 'When he speaks, / The air, a chartered libertine, is still.' The lines introducing the scene of Suffolk's murder in *2 Henry VI*,

> The gaudy, blabbing and remorseful day
> Is crept into the bosom of the sea,

also won his praise:

> The epithet "blabbing" applied to the day by a man about to commit murder, is exquisitely beautiful. Guilt is afraid of light, considers darkness as a natural shelter, and makes night the confidante of those actions which cannot be trusted to the "tell-tale day".

Often, however, Johnson's pursuit of the necessary 'resemblance' is less happy than this. In a note on King John's words to the ambassador Chatillon,

> Be thou as lightning in the eyes of France,
> For ere thou canst report I will be there,
> The thunder of my cannon shall be heard,

he writes: 'The simile does not suit well: the lightning indeed appears before the thunder is heard, but the lightning is destructive, and the thunder innocent.' Here Shakespeare's 'fulness of idea' is more expressive than his editor allows, for the King's 'thunder' is surely intended to overwhelm Chatillon's 'report'. Again, on Richard II's words to Bolingbroke as they hold the crown between them,

> Now is this golden crown like a deep well,
> That owes two buckets filling one another;
> The emptier ever dancing in the air,
> The other down, unseen and full of water;
> That bucket down and full of tears am I,
> Drinking my griefs, whilst you mount up on high,

Johnson's note is: 'This is a comparison not easily accommodated to the subject, nor very naturally introduced. The best part is this line, in which he makes the usurper the "empty" bucket.' It is, however, the last few lines which, in the larger context of the play, illustrate most tellingly the kind of self-absorption, histrionic and self-regarding, that makes it impossible for the King to survive against Bolingbroke.

The last two examples in particular illustrate the attention that was given to 'properties' – as though the 'propriety' of a figure also involved these. Johnson objected to the description of Antony's heart as 'the bellows and the fan, /To cool a Gypsy's lust':

> In this passage something seems to be wanting. The "bellows" and "fan" being commonly used for contrary purposes, were probably opposed by the author, who might perhaps have written, "is become the bellows and the fan, / *To kindle and* to cool a Gypsy's lust".

Up to Johnson's time and beyond, 'trees' could be 'mossed', though not (as in *Timon*) 'moist'; it was not until 1794 that Walter Whiter challenged the prevailing verbal criticism by invoking another Lockian principle, 'the association of ideas', to explain Shakespeare's seemingly unfamiliar choice of words.[15] Yet perhaps there was a further reason why Johnson insisted on such descriptions as included recognizable 'properties'. He was the first to use 'unideal' in the sense of 'lacking in ideas', 'conveying no clear mental picture' (*Rambler* 135, 'Life of Dryden'), and his preference for a clear or definite 'image' (a word he used more frequently than any of his contemporaries) is generally evident from his criticism. He disliked 'the enumeration of the choughs and crows, the samphire-man and the fishers' in the description of Dover Cliff, and also the mention of 'the beetle and the bat' in *Macbeth*, which he once said detracted 'from the general idea of darkness – inspissated gloom'. What these examples in part suggest is that he had a strong visualizing tendency in reading poetry. Johnson objected to a use of metaphor – as in Wolsey's famous speech where he bids 'farewell' to his greatness – which included details that did not 'correspond exactly with nature' ('Vernal frosts indeed do not kill the "root"'); but, perhaps even more significantly, he also objected to Wolsey's phrase 'a tomb of orphans' tears', remarking, 'A "tomb of tears" is very harsh.'

Examples of this sort could be multiplied, but the point will already be clear. It would, however, be unfair to represent Johnson entirely by notes like these. In his willingness to grapple with the actual text (whereas Warburton had for the most part expended his ingenuity in proposing other readings), he shows a greater intelligence in coming to grips with Shakespeare's meaning. We have already noted the debt of modern editors to his attempts at paraphrase; and his superiority to Warburton can also be demonstrated from their respective comments on one of Shakespeare's 'harsh' metaphors. In the first scene of *Measure for Measure*, the Duke makes 'a leavened and prepared choice' in proceeding to bestow his commission on Angelo. For 'leavened' Warburton had proposed 'levelled', claiming that 'the allusion is to archery, when a man has fixed upon his object after taking good aim'; but Johnson rejects this suggestion:

> No emendation is necessary. 'Leavened choice' is one of Shakespeare's harsh metaphors. His train of ideas seems to be this. 'I have proceeded to you with choice *mature*, *concocted*, *fermented*, leavened.' When bread is 'leavened', it is left to ferment: a 'leavened' choice is therefore a choice not hasty, but considerate, not declared as soon as it fell into the imagination, but suffered to work long in the mind. Thus explained it suits better with 'prepared' than 'levelled'.

It is a pity that Johnson takes it no further than this. Because of his note, however, we might be prompted to ask whether Angelo needs leavening, or whether the Duke's language here does not suggest something about his manner of proceeding. He has 'prepared' things to a certain point and proposes to leave them to work; but how they will turn out has still, in a sense, to be guessed at: 'What figure of us think you he will bear?'

On the use to which such notes are to be put, Johnson himself should be given the last word. At the end of the Preface, in weighing his edition as a whole, he is inclined to regard them as 'necessary evils'. 'Let him', he continues, 'that is yet unacquainted with the powers of Shakespeare, and who desires to feel the highest pleasure that the drama can give, read every play from the first scene to the last, with utter negligence of all his commentators.' Johnson realizes how, by coming between the reader and the work, such notes can inhibit imaginative involvement: 'Particular passages are cleared by notes, but the general effect of the work is weakened. The mind is refrigerated by interruption; the thoughts are diverted from the particular subject.' He then makes an interesting point about what is involved in the very act of criticism: 'There is', he says, 'a kind of intellectual remoteness necessary for the comprehension of any great work in its full design and its true proportions.' Here he recognizes that criticism is ultimately a complex act of imagination and analysis, which requires the critic to remain alive to his experience of a work, and yet somehow achieve enough detachment to be able to articulate his response in a way that is faithful to the work in all its compelling detail. In his own criticism of Shakespeare Johnson often succeeds in doing this; at its best it illuminates the plays. And because Shakespeare touched him at the deepest levels of experience, he cannot write about the plays without also revealing something about himself.

8

Lives of the Poets

I

During the 1760s Johnson's life changed in a number of ways. From 1762 onwards his pension gave him a measure of financial security; the next year he met Boswell; and early in 1765 a friendship began which lasted until Henry Thrale's death in 1781 and his wife's remarriage in the last year of Johnson's life. During the summer of 1766 he spent more than three months in the Thrales' house at Streatham, and in the years that followed he was regularly their companion, almost a member of their family, not only in London but at Brighton and Bath, and on their tours to Wales (1774) and France (1775). He was also looking forward to a proposed trip to Italy with them – a country he particularly wished to see since he looked to 'the shores of the Mediterranean' as the birthplace of Western civilization – when the sudden death of their son caused the trip to be cancelled. Relieved from the necessity of providing himself with an income, Johnson was ready enough to travel. Though his most important ramble was with Boswell, to the Highlands of Scotland, after his *Shakespeare* appeared scarcely a year went by when he did not visit his native Midlands.

With his edition behind him, Johnson seems to have contemplated a rest from writing. When it was due to appear, he wrote (9 October 1765) to Joseph Warton: 'As I felt no solicitude about this work, I receive no great comfort from its conclusion; but yet am well enough pleased that the public has no further claim upon me.' Though he was doubtless thinking of the claims of those subscribers who had waited so long for their volumes, he seems also to have been expressing a conviction that he had done his fair share of writing. During the early 1770s he largely confined himself to revising his *Shakespeare* (with the help of George Steevens) and his *Dictionary*, and writing his four political tracts; apart from his *Journey*, these were his only major pieces until he began publishing, at the end of the decade, his *Lives of the Poets*.

The attitude Johnson expressed in his letter to Warton is also reflected in what he said to Boswell and Goldsmith early the following year. When Boswell pressed him to write something else, and Goldsmith chipped in with, 'Ay, Sir, we have a claim upon you', Johnson retorted:

> 'No, Sir, I am not obliged to do any more. No man is obliged to do as much as he can do. A man is to have part of his life to himself. If a soldier has fought a good many campaigns, he is not to be blamed if he retires to ease and tranquillity. A physician, who has practised long in a great city, may be excused if he retires to a small town and takes less practice. Now, Sir, the good I can do by my conversation bears the same proportion to the good I can do by my writings, that the practice of a physician, retired to a small town, does to his practice in a great city.'

What this reply, however, also suggests is that Johnson had a very deep sense of vocational commitment. Boswell notes that

> the solemn text 'of him to whom much is given, much will be required' seems to have been ever present to his mind, in a rigorous sense, and to have made him dissatisfied with his labours and acts of goodness, however comparatively great; so that the unavoidable consciousness of his superiority was, in that respect, a cause of disquiet.

Despite his more relaxed way of life after his *Shakespeare* had appeared, Johnson could never convince himself that he had done enough to be saved, and his disquiet is everywhere apparent in his prayers and meditations (including those he wrote while engaged on the *Lives*). It was, therefore, understandable that he should accept this new challenge when it came, especially since poetry had been with him such a lifelong interest. As we read his last great work, we become aware that a lifetime of thinking and talking about poetry has been fed into its pages.

It was on Easter Saturday, 1777, that Johnson met a deputation of booksellers and agreed to undertake it, and Edward Dilly, one of the partners in the venture, gives in a letter to Boswell an account of this meeting. An edition of the English poets was being printed at Edinburgh, and since this was taken by the London booksellers to be an invasion of what they thought of as their 'literary property', they planned to publish 'an elegant and accurate edition of all the English poets of reputation, from Chaucer to the present time', with 'a concise account of the life of each author by Dr. Samuel Johnson'. Accordingly, three of them waited on him to solicit his help, and he 'very politely undertook it, and seemed exceedingly pleased with the proposal'. 'As to the terms', continues Dilly, 'it was left entirely to the Doctor to name his own; he mentioned two hundred guineas; it was immediately agreed to, and a farther compliment, I believe, will be made to him.'

The *Prefaces, Biographical and Critical* began not with Chaucer but with Abraham Cowley; they were in that sense less extensive in scope than the booksellers had planned. But from Cowley onwards the fifty-two 'Lives' provide a comprehensive account of English poetry from the 'metaphysical' school of Donne to Gray and his contemporaries. This appeared in two instalments. Twenty-two poets (Cowley to John Hughes) occupied the first four volumes published in March 1779, and thirty (Addison to Gray) the last six published in May 1781. The name of Hughes suggests a feature of the work that is even more obvious in respect of other names: in the poets it includes it is uneven, sweeping like a dragnet great and small. What Johnson says of George Stepney may be applied to several others whose 'Lives' he wrote: 'One cannot always find the reason for which the world has sometimes conspired to squander praise.' Despite the booksellers' inclusion of names like these, it was left to Johnson to suggest the addition, not only of John Pomfret, Sir Richard Blackmore, Thomas Yalden and Isaac Watts, but of Thomson. We are liable to forget that *The Choice or Wish* by Pomfret was among the most popular poems of its time, or that Blackmore (remembered from the pages of *The Dunciad*) was an inveterate writer of epics. Without the Scot Thomson, however, there would have been a discernible gap, even in an edition of the *English* poets.

II

In a letter to Boswell soon after his meeting with the booksellers, Johnson referred breezily to his being 'engaged to write little Lives, and little Prefaces, to a little edition of the English Poets'. The work, however, expanded under his hands, and in his foreword to the first four volumes Johnson explains how this came to happen:

> My purpose was only to have allotted to every poet an advertisement, like those which we find in the French Miscellanies, containing a few dates and a general character; but I have been led beyond my intention, I hope by the honest desire of giving useful pleasure.

The task he set himself was, then, a formidable one, and his later diary entry for Good Friday, 1781, records that he had performed it 'in my usual way, dilatorily and hastily, unwillingly to work, and working with vigour and haste'. During the late summer of 1777 he made an extended visit to the Midlands – though while in Oxford he gleaned some material for his *Lives* from the Bodleian. By the following Easter he had, as he tells us, 'written a little of the lives of the poets'; and during the early summer the work was clearly going forward, for his letter (27 July) to the printer John Nichols mentions that Cowley, Denham, Butler and Waller have been finished, Dryden is mostly written, and Milton is next on the list.

After the first four volumes came out, Johnson seems to have been slow in making a further effort. By April 1780, however, he was at work, with Addison and Prior behind him and a start made on Rowe. On 11 April he wrote to Mrs Thrale at Bath:

> You are at all places of high resort, and bring home hearts by dozens; while I am seeking for something to say about men of whom I know nothing but their verses, and sometimes very little of them. Now I have begun, however, I do not despair of making an end.

Colds and a persistent cough were to trouble him during the spring and early summer; on 15 April he wrote again to Mrs Thrale: 'I thought to have finished Rowe's life today, but I have five or six visitors who hindered me, and I have not been quite well. Next week I hope to dispatch four or five of them.' By late August, when he wrote to Boswell, he was inclined to express dissatisfaction with what he had accomplished during his working-summer in London: 'I have sat at home in Bolt Court all the summer, thinking to write the Lives, and a great part of the time only thinking.' His pen, nevertheless, must have been moving rapidly enough. At the beginning of September, probably only the longer 'Lives' of Swift and Pope had still to be written; and the whole work was finished early the following year.

In writing the *Lives* Johnson obtained different kinds of assistance from numerous people. Nichols provided not only books, but many factual details as well. Boswell (and probably Lord Hailes) supplied information about Thomson. Details of Watts's life were sought from William Sharp, who had some of the poet's letters in his possession. To Richard Farmer of Cambridge Johnson wrote on a couple of occasions, saying that if suitable material were available there he would get the booksellers to employ someone to transcribe it, or even make the journey himself. From Garrick he received Dryden's notes on Rymer, and from Dr William Vyse, rector of Lambeth, Dryden's letter to his sons in Rome; while from the Sheriff of London he hoped for information concerning Elkanah Settle's office of 'city poet'. A good deal of knowledge, especially of his nearer contemporaries, must have come from what he had been told. Richard Savage is acknowledged as one such source; and from Lord Marchmont he was to learn details of Pope. His most important single source for this 'Life' was, however, the manuscript of Joseph Spence's *Anecdotes*, which was lent to him by courtesy of the Duke of Newcastle. Others, including his friends Joseph Warton, Charles Burney, Mrs Thrale and George Steevens, helped in various ways, though Steevens was the only one of these he later thanked by name.

In the *Lives* Johnson reprinted some of his earlier work: the *Life of Savage*, a 'Dissertation' on Pope's epitaphs (1756), and an account of Collins (1763). He also included William

Oldisworth's memoir of Edmund Smith, and a life of Edward Young by Herbert Croft of Lincoln's Inn, a friend of the poet's son. He tried to get Lord Westcote to write his brother Lyttelton's life, intending to confine himself to comments on the poetry. Westcote, however, declined, and within the week Johnson was to write ruefully to Mrs Thrale:

> I sent to Lord Westcote about his brother's life, but he says he knows not whom to employ, and is sure I shall do him no injury. There is an ingenious scheme to save a day's work or part of a day utterly defeated.

In replying to Westcote Johnson had observed: 'For the life of Lord Lyttelton I shall need no help – it was very public, and I have no need to be minute.' Yet he was soon writing to Nichols: 'I expected to have found a Life of Lord Lyttelton prefixed to his works. Is there not one before the quarto edition? I think there is – if not I am, with respect to him, quite aground.' This remark applied to an exact contemporary and a man he had once met shows how difficult, in one sense, Johnson's undertaking was. Where he could make use of printed sources, his practice was to work from these – though what he produced by compressing and reshaping available material became distinctively his own.

Conscious of the shortcomings of the undiscriminating and partial estimates that generally went under the name of biography, Johnson sought to give prominence to such details as would clearly highlight the individual character. His *Lives* have the kind of vividness that makes us return to them. We still want to read about Pope in Johnson's pages; while his account of the horror and pathos of Swift's last days has never been surpassed. In general, the insights he brings to his material are peculiarly shrewd and penetrating – though sometimes he seems to take too much upon himself in expressing his forthright personality and opinions. His account of Milton, in particular, provoked an outcry; yet even here Johnson's concern is not just with the man, but with the connection he senses between the man and his poetry. Though the verse often seemed to him as uncompromizing as Milton's own attitudes and beliefs, he recognizes that its author 'was born for whatever is arduous'. In discussing Milton's supposed neglect of stated periods of worship, he writes: 'That he lived without prayer can hardly be affirmed; his studies and meditations were an habitual prayer.' We might not choose to put it like this, but Johnson's remark at least illustrates what Bate has rightly noticed, that 'he almost instinctively stretched these biographical prefaces into a form of literary criticism'. 'They are', he adds, 'biography turning into criticism, not criticism withdrawing into biography.'[1]

III

The *Lives* is, of all Johnson's works, perhaps the most widely read. Like his *Shakespeare*, it not only reflects assumptions he shared with his age, but has, nevertheless, a personally realized quality that represents a vivid response to different kinds of poetry. One might expect Johnson to have been most at home in dealing with the poets who wrote in the neoclassical mode. Certainly this has been said.[2] Yet such a claim needs to be qualified, not only because the criticism in the 'Life of Dryden' is arguably so much better than that in the 'Life of Pope', but also because he responded so positively to poets as different as Donne and Thomson. Such was the catholicity of Johnson's taste that he recognized real originality in whatever mode.

He himself thought the 'Life of Cowley' the best of his *Lives* because of its account of 'metaphysical' poetry. Though Dryden had said that Donne 'affects the metaphysics',[3] it was left to Johnson to make the term current. What he meant by it – rather different from what it means today – can be seen from his praise of Cowley's 'two metrical disquisitions *for* and *against* Reason' as 'no mean specimens of metaphysical poetry'. In 'Reason' and 'The Tree of Knowledge' (considered as a pair of poems, or companion poems), the poet seemed to be arguing ingeniously on opposite sides of the same question as though acting out the roles of the opposing speakers in a scholastic or 'schools'-type disputation. Cowley's 'For Hope' and 'Against Hope' were taken to provide another example of this, and Johnson quoted from the latter to illustrate the kind of 'scholastic speculation' which showed 'an unequalled fertility of invention'. By an easy transference, 'metaphysical' came to be applied to any such attempt at ingenuity. Dryden had noted how inappropriate this was in love poetry, and Johnson condemned such cleverness in other kinds of poetry as well (including Cowley's epic on King David). Yet despite this widely shared presupposition, he also found the 'wit' of the metaphysical poets genuinely stimulating. And it is this which makes the 'Life of Cowley' so interesting. What it reveals is a complex attempt at critical placing.

In the previous chapter we saw how Johnson associated the 'natural' in art with what he considered 'natural' in real life, and ideally he set fairly narrow limits to how love or grief should be expressed in poetry. Neither Milton's 'Lycidas' nor metaphysical love poetry seemed to him a convincing 'representation' of genuine emotion; in each instance the professed emotion appeared counterfeit because of the kind of language or imagery used to express it. Since he accepted as his yardstick what seemed to him normal in real life, his criticism of the metaphysical mode seems a blanket one, in practice allowing too little opportunity for a discriminating analysis of the experience presented in a given poem. Nevertheless, he seems to have been aware of the difference between Cowley's love poetry and Donne's, and is right to feel that *The Mistress* 'has no power of seduction', for many of Cowley's verses fall dead from the page. His criticism of Donne is at times rather lazy, but not necessarily negative. Of the extension of lovers' tears 'into worlds' (in 'A Valediction: of Weeping'), he says, 'If the lines are not easily understood, they may be read again.' Johnson seems to be putting some onus on the reader to understand the lines, however difficult they may at first appear to be. Of the celebrated compass image in 'A Valediction: forbidding Mourning', he says, 'It may be doubted whether absurdity or ingenuity has the better claim'. This seems hardly praise; yet 'ingenuity' here may well indicate something positive – a recognition that to bring such a figure, however 'far-fetched', into existence at all is a sign of poetic 'invention' or 'genius'. Two examples quoted in the *Dictionary* support this view: 'These are but the frigidities of wit and become not the genius of manly ingenuities' (Sir Thomas Browne); 'Such sots have neither parts nor wit, ingenuity of discourse, nor fineness of conversation, to entertain or delight anyone' (Robert South).

Johnson did not object to metaphysical poetry merely because it yoked together 'the most heterogeneous ideas'. He objected also to the 'laboured particularities' of its conceits since its attempt to be 'analytic' inevitably cut across his own expectations as a reader of poetry:

> One of the great sources of poetical delight is description, or the power of presenting pictures to the mind. Cowley gives inferences instead of images, and shows not what may be supposed to have been seen, but what thoughts the sight might have suggested.

This passage again alerts us to what seems to have been Johnson's habit of visualizing poetry: he complains that the metaphysical poets 'broke every image into fragments'. Donne's compass image must have seemed both far-fetched and too detailed or particularized; not surprisingly, it is in this 'Life' that Johnson makes his famous reference to the 'grandeur of generality' as a desirable poetic criterion. Clearly he is right to object to the fussy and otiose details of Cowley's ode 'The Muse'. While the description of Gabriel in the *Davideis* is more successful, Johnson was offended not only by the detail (which somehow seemed to confine the reader's imagination too narrowly), but also by the associations that certain of the words carried for him:

> That Gabriel was invested with the softest or brightest colours of the sky we might have been told, and been dismissed to improve the idea in our different proportions of conception; but Cowley could not let us go till he had related where Gabriel got first his skin, and then his mantle, then his lace, and then his scarf, and related it in the terms of the mercer and tailor.

Perhaps most revealing, however, is his comment that the poet 'gives inferences instead of images'. After quoting Virgil's description of the stone Turnus lifts against Aeneas ('*saxum circumspicit ingens, / saxum antiquum, ingens*'), Johnson contrasts with it the lines in which Cowley describes Cain's slaying of his brother:

> I saw him fling the stone, as if he meant
> At once his murder and his monument.

What this example suggests is that Johnson's response to imagery tended to be somewhat static – as though he was unable or unwilling to take in whole, as it were instantaneously, the play of wit so characteristic of metaphysical poetry.

Yet there is a reverse, and thoroughly positive, side to what Johnson blamed the metaphysical poets for. Their conceits might have seemed outlandish when judged according to Augustan standards of propriety, but they also served to point up the shortcomings of some later poetry which, however 'correct', was also dull and lifeless:

> If they frequently threw away their wit upon false conceits, they likewise sometimes struck out unexpected truth; if their conceits were far-fetched, they were often worth the carriage. To write on their plan it was at least necessary to read and think. No man could be born a metaphysical poet, nor assume the dignity of a writer, by descriptions copied from descriptions, by imitations borrowed from imitations, by traditional imagery and hereditary similies, by readiness of rhyme and volubility of syllables.

The metaphysicals clearly provided a welcome contrast to such verses as were lacking in all originality, or were (in the words of *An Essay on Criticism*) 'Correctly cold, and regularly low'. Their poetry, in fact, prompted Johnson to re-examine Pope's famous definition of 'wit', 'What oft was thought, but ne'er so well expressed': 'Pope's account of wit', he writes, 'is undoubtedly erroneous: he depresses it below its natural dignity, and reduces it from strength of thought to happiness of language.' Implicit in Pope's definition is the prevailing theory of language – that 'language' is 'the dress of thought' (as is said elsewhere in this 'Life') rather than the actual embodiment of it; that what is said can somehow be separated from how it is expressed. While this same distinction often allows Johnson to deploy his argument with a good deal of flexibility to serve different ends, he also seems to have recognized that 'thought' and 'expression' cannot be separated in this way. By contrast, say, with Addison, the metaphysical poets 'exercised' his mind ('by recollection or inquiry'), and they constantly 'surprised' him with their 'novelty'. And 'novelty', as Johnson saw, could not be dispensed with if what was presumed to be 'wit' was to have the required sharpness of impact. Of Addison's poetry, on the other hand, he was compelled to say: 'He thinks justly, but he thinks faintly.'

IV

When Johnson, who had a lifelong ambition to write a life of Dryden, came to review his poetry in the *Lives*, he measured him against his seventeenth-century predecessors in the following terms: 'He had more music than Waller, more vigour than Denham, and more nature than Cowley.' This comparison not only ascribes to Dryden 'nature', 'vigour' and 'music', but does so in a way that lays claim to his possessing all these qualities in large measure. Denham had more 'vigour' than Waller, but Dryden had more than both; and if, in the abstract, he did not have more than Cowley, his 'vigour' was ultimately seen as more impressive in being put to better use. Denham had infinitely more 'music' than Cowley, and Waller more than Denham, but Dryden had more even than Waller. Ultimately, of course, such qualities cannot be measured separately, the implication clearly being that they enhance one another because of the way in which Dryden combines them. Yet Johnson's terms are suggestive: he sees that the line of wit extends from the metaphysicals to Dryden and beyond (in the 'Life of Denham' he traces the use of a striking image from Denham, through the Earl of Orrery, to Pope); and he recognizes Dryden's historical importance in 'improving' English versification.

Johnson's remarks on Dryden's early poems recall his response to the metaphysicals. In the verses *To my Lord Chancellor* he notes (in ll. 31–42)

> a conceit so hopeless at the first view that few would have attempted it, and so successfully laboured that though at last it gives the reader more perplexity than pleasure, and seems hardly worth the study that it costs, yet it must be valued as a proof of a mind at once subtle and comprehensive.

The general admiration he felt for Dryden was prompted in no small measure by his sense of coming into contact with a mind 'in full possession of great stores of intellectual wealth': 'His works', he says, 'abound with knowledge, and sparkle with illustrations.' His reference, too, to a conceit 'so successfully laboured' points to the advance he thought Dryden had made on metaphysical wit by bringing together, in an expressive and functional way, the different elements of his image or analogy. Johnson acknowledges that in his later poems 'he did not often bring upon his anvil such stubborn and unmalleable thoughts'; even so, his ability 'to *unite* the most unsociable matter' (my italics) constituted an important part of what Johnson saw was Dryden's achievement.

Dryden inherited and improved on a developing seventeenth-century tradition; and from where Johnson as critic stood, he could only have praise for his discrimination in making such poetic choices as seemed subsequently to have been vindicated. These he regarded as absolutes rather than the virtues of a particular style or period:

> To him we owe the improvement, perhaps the completion of our metre, the refinement of our language, and much of the correctness of our sentiments. By him we were taught *sapere et fari*, to think naturally and express forcibly. . . . What was said of Rome adorned by Augustus, may be applied by an easy metaphor to English poetry embellished by Dryden – *lateritiam invenit, marmoream reliquit*, he found it brick, and he left it marble.

This passage is suggestive: much of Dryden's work can be related to an idea or theme that he helped formally to inaugurate – 'the myth and ideal of Augustanism as applied to Britain, with its hope for strong and harmonious rule, a flourishing of the arts of peace, and the favour of providence on both'.[4] The idea is broached in *Astraea Redux*, and Johnson notes, in respect of its change of allegiance from the earlier *Heroique Stanzas* on Cromwell, that here the poet 'changed with the nation'. In their context, however, Johnson's remarks on Dryden's Augustanism are to be more precisely related to his contribution in achieving for English poetry 'propriety in word and thought'.

It was Dryden's use of diction that won Johnson's special praise:

> There was before the time of Dryden no poetical diction, no

> system of words at once refined from the grossness of domestic use and free from the harshness of terms appropriated to particular arts. Words too familiar or too remote defeat the purpose of a poet. From those sounds which we hear on small or on coarse occasions, we do not easily receive strong impressions or delightful images; and words to which we are nearly strangers, whenever they occur, draw that attention on themselves which they should transmit to things.
>
> Those happy combinations of words which distinguish poetry from prose had been rarely attempted; we had few elegances or flowers of speech: the roses had not yet been plucked from the bramble, or different colours had not been joined to enliven one another.

The first assumption made here is that some words are inappropriate to poetry; the second, less obvious, assumption is that certain 'combinations of language' distinguish poetry from prose. Yet these assumptions are basically at odds. If the suitableness of words depends on their immediate context, how can a different criterion for determining the vocabulary of poetry be supposed to operate?

Johnson's best known discussion of this question occurs in *Rambler* 168. There he comments on the language of Lady Macbeth's famous soliloquy, where she anticipates 'the fatal entrance of Duncan/Under my battlements':

> Come, thick Night,
> And pall thee in the dunnest smoke of Hell,
> That my keen knife see not the wound it makes,
> Nor Heaven peep through the blanket of the dark,
> To cry, 'Hold, hold!'

'In this passage', writes Johnson, 'is exerted all the force of poetry, that force which calls new powers into being, which embodies sentiments and animates matter; yet perhaps scarce any man now peruses it without some disturbance of his attention from the counteraction of the words to the ideas.' Lady Macbeth's use of 'knife' provides for him one instance of this: 'We do not immediately conceive that any crime of importance is to be committed with a *knife* – "an instrument", he notes, 'used by butchers and cooks in the meanest employments.' Given this comment, it is interesting to note Suffolk's reply to the Queen's words, 'Are you the butcher, Suffolk? Where's your knife?', in *2 Henry VI*:

> I wear no knife to slaughter sleeping men;
> But here's a vengeful sword, rusted with ease,
> That shall be scoured in his rancorous heart
> That slanders me with murder's crimson badge.

There is, nevertheless, a further point to be made. Lady Macbeth wants to conceal her imagined deed, yet she uses a word traditionally associated with blood-letting. Is it, in this instance at least, the context as much as the word itself which prompts Johnson's objection?

Dryden used 'knife' frequently, in a variety of contexts – as a pruning-knife, a knife for eating (also the artisan's tool of trade), a means of suicide as ignoble as 'ratsbane' or 'halter', the weapon of the madman, the weapon feared by the guilty 'wretch', the 'persecuting knife', and the sacrificial or priestly 'butcher's' knife (once, appropriately, in *The Hind and the Panther*). He also used it in translating Ovid's description of the intended sacrifice of Iphigenia ('The royal victim bound, the knife already reared'), where it is the sacrificial knife of those unwilling to commit the brutal act ('The weeping priests, in linen-robes arrayed'). Since Johnson apparently did not object to any of these examples, his criterion for judging 'poetical diction' would seem to have been context rather than simply vocabulary. At the same time, his reference to 'roses' and 'brambles' suggests that he regarded some words as inherently more 'splendid' or 'poetical' than others; and it seems therefore significant that he praised Dryden as the English Virgil, whose 'splendour of diction' had enriched his native poetry.

For the most part, however, Johnson's engagement as reader seems to have been with 'thoughts' or 'sentiments' as these are 'embodied' in language. In particular, he recognized how Dryden joins words 'to enliven one another'; and in comparing him with Pope, he voted him a greater share of 'poetical vigour', of 'that energy which collects, combines, amplifies and animates'. Unfortunately Johnson too rarely descends to particulars; and too often his quotations are designed to illustrate faults. But one passage he singles out (to illustrate Dryden's knowledge of human nature) is the description of Shaftesbury in *The Medal*. This he considers a 'very skilfully delineated and strongly coloured' portrait of one 'whose propensions to mischief are such that his best actions are but inability of wickedness'. Aristotle used ἐνέργεα 'for the species of metaphor which calls up a mental picture of something "acting" or moving' (*OED*), and Johnson, when he refers to Dryden's 'energy', seems to mean by it the whole creative vigour of the poet as this is displayed in his 'strength of expression' (one of the definitions of *energy* in the *Dictionary*). Certainly the opening lines of the portrait of Shaftesbury are especially vivid:

> Power was his aim: but, thrown from that pretence,
> The wretch turned loyal in his own defence,
> And malice reconciled him to his prince.

The very language ('wretch turned loyal', 'malice reconciled'), suggests the inner, disruptive turmoil of Shaftesbury's own mind and motives.

Johnson recognized Dryden's genius for language and the overall vigour of his poetry, but though he claimed he had 'brighter paragraphs' than Pope, he did not allow him to have 'better poems'. He objected, for example, to the 'constitutional absurdity' of the use of the beast fable in *The Hind and the Panther*: 'The scheme of the work is injudicious and incommodious, for what can be more absurd than that one beast should counsel another to rest her faith upon a pope and council?' More interesting is his criticism of *Absalom and Achitophel*, where he notes 'an unpleasing disproportion between the beginning and the end':

> We are alarmed by a faction formed out of many sects various in their principles but agreeing in their purpose of mischief, formidable for their numbers and strong by their supports, while the King's friends are few and weak. The chiefs on either part are set forth to view; but when expectation is at the height, the King makes a speech, and
>
> 'Henceforth a series of new times began.'

> Who can forbear to think of an enchanted castle, with a wide moat and lofty battlements, walls of marble and gates of brass, which vanishes at once into air when the destined knight blows his horn before it?

The poem's structure has been defended on the grounds that 'the conservative myth' – that set of assumptions which any reasonable man would have entertained concerning the 'divinity of order' and the 'danger' of all forms of unlicensed behaviour – makes it inevitable that the poem should end as it does. According to this view, the 'physical disproportion becomes itself functional in showing what is right is so clear and simple'.[5] Perhaps, however, Johnson was rightly troubled; though it is questionable whether the 'disproportion' he noted is ultimately so 'unpleasing'. A telling point is made by Howard Erskine-Hill:

> For me it is a merit of the poem that its conclusion begs just half a question. Will the 'moody, murmuring' people stay 'willing' long? With Heaven's consent perhaps so, but we are reminded that the Augustan edifice of order stood on a precarious foundation. This insight is fundamental to the character of the poem; unlike Shakespeare's great tragedies of state it dramatizes not the working out but the containment of conflict. It is to this end that its abounding vigour of statement, its audacious satiric life, its glowing rhetorical richness, and its splendid formal architecture all move.[6]

It is in his criticism of *Annus Mirabilis* that Johnson anticipates his most telling reservation about Dryden:

> His description of the Fire is painted by resolute meditation, out of a mind better formed to reason than to feel. The conflagration of a city, with all its tumults of concomitant distress, is one of the most dreadful spectacles which this world can offer to human eyes; yet it seems to raise little emotion in the breast of the poet: he watches the flame coolly from street to street, with now a reflection, and now a simile, till at last he meets the King, for whom he makes a speech rather tedious in a time so busy, and then follows again the progress of the fire.

Dryden's witty detachment from the scene is condemned as a failure of sensibility, as an inability to feel that distress at human suffering which his critic can himself so vividly imagine. Why should Boswell have supposed that, in drawing Dryden's character, Johnson was, in effect, composing a self-portrait? 'It may indeed be observed', he writes, 'that in all the numerous writings of Johnson, whether in prose or verse, and even in his tragedy, of which the subject is the distress of an unfortunate princess, there is not a single passage that ever drew a tear.' We can accept this judgment of *Irene*, but we cannot allow it to apply, say, to the elegy on Levet or *The Vanity of Human Wishes*; as Mrs Piozzi tells us, when Johnson was one day reading his lines on the scholar 'he burst into a passion of tears'. To put these poems beside Dryden's is to make the difference between the two men obvious. And that Johnson himself was aware of it is clear from his summing-up: 'With the simple and elemental passions as they spring separate in the human mind, he seems not much acquainted'; 'Dryden's was not one of the "gentle bosoms"' (a quotation from *Tyrannic Love*); 'He is therefore with all his variety of excellence not often pathetic'. Johnson was perhaps thinking primarily of the plays, but his remark can also be applied to much of the poetry. Finding there little evidence of the mind that suffers or the heart that feels, he is forced to conclude: 'He could more easily fill the ear with some splendid novelty than awaken those ideas that slumber in the heart.' This is not, of course, true of Dryden's lines on Oldham, or of his epistle to Congreve, but these were poems which Johnson did not have in front of him when he wrote this 'Life' (and they did not appear in the booksellers' edition).

V

If the 'Life of Dryden' deserves to be regarded as a critical classic, the same cannot be said of the 'Life of Pope', even though it frequently has been. Scholars have praised these two works in the same breath, or even singled out the latter as Johnson's 'masterpiece'.[7] What is said, however, of individual poems surely suggets that the criticism here falls below his best. Though Johnson praises *Windsor Forest* for its 'art of interchanging description, narrative and morality', and traces its ancestry to Denham's *Cooper's Hill* and Waller's *On St. James's Park, as lately Improved by his Majesty*, he seems to have little or no sense of the tensions latent in it, or the means by which Pope attempts their resolution. The 'Elegy to the Memory of an Unfortunate Lady', though allowed to show at times a 'vigorous animation', receives less than its due because it treats suicide 'with respect'. *An Essay on Criticism*, on the other hand, is overpraised as one of Pope's 'greatest' works, sufficient in itself to place him in the first rank of poets. *The Rape of the Lock* admittedly calls forth some of Johnson's best comments; but even here there is the puzzling suggestion that 'the game at ombre might be spared' (apparently he thought its inclusion would have been more defensible 'if the lady had lost her hair while she was intent upon her cards', for then 'it might have been inferred that those who are too fond of play will be in danger of neglecting more important truths'). The least convincing part of *An Epistle to Dr Arbuthnot* – 'the poet's vindication of his own character' – is said to be the best, while the portrait of Sporus is dismissed without further comment as 'the meanest passage' in the poem. Johnson's response to *The Dunciad* is curiously mixed: while acknowledging its debt to *MacFlecknoe* in a way that nevertheless allows it 'to claim the praise of an original', he is offended by 'the grossness of its images'. Though he mentions 'the excellence' of some passages (numbering, in all, about a hundred lines), he seems unable to appreciate the peculiar quality and intensity of its larger imaginative vision.

Yet despite judgments like these, Johnson could say that Pope's poetry is read 'with perpetual delight'. Obviously he regarded him as having perfected the art of versification which Dryden had done so much to establish. Boswell, indeed, once heard him say: 'Sir, a thousand years may elapse before there shall appear another man with a power of versification equal to that of Pope.' Johnson was put off by 'the lax and lawless versification' of Cowley's attempt to write Pindarics – an attempt that spawned a host of puerile imitations; these so turned him against the form that his attitude carried over to Gray's two 'Pindaric' odes. Mostly his criticism is, of course, directed against Gray's use of language in these (and other) poems, but the versification is also criticized ('the ode is finished before the ear has learned its measures'), and the reference to 'a kind of cumbrous splendour which we wish away' seems a condemnation of both Gray's diction and versification, almost as though one derived an undue licence from the other. Similarly Johnson rejected the attempts at blank verse which the example of Milton had so much encouraged. It was as though he saw English poetry being threatened by an amorphousness of one sort or another, and he therefore upheld the heroic couplet as the norm to be followed. In its 'stated recurrence of settled numbers' his ear detected a welcome harmony and discipline.

Johnson seems to have been particularly responsive to what might loosely be termed 'verbal melody', and for him it was pre-eminently Pope who applied his 'colours of language' in a way that 'tuned the English tongue'. This phrase occurs in his remarks on the translations of Homer; there he found 'lines so elaborately corrected and so sweetly modulated' that they 'took possession of the public ear'. This aspect of Johnson's criticism gives, in fact, further meaning to his censure of 'harsh' diction and 'harsh' metaphors; clearly he sought in poetry a use of language that not only did not violate the accepted meanings of words, but combined them with a recognizable 'sweetness of melody' (a phrase applied to the verse of *An Essay on Man*). Yet it is also important to note his positive delight at Pope's 'colours of language'. Just as in his praise of Dryden's 'poetical diction' Johnson insists on the importance to poetry of certain 'elegances or flowers of speech', so his judgment of Pope displays an awareness of the poet's incredibly rich and fertile imagery. He says of *Eloisa to Abelard*: 'Here is particularly observable the *curiosa felicitas*, a fruitful soil and careful cultivation. Here is no crudeness of sense nor asperity of language.' And of Pope's intention to enlarge, against Addison's advice, the original two-canto *Rape*, Johnson says:

> Pope foresaw the future efflorescence of imagery then budding in his mind, and resolved to spare no art or industry of cultivation. The soft luxuriance of his fancy was already shooting, and all the gay varieties of diction were ready at his hand to colour and embellish it.

It is now a commonplace that in this 'Life' Johnson was not so much initiating criticism as adjudicating on the estimates of

Pope that had already appeared. These were principally two: Joseph Warton's *Essay on the Writings and Genius of Pope* (1756), which Johnson had reviewed in *The Literary Magazine* when it came out, and Owen Ruffhead's 'Critical Essay on his Writings and Genius', which, included in his *Life of Pope* (1769), was directed against Warton. Perhaps Johnson's 'Life' could have been a masterpiece if he had set out seriously to answer Warton. Instead he rather shrugged him off without sufficiently probing the details of his argument: 'After all this it is surely superfluous to answer the question that has once been asked, whether Pope was a poet, otherwise than by asking in return: "If Pope be not a poet where is poetry to be found?"' It has been claimed, not only that this concluding section of the 'Life' represents Johnson's 'best criticism', but that it is essentially his own.[8] If, however, the 'all this' is not quite perfunctory (since it refers to an earlier passage listing 'all the qualities' that go to make up Pope's 'genius'), it is nevertheless true that this central paragraph, which praises Pope's 'invention', 'imagination', 'judgment', and 'colours of language', is, even to certain verbal parallels, based on a more diffuse passage in Ruffhead's work.

Warton had sought to make a distinction between 'pure poetry' and the work of Pope by adopting a 'process of critical chemistry' learnt from Horace. His proposed method for judging a poem was 'to drop the measures and numbers, and transpose and invert the order of words' and read it as prose. 'If', he continues, 'there be really in it a true poetical spirit, all your inversions and transpositions will not disguise and extinguish it.' According to this test, the first fourteen lines of Pope's *Epistle to Cobham* were taken to fare badly by comparison with 'ten lines of the *Iliad, Paradise Lost*, or even of the *Georgics* of Virgil'.[9]

In neither his review of Warton nor his 'Life of Pope' did Johnson directly challenge this assumption. Instead it was left to the relatively minor figure (and neighbour of his) Percival Stockdale to argue that a poet's work could properly be approached only on its own terms:

> While he is heated with the warmth of inspiration, he is attentive to propriety, to order, and embellishment; not only

> to the most pertinent selection of words, but likewise to their position; to the strength, and harmony which are produced by their judicious, and fortunate arrangement. For these are indisputable and powerful constituents of poetry. A particle may be so placed in a verse, that the sense of the author may be clear, and the idiom of our language may not be violated; yet even that particle, by a happy transposition, might acquire life, and energy, and give more animation, and lustre to the line. In the productions of the fine arts, nothing is indifferent; the minutest parts have their great importance and influence; they reflect proportion, and expression on the other parts, from which *they* likewise draw those advantages; and all the parts, as they are disposed, and compacted by the artist, form a striking whole.[10]

Had Johnson chosen to descend to particulars (and Stockdale's work to this extent furnished a precedent for doing so), he might well have engaged in some illuminating practical criticism. Instead he writes his defence – if that is what it can be called – with but half an eye cocked on Warton's charge that Pope lacked imagination and originality.

Warton expressed a preference for the 'wild and romantic', for that 'Gothic' element (as in Gray's *Bard*) which seemed to him so much above what Pope could generally rise to – except in parts of *Eloisa*. For the most part Johnson's sensibility did not run on such scenes, even though we get from him a clearer impression of the 'magnificence' of Young's *Night Thoughts* (which he praised as 'original') than we get from Warton. Yet phrases in the *Essay* like 'a creative and glowing imagination', 'a lively and plastic imagination', put more emphasis on the creative power of the imagination than Johnson ever did in using the word. Like Warton, Young, in his *Conjectures on Original Composition* (1759), had denied that Pope, 'pre-engaged in imitation', was an 'original' author. And Richard Hurd, in his *Letters on Chivalry and Romance* (1762), was to object to the maxim 'follow Nature' (where 'nature' could only mean 'the known and experienced course of affairs in the world') on the grounds that 'the poet has a world of his own, where experience has less to do, than consistent imagination'.[11] In Johnson's more traditional view, imagination could draw only on previous experience: 'Imagination is useless without knowledge: nature gives in vain the power of combination unless study and observation supply materials to be combined' ('Life of Butler'). Even though in *The Rambler* he had regarded imagination as 'a licentious and vagrant faculty, unsusceptible of limitations, and impatient of restraint' (no. 125), his plea for literary originality had there been based on the contention that 'in the boundless regions of possibility, which fiction claims for her dominion, there are surely a thousand recesses unexplored, a thousand flowers unplucked, a thousand fountains unexhausted, combinations of imagery yet unobserved, and races of ideal inhabitants not hitherto described' (no. 121).

This sentence was perhaps written with *The Rape of the Lock* in mind, and it is in meeting Warton's objection to this poem that Johnson makes his most telling point. Warton, too, had praised this poem highly: 'It is in this composition, Pope principally appears a POET; in which he has displayed more imagination than in all his other works taken together.' Warton, however, adds that although Pope's 'claim to imagination is chiefly founded' on the sylphs, he did not invent them but 'found them existing ready to his hand'.[12] Johnson seeks to scotch this objection by representing it as 'a charge which might with more justice have been brought against the author of the *Iliad*, who doubtless adopted the religious system of his country'. 'What is there', he asks, 'but the names of his agents which Pope has not invented?' 'Has he not assigned them characters and operations never heard of before. Has he not, at least, given them their first poetical existence? If this is not sufficient to denominate his work original, nothing original ever can be written.' In summing up later Pope's 'qualities' of 'genius', Johnson distinguishes between 'invention', 'by which new trains of events are formed and new scenes of imagery displayed, as in *The Rape of the Lock*', and 'imagination', 'which strongly impresses on the writer's mind, and enables him to convey to the reader, the various forms of nature, incidents of life, and energies of passion'. Warton, we may assume, would have objected to this distinction between 'imagination' and 'invention', and quibbled over the meaning to be given to 'new'. Yet the significance of Johnson's comments on *The Rape of the Lock* is that he overlooks this distinction in favour of something more important – the realizing power of poetry: 'In this work are exhibited in a very high degree the two most engaging powers of an author. New things are made familiar, and familiar things are made new.' Though Johnson here talks of 'the *two* most engaging powers of an author', his language, at least, seems to recognize the all-important sense in which Pope is a 'maker': 'New things are *made* familiar, and familiar things are *made* new.' And this is where his real difference from Warton lies, who, in seeking to define 'pure poetry', had criticized Pope for not writing like a Milton. Johnson's perception of what is poetry allows him to interpret 'imagination' in a more flexible way. He is able to approach different poets, Pope no less than Milton, with a more inclusive sensibility and a more discriminating critical intelligence.

VI

As one might expect, more space in the *Lives* is devoted to *Paradise Lost* than to any other work. Johnson declared it to be 'a poem which, considered with respect to design, may claim the first place, and with respect to performance, the second among the productions of the human mind.' Here again we see the importance he attached to 'invention', and his comment is reminiscent of his saying to Boswell that 'Virgil was not the greatest of heroic poets only because he was not the first'. On another occasion Johnson said: 'We must consider whether Homer was not the greatest poet, though Virgil may have produced the finest poem. Virgil was indebted to Homer for the whole invention of the structure of an epic poem.' Yet his remarks on *Paradise Lost* involve more than this. Not only do they indicate his engagement with the poem's subject-matter, but they include a judgment that later seems to deny this when he records the poem's 'want of human interest': 'The plan of *Paradise Lost* has this inconvenience, that it comprises neither human actions nor human manners.' If, then, we are to give a proper estimate of his criticism, we must ultimately take account of such a contradiction. Indeed, it could be said that this is but the central contradiction in an argument fraught with inconsistencies, and that what makes these so interesting is that they reflect his complex and even divided response to the poem.

Johnson's remarks on Milton's 'fable' recall Addison's: in an age that accepted the literal truth of Scripture, the story of Eden and the Fall was regarded as sacred history. Addison, in his essays on the poem in *The Spectator*, contrasts it with the *Iliad* and the *Aeneid*: 'Milton's subject was still greater than either of the former; it does not determine the fate of single persons or nations, but of a whole species' (no. 267). Johnson takes the same view:

> The subject of an epic poem is naturally an event of great importance. That of Milton is not the destruction of a city, the conduct of a colony, or the foundation of an empire. His subject is the fate of worlds, the revolutions of heaven and of earth; rebellion against the Supreme King raised by the highest order of created beings; the overthrow of their host and the punishment of their crime; the creation of a new race of reasonable creatures; their original happiness and innocence, their forfeiture of immortality, and their restoration to hope and peace.

Johnson writes of heaven and the fallen angels in the present tense ('we have restless and insidious enemies in the fallen angels'). He can claim that the subject of the poem is 'universally and perpetually interesting' because, as Addison says, all men are 'related to the persons who are the principal actors in it' (*Spectator* 273). And since he regards everything that happens in it as having taken place 'under the immediate and visible direction of Heaven', it becomes no longer relevant to talk of epic 'machinery': 'It contains the history of a miracle, of Creation and Redemption; it displays the power and the mercy of the Supreme Being; the probable therefore is marvellous, and the marvellous is probable.'

Milton's subject was for Johnson the greatest imaginable. It was founded on fixed and immutable truth and described how man came to be in his present fallen condition. For this reason it received his unqualified assent. And Johnson's imagination was also excited by the 'sublimity' of its presentation: Milton brought to his subject 'an imagination in the highest degree fervid and active' – 'the power of displaying the vast, illuminating the splendid, enforcing the awful, darkening the gloomy and aggravating the dreadful'. 'Whatever be his subject', writes Johnson, 'he never fails to fill the imagination.' This phrasing is significant, coming as it does from one so conscious of the 'hunger of imagination', and so willing to have the 'vacuity of life' filled up with something real and solid.

The irony, however, was that *Paradise Lost* impinged so nearly on Johnson's sensibility that he could not contemplate it with equanimity, let alone aesthetic pleasure. His response to its religious theme is best described by himself:

> Of the ideas suggested by these awful scenes, from some we recede with reverence except when stated hours require their association, and from others we shrink with horror, or admit them only as salutary inflictions, as counterpoises to our interests and passions. Such images rather obstruct the career of fancy than incite it.
>
> Pleasure and terror are indeed the genuine sources of poetry, but poetical pleasure must be such as human imagination can at least conceive, and poetical terror such as human strength and fortitude can combat. The good and evil of eternity are too ponderous for the wings of wit; the mind sinks under them in passive helplessness, content with calm belief and humble adoration.

It had been traditional to regard the 'sublime' as inseparable from the intensity of its emotional effect. Johnson's friend Edmund Burke had proposed a psychological explanation of this, and what his account stressed was that whatever was 'terrible' should be far enough removed to seem also pleasurable:

> Whatever is fitted in any sort to excite the idea of pain, and danger, that is to say, whatever is in any sort terrible, or is conversant about terrible objects, or operates in a manner analogous to terror, is a source of the *sublime*; that is, it is productive of the strongest emotion which the mind is capable of feeling. . . . When danger or pain press too nearly, they are incapable of giving any delight, and are simply terrible; but at certain distances, and with certain modifications, they may be, and they are delightful, as we every day experience.[13]

Given Johnson's criticism of *Paradise Lost*, this account is suggestive. Despite what he says of 'calm belief and humble adoration', the poem's 'awful scenes' often remained for him 'simply terrible'.

Johnson was, nevertheless, clearly impressed by the extent of Milton's knowledge and his astounding powers of imagination: 'Here', he says, 'is a full display of the united force of study and genius, of a great accumulation of materials, with judgment to digest and fancy to combine them.' There is even a hint that the 'accumulation of knowledge' which 'impregnated' the poet's mind, and which therefore contributed so powerfully to the realization of his 'awful scenes', could in itself provide for Johnson a measure of relief. He notes as follows the 'amplitude' of the poem's similies: 'Thus, comparing the shield of Satan to the orb of the moon, he crowds the imagination with the discovery of the telescope, and all the wonders which the telescope discovers.' Surely it is significant that he here cites a passage which, occurring in the midst of a description of the torments of the 'lake of fire', allows his imagination to dwell instead on

> the moon, whose orb
> Through optic glass the Tuscan artist views
> At evening from the top of Fesole,
> Or in Valdarno, to descry new lands,
> Rivers or mountains in her spotty globe.

Johnson's response to Milton's poem was, then, a complex one, and nowhere is this more evident than in the central contradiction already noted. Even in merely formal terms this involves a distinct break with what as critic he had ostensibly set out to do – to consider Milton's poem, as Addison had done before him, according to the neo-Aristotelian headings of fable, characters, sentiments and diction. But once he has recorded, in his discussion of the 'sentiments', the poem's 'want of human interest', no account of its 'diction' follows in the section devoted to it. Instead Johnson first comments on *Paradise Regained* and *Samson Agonistes*, and then, with *Paradise Lost* very much in mind, offers general remarks on Milton's diction. Perhaps this seemed to him a more economical way of proceeding; he claimed, after all, that 'Milton's style was not modified by his subject: what is shown with greater extent in *Paradise Lost* may be found in *Comus*'. Yet it seems more likely that the significance of this arrangement lies elsewhere. Unlike Addison, he discusses 'the defects and faults' of the poem before the language, and this order seems to have been forced on him by what he felt compelled to say about it. After he has remarked on 'the want of human interest', the words flow more equably from his pen. He considers in turn the inconsistency of attributing materiality to spirits, the unskilfulness of the allegory of Sin and Death, the erroneous reference to prelapsarian 'timorous deer', the unsuitable levity of the Paradise of Fools, and Richard Bentley's defence of Milton's word-play. He becomes, in fact, rather like any other eighteenth-century critic, and even though he says that the 'unskilful allegory' appears 'one of the greatest faults of the poem', the reader does not feel this objection to have, by comparison with the earlier one, any real weight.

Johnson's central criticism of the poem not only forms the climax of his argument, but is put forward, seemingly, only after something of a struggle. The stages by which he leads up to it suggest his readiness to make excuses for Milton's epic: 'As human passions did not enter the world before the Fall, there is in the *Paradise Lost* little opportunity for the pathetic, but what little there is has not been lost.' 'The defects and faults of *Paradise Lost*, for faults and defects every work of man must have, it is the business of impartial criticism to discover.' 'The plan of *Paradise Lost* has this inconvenience, that it comprises neither human actions nor human manners.' After he has introduced this point, Johnson goes on to record both his own response to 'the ideas suggested by these awful scenes' and Milton's 'great accumulation of materials'; and only then does he bring himself to elaborate on his central objection: 'But original deficience cannot be supplied. The want of human interest is always felt. *Paradise Lost* is one of the books which the reader admires and lays down, and forgets to take up again.'

It seems not merely inadequate but misleading to regard this and other potential contradictions either as evidence of 'Johnson the judge' stepping aside to permit a word from 'Johnson the reader',[14] or as indicative of his more formal critical method. It has been said, for example, that in his remarks on *Paradise Lost* he acts as a 'moderator, considering both sides of the argument to reach his judgment', and that 'we do not see the moderator *within* the criticism', where 'he is almost wholly concerned to argue for and against'.[15] On the contrary, it is only by seeing Johnson in the criticism that we can begin to see it in all its fascinating complexity. So painfully unsure was he of his own salvation that he found parts of the poem almost overwhelming. Yet aware of its imaginative power, he was also captivated by the grandeur of its moral design. Milton's purpose was, he says, 'to show the reasonableness of religion, and the necessity of obedience to the Divine Law.' *Paradise Lost* moved Johnson in some ways, inexorably, but not, apparently, in others. He notes that 'the anguish arising from the consciousness of transgression, and the horrors attending the sense of divine displeasure, are very justly described and forcibly impressed'; yet he adds that 'the passions are moved only on one occasion'. Even though he was often in his life heard to repeat Belial's words,

> for who would lose,
> Though full of pain, this intellectual being,

what he seems to have had in mind was the 'sore beset' Adam of book X. If, however, Johnson could have brought himself to comment on the great speech in book IX, where Adam resolves 'to die' with Eve, he might have come even closer to the central problem that the poem raises.

This is, however, raised (even if in a less acute form) in Raphael's warning to Adam in book VIII. Johnson says that 'Raphael's reproof of Adam's curiosity after the planetary motions, with the answer returned by Adam, may be confidently opposed to any rule of life which any poet has delivered'. As we have seen, the question raised by this episode – the proper limits to be set to human curiosity – was one Johnson could never satisfactorily resolve. He could, in theory at least, play Adam to God's Raphael, but his central dilemma was in wishing to be a passionate believer at the same time as he was a confirmed and passionate humanist. Here especially he found his mind embattled against itself, and the strength of his criticism of Milton's poem is precisely this – that his mind had the capacity to be embattled in this way.

Perhaps no other work elicited so clearly from Johnson a divided response; yet it must also be said that the presence of conflicting impulses is an important feature of his criticism generally. What makes this distinctive is his ability to respond so often, and with such immediacy, to the genuine complexities of the work before him. Of course, the form and content of 'Lycidas' so offended him that he was unable to do this, blankly refusing to take the poem on its own terms. This is, however, the exception that proves the rule. Elsewhere, as in his remarks on *Paradise Lost* or *King Lear*, Johnson shows his critical intelligence by pointing so acutely to the central problem or achievement. In each instance his seeming reservations are but proof of the fulness of his imaginative involvement. He speaks what he feels. And because he does this, he says what he ought to say.

Epilogue

I

When Johnson's last great work was finished, he was over seventy and had less than four years to live. Sickness and disappointment were soon to take their toll, and Henry Thrale's death in 1781 was confessedly a bitter blow. A little more than a week later he wrote in his diary: 'The decease of him from whose friendship I had obtained many opportunities of amusement, and to whom I turned my thoughts as to a refuge from misfortunes, has left me heavy.'

Late in 1781 Johnson spent some time in the Midlands, but returned to London in indifferent health. In his diary (18 March 1782) he records that he has been 'from the middle of January, distressed by a cold which made my respiration very laborious, and from which I was but little relieved by being blooded three times, having tried to ease the oppression of my breast by frequent opiates'. A fortnight or so earlier he had written to his step-daughter Lucy Porter, telling her that he had been ill since he left Lichfield the previous December, and that his household was 'but melancholy': other inmates were, like himself, 'very sickly', and Levet had already died of a stroke. As he wrote in a letter (27 February) to Edmond Malone, 'I have for many weeks been so much out of order, that I have gone out only in a coach to Mrs Thrale's where I can use all the freedom that sickness requires.'

Though Johnson was still to spend some time in her company, it seems that Mrs Thrale was already becoming attached to Piozzi. Her old friend probably sensed it too, for towards the end of April he wrote to her in a teasing vein between jest and earnest:

> I have been very much out of order since you sent me away; but why should I tell you, who do not care, nor desire to know? . . . Do not let Mr. Piozzi nor any body else put me quite out of your head, and do not think that any body will love you like – Sam. Johnson.

He stayed with her the following month at Streatham, and was there, too, in October, when he said his final farewell to the place. Mrs Thrale had let the house for three years to Lord Shelburne, but, even so, Johnson was to spend the next six weeks with her at Brighton; and it was not until April 1783 that he was to see her (though neither was then aware of the fact) for the last time. By then she clearly knew the strength of her passion for Piozzi, though she kept it a close secret. Yet Johnson must have suspected something; at least he discerned some change in her attitude towards him, and spoke in a letter (19 June 1783) of her 'diminution of regard'.

In this letter Johnson gives her an account of the stroke which, a couple of days earlier, had temporarily deprived him of the power of speech. Mrs Thrale was at Bath, and what she wrote in her diary (under 24 June) shows how her attachment to him had waned, and how much her attention was consumed by thoughts of another:

> I sincerely wish the continuance of a health so valuable; but have no desire that he should come to Bath, as my plan is mere retirement and economy which alone can shorten the absence that destroys my health, consumes my soul, and keeps me to mourn *his* distance to whom only I wish to be near.

When Johnson first suffered his apoplexy he composed a prayer asking that, however he might be afflicted physically, God would spare his understanding. 'This prayer', he tells Mrs Thrale, 'that I might try the integrity of my faculties, I made in Latin verse. The lines were not very good, but I knew them not to be very good, I made them easily, and concluded myself to be unimpaired in my faculties.' He was soon up and about, and a fortnight later was able to go out and dine with members of the Club.

Johnson was never one to submit tamely to illness. He was as keen as he ever was to go abroad and meet his friends and acquaintances, and his conversation remained vigorous to the end. Thoroughly characteristic are the remarks attributed to him during his last illness. 'Such', Boswell notes, 'was his intellectual ardour, even at this time, that he said to one friend, "Sir, I look upon every day to be lost in which I do not make a new acquaintance"; and to another, when talking of his illness, "I will be conquered; I will not capitulate".' Less than a month after his stroke, Johnson went to Rochester to visit Langton (who was stationed there with his regiment), and a fortnight later he was back in London apparently much refreshed. Within six weeks he was off again to visit a friend in Salisbury, and wrote (29 August) to his physician Richard Brocklesby: 'I was no more wearied with the journey, though it was a high-hung rough coach, than I should have been forty years ago.' While there he first took in Stonehenge, which he later compared with Salisbury Cathedral as 'the first essay and the last perfection in architecture'.

Johnson had revised the *Lives of the Poets* in 1782, and after that undertook no sustained piece of work for publication – though he did plan to compile, in the last six months or so of his life, a book of devotions. He amused himself in the summer of 1783 by translating Sallust's *Catiline*, and despite being troubled in the later part of the year with a sarcocele, gout and recurrent asthma, had enough vigour left to found with Brocklesby the Essex Head Club, which, as Boswell says, provided him with 'society in the evening for three days in the week'. A number of learned men were members, including Arthur Murphy, John Nichols, William Windham (whom, though a Whig, Johnson valued highly), and Dr Samuel Horsley (successively bishop of St David's, Rochester, and St Asaph). Boswell, too, became a member, and it was on this occasion that Johnson produced his well-known remark that his friend was 'a very *clubable* man'. But despite his wish, still, to savour company, illness and severe dropsy confined him to his house from December until the following April. At Easter he found himself almost miraculously better, and was strongly inclined to attribute his improvement to divine help. For the rest of his life, however, he remained solicitous about his intake of fluids, and kept a close watch on his health.

Feeling for the time so much better, Johnson was soon going abroad again, and during May, when Boswell was in London, dined out six nights in one week. In June he went to Oxford with Boswell, and spent a fortnight with Dr Adams. Later in the summer he went to Ashbourne to stay with his old friend Taylor. His nights, however, were so troubled that he was often forced to prop himself in a chair in order to get some sleep. Though at times he felt himself to be better, he seems to have gone visibly downhill during the summer. While staying for some weeks at Lichfield with his step-daughter, he wrote to Boswell (3 November): 'I have this summer sometimes amended and sometimes relapsed, but upon the whole, have lost ground very much. My legs are extremely weak, and my breath very short, and the water is now encreasing upon me.' He had given much the same account to his friend William Hamilton two weeks earlier; and yet so great was his zest for life that he could look forward to seeing Hamilton again 'to talk over what we have often talked, and perhaps to find new topics of merriment, or new incitements to curiosity'.

Johnson lived less than a month after he returned to London. He spent his last weeks receiving the friends who visited him, and in making translations from the Greek Anthology. In general he made preparations for death. He sent an epitaph on his father, mother and brother to be put in the church at Lichfield, gave a collection of his works to his old college, Pembroke, burned a good many of his private papers, and was prompted by Sir John Hawkins to make a will (in which he left a handsome legacy to his negro servant Francis Barber). On being told by his physicians that he could not recover 'without a miracle', he resolved to take no more medicine, 'not even my opiates, for I have prayed', said he, 'that I may render up my soul to God unclouded.' He died on 13 December, and a week later was buried in Westminster Abbey.

II

Johnson's most striking obituary was pronounced by William Hamilton: 'He has made a chasm, which not only nothing can fill up, but which nothing has a tendency to fill up. – Johnson is dead. – Let us go to the next best: – there is nobody; – no man can be said to put you in mind of Johnson.' This eloquently testifies to the sense of loss which his friends must have felt at his death; but to what extent does it reinforce our estimate of the man and his work? While Boswell's *Life* presents us with a personality and intellect of such mammoth proportions, Johnson's own writings also bear witness to his impressive intelligence and largeness as a person.

If he had himself been asked to provide a text for his life and writings, he would have been justified in proffering Terence's famous line, *Homo sum: humani nil a me alienum puto* ('I am a man and hold that what affects another man affects me'). More likely, however, he would have responded in the words of an early *Rambler*: 'Men more frequently require to be reminded than informed' (no. 2). Yet if we are inclined to take this as our text, we must also remember that Johnson's kind of 'reminding' goes very deep. It challenges easy assumptions about the possibility of earthly happiness; but ultimately it involves much more than this in holding up to scrutiny all forms of human complacency.

'Clear your mind of cant' is one of Johnson's best known sayings, and its force is neither blunted nor misrepresented by having it set in the widest possible context. His concern extended not just to those he knew but to the whole of humanity; and in amounting, almost, to a kind of compulsion, this was not unconnected with what he took a Christian's duty to be. In offering to 'remind' his readers of their nature and duty, he naturally drew attention to human weaknesses and limitations; yet he also had an abiding sense of the importance and dignity of human aspirations. At the same time as he insisted on man's obligations, he was also keenly aware of what was properly due to him as a human being.

A civilization was, in Johnson's view, to be judged by the way it treated its poor. Moreover, he spoke out more strongly against slavery than any other person of his generation. Perhaps nowhere is his attitude on this question more clearly stated than in the notes he dictated to Boswell on the case of the negro who was seeking his liberty before the Scottish Court of Session. Boswell himself held that slavery was 'a status which in all ages GOD has sanctioned', and that to abolish it would not only defraud the slave-owners ('an innumerable class of our fellow-subjects'), but be 'extreme cruelty to the African Savages, a portion of whom it saves from massacre'. Had Johnson been able to read this complacent rationalization, it would have provoked him to wrath. Angered by every kind of human exploitation, his own words move unerringly to the central issue: 'The sum of the argument is this: – No man is by nature the property of another.' Here we have summed up both his sense of human dignity, of the independence of the human spirit, and his hatred of all forms of cruelty, of whatever constitutes a threat to individual freedom. Johnson's words vividly remind us of his genuine and fundamental humanity, of a style of thinking that, one hopes with Carlyle, will never become obsolete.

Notes

Chapter 1 Johnson and His Age

1 Cited by M. J. Quinlan, 'Johnson's American Acquaintances', in *Johnson, Boswell and their Circle*, ed. M. M. Lascelles, J. L. Clifford, J. D. Fleeman, J. P. Hardy (1965), p. 198.

2 *The Correspondence and other Papers of James Boswell relating to the Making of the Life of Johnson*, ed. Marshall Waingrow (1969), p. 31.

3 'Johnson and the Enlightenment', in *Johnson, Boswell and their Circle* (1965), pp. 87 ff.

4 Cf. C. F. Chapin, *The Religious Thought of Samuel Johnson* (1968), pp. 113 ff.

5 '*Rasselas* Reconsidered', *Essays and Studies*, N.S. IV (1951), 46.

6 Cf. René Pomeau, *La Religion de Voltaire*, cited in *Voltaire: 'Candide', A New Translation*, ed. R. A. Adams (1966), p. 140.

7 A lead cast of the original is in the Victoria and Albert Museum, and a copy in marble in the National Portrait Gallery.

8 *Praeterita*, ed. Kenneth Clark (1949), pp. 210–11.

9 *Samuel Johnson the Moralist* (1961), p. 12.

Chapter 2 Beginnings

1 The actual date was 7 September, the equivalent now of 18 September (when the calendar was reformed in 1752, eleven days were removed). The house in which Johnson was born and lived the first part of his life is now The Samuel Johnson Birthplace Museum.

2 'M' is not, of course, used as a consistent symbol in the *Diaries*. For example, the entry under 18 March 1765, 'M.3 in bed in the morning with little difficulty', probably refers to bowel movements (Johnson had been drinking wine the night before), whereas 'Strongly tempted in a dream to M.' must clearly refer to something else. There is also the entry under 25 August 1771: 'I have M. once by accident'. In James's *Medicinal Dictionary* under *oneirosmos*, the noctural emission is explicitly described as a presage of insanity. A few months before his death, Johnson prayed for 'repentance', designating the faults he wished to remember by

abbreviations of Greek words that are probably to be translated as 'melancholy', 'shameful thoughts', 'vain imaginations'. An 'M' closes the list, and it seems unlikely, given the wording of Johnson's prayer, that this stands (as the Yale editors suggest) for 'Remember'. Probably, however, they are right to interpret as *memento* ('Remember') the 'M' which occurs in the second entry of the Latin diary Johnson kept while at Pembroke: 'Oct. 22. M quod feci Sept. 9 et 12 et 17 et 19 et 22 et 28 et 26.'

3 Cf. J. L. Clifford, *Young Samuel Johnson* (1955), p. 124 and n.
4 D. J. Greene, *The Politics of Samuel Johnson* (1960), p. 99.

Chapter 3 Poetry

1 Quoted by John Butt, 'Johnson's Practice in the Poetical Imitation', in *New Light on Dr. Johnson*, ed. F. W. Hilles (1959), p. 19.
2 Edward Herbert (of Cherbury), *The Life and Reigne of King Henry the Eighth* (1649), p. 266.
3 Cf. J. H. Plumb, *Sir Robert Walpole: The King's Minister* (1961), pp. 85–6.
4 Cf. *Poems* (1964) ed. E. L. Adam Jr, with George Milne, p. 108 n.; Donald Greene, *Samuel Johnson* (1970), p. 57.
5 Stephen Vincent Benét's phrase, quoted by F. W. Hilles, 'Johnson's Poetic Fire', in *From Sensibility to Romanticism*, ed. F. W. Hilles and Harold Bloom (1965), p. 76 and n.
6 'Johnson's Poetry', *New Statesman*, 6 August 1965, p. 190.
7 Cf. Paul Fussell, *Samuel Johnson and the Life of Writing* (1971), p. 130.
8 M. J. Quinlan, *Samuel Johnson: A Layman's Religion* (1964), p. 11.

Chapter 4 Periodical Essays

1 *'The Idler' and 'The Adventurer'* ed. W. J. Bate, J. M. Bullett, L. F. Powell (1963), p. xv.
2 See Katharine C. Balderston, 'Doctor Johnson and William Law', *Publications of the Modern Language Association of America*, lxxv (1960), 384.
3 *The Achievement of Samuel Johnson* (1955), p. 95.
4 *Diaries, Prayers, and Annals*, ed. E. L. McAdam, Jr, with Donald and Mary Hyde (1958), pp. 143, 160.
5 See E. A. Bloom, 'Symbolic Names in Johnson's Periodical Essays', *Modern Language Quarterly*, XIII (1952), 333–52.
6 The numbering of *The Idler* follows that of the Yale edition, which is also that of the first collected edition.

Chapter 5 *Dictionary*

1 This portrait, given to Boswell by Reynolds, is now in the National Portrait

Gallery. An engraving of it was prefixed to the first volume of Boswell's *Life*, and it also appears as the frontispiece to the standard Oxford edition, revised by L. F. Powell.

2 J. W. Krutch, *Samuel Johnson* (1944), p. 129.

3 Cf. Thomas Sprat, *The History of the Royal-Society of London* (1667), p. 112; and Stephen Skinner, *Etymologicon linguae* (1671), sig. a2^{v}, cited by J. H. Sledd and G. J. Kolb, *Dr. Johnson's Dictionary: Essays in the Biography of a Book* (1955), p. 5.

4 *Dr. Johnson's Dictionary* (1955), pp. 102–3.

5 Niall Rudd, 'Donne and Horace', *The Times Literary Supplement*, 22 March 1963, p. 208.

6 See H. L. Levy, 'H. P. Sturz and Dr. Johnson', *The Times Literary Supplement*, 10 February 1940, p. 40.

7 For a list of some of the authors whose works on particular branches of knowledge Johnson cited, see *A Bibliography of Samuel Johnson*, ed. W. P. Courtney, rev. D. N. Smith (1915), pp. 45–6.

8 *Philosophic Words: A Study of Style and Meaning in the 'Rambler' and 'Dictionary' of Samuel Johnson* (1948), p. 37.

9 *Samuel Johnson* (1974), p. 183.

10 *Philosophic Words*, (1948), p. xiv.

11 Terry Coleman, 'Best, but not Greatest', *Guardian*, 16 Oct 1971, p. 22.

Chapter 6 *Rasselas*

1 'In Praise of *Rasselas*: Four Notes (Converging)', in *Imagined Worlds*, ed. Maynard Mack and Ian Gregson (1968), p. 124.

2 E. R. Wasserman, 'Johnson's *Rasselas*: Implicit Contexts', *Journal of English and Germanic Philology*, LXXIV (1975), 14.

3 See Emrys Jones, 'The Artistic Form of *Rasselas*', *Review of English Studies*, N.S. XVIII (1967), 393.

4 H. M. Chapone, *Posthumous Works* (1807), vol. I, p. 108.

5 In the revised edition of 1773 he added two more, from Dryden and Wesley.

6 Carey McIntosh, *The Choice of Life: Samuel Johnson and the World of Fiction* (1973), p. 193.

Chapter 7 Edition of Shakespeare

1 *Dr Johnson on Shakespeare*, ed. W. K. Wimsatt (1960), p. 18.

2 René Wellek, *A History of Modern Criticism: 1750–1950*, I *The Later Eighteenth Century* (1955), pp. 86–7.

3 John Dryden: *Of Dramatic Poesy and other Critical Essays*, ed. George Watson (1962), vol. I, p. 146.

4 M. H. Abrams, *The Mirror and the Lamp* (1953), p. 38.

5 *Characteristics of Men, Manners, Opinions, Times*, ed. J. M. Robertson (1964), pp. 114, 180; *An Essay upon English Tragedy* (? 1757), pp. 18, 26;

Elements of Criticism (1762), vol. II, pp. 153, 155, 159; *An Essay on the Writings and Genius of Shakespeare compared with the Greek and French Dramatic Poets* (1769), p. 37; *A Philosophical Analysis and Illustration of some of Shakespeare's Remarkable Characters* (1774), pp. 8 ff.

6 M. A. Quinlan, *Poetic Justice in the Drama: The History of an Ethical Principle in Literary Criticism* (1912), p. 202; Donald Greene (ed.), *Samuel Johnson* (1965), p. 198.

7 *The Critical Works of Thomas Rymer*, ed. C. A. Zimansky (1956), p. 27; *The Critical Works of John Dennis*, ed. E. N. Hooker (1939–43), vol. II, pp. 6, 20–1.

8 Cf. F. V. Bernard, 'Johnson and *Lear*', *Johnsonian News Letter*, ed. J. L. Clifford and J. H. Middendorf, XVII (1957), i, 7–8.

9 *Monsieur Bossu's Treatise of the Epick Poem . . . done into English . . . by W. J.* (1695), pp. 113–14.

10 *An Essay on Pope's Odyssey* (1726–7), vol. I, p. 25; *Elements of Criticism*, vol. III, p. 29, 132; *Of Dramatic Poesy and Other Critical Essays*, vol. I, pp. 99, 256–7.

11 Arthur Sherbo, *Johnson's Notes to Shakespeare*, Augustan Reprint Society, vol. XIX (1956), p. viii.

12 Cf. F. H. Langman, '*The Winter's Tale*', *Southern Review*, IX, iii (1976), 198.

13 *Critical Observations on Shakespeare* (1746), p. 137.

14 *A Treatise concerning the Principles of Human Knowledge, The Works of George Berkeley*, ed. A. A. Luce and T. E. Jessop (1948–57), vol. II, p. 56; *Of Dramatic Poesy and other Critical Essays*, vol. I, p. 171; *An Essay upon Projects* (1697), pp. 244–5; *Elements of Criticism*, vol. III, pp. 137, 155.

15 Cf. *A Specimen of a Commentary on Shakespeare* (1794), esp. pp. 81–2.

Chapter 8 *Lives of the Poets*

1 *The Achievement of Samuel Johnson* (1955), p. 185.

2 Cf. George Watson, *The Literary Critics* (1964, rev. ed.), p. 94; John Wain, *Samuel Johnson* (1974), pp. 345–6.

3 *Of Dramatic Poesy and other Critical Essays*, vol. II, p. 76.

4 Howard Erskine-Hill, 'John Dryden: The Poet and Critic', in *Dryden to Johnson*, ed. Roger Lonsdale (1971), p. 26.

5 B. N. Schilling, *Dryden and the Conservative Myth: A Reading of 'Absalom and Achitophel'* (1961), p. 291.

6 *Dryden to Johnson* (1971), p. 41.

7 M. J. C. Hodgart, *Samuel Johnson and his Times* (1962), p. 98.

8 F. W. Hilles, 'The Making of *The Life of Pope*', in *New Light on Dr. Johnson* (1959), p. 272; Benjamin Boyce, 'Samuel Johnson's Criticism of Pope', *Review of English Studies*, N.S. V (1954), 43.

9 *An Essay on the Genius and Writings of Pope* (1762, 2nd ed., corrected), p. ix.

10 *An Inquiry into the Nature and Genuine Laws of Poetry, including a*

particular Defence of the Writings and Genius of Mr. Pope (1778), pp. 6–8.

11 *An Essay on Pope* (1762), pp. v, 42, 108; *Conjectures on Original Composition* (1759), pp. 67–8; *Letters on Chivalry and Romance* (1762), p. 93.

12 *An Essay on Pope* (1762), p. 246.

13 *A Philosophical Enquiry into the Origin of our Ideas of the Sublime and Beautiful* (1759, 2nd ed., corrected), pp. 58–9, 60.

14 J. W. Krutch, *Samuel Johnson* (1944), p. 484.

15 D. M. Hill, 'Johnson as Moderator', *Notes and Queries*, CCI (1956), 522.

Select Bibliography

Collected Works

Of the early editions the first two are most reliable textually:

The Works of Samuel Johnson, LL.D. Together with his Life . . . by Sir John Hawkins, 11 vols, London, 1787.

The Works of Samuel Johnson, LL.D. A New Edition . . . with An Essay on his Life and Genius, by Arthur Murphy, 12 vols, London, 1792.

The standard modern edition (still in preparation) is the Yale Edition of the Works of Samuel Johnson (gen. ed. formerly A. T. Hazen, presently J. H. Middendorf) of which the following volumes have so far appeared:

i *Diaries, Prayers, and Annals*, ed. E. L. McAdam, Jr, with Donald and Mary Hyde, 1958

ii *'The Idler' and 'The Adventurer'*, ed. W. J. Bate, J. M. Bullitt, and L. F. Powell, 1963

iii–v *The Rambler*, ed. W. J. Bate and A. B. Strauss, 1969

vi *Poems*, ed. E. L. McAdam, Jr, with George Milne, 1964

vii–viii *Johnson on Shakespeare*, ed. Arthur Sherbo, with an introduction by B. H. Bronson, 1968

ix *A Journey to the Western Islands of Scotland*, ed. Mary Lascelles, 1971

x *Political Writings*, ed. D. J. Greene, 1977.

Individual Works and Selections

The Critical Opinions of Samuel Johnson, ed. J. E. Brown, Princeton, 1926 (reissued New York, 1961).

Johnson's Dictionary: A Modern Selection, ed. E. L. McAdam, Jr and George Milne, New York, 1963.

Johnson's Journey to the Western Islands of Scotland, and *Boswell's Journal of a Tour to the Hebrides with Samuel Johnson, LL.D.*, ed. R. W. Chapman, London, 1924, 1930; paperback edn, 1970.

The Letters of Samuel Johnson, ed. R. W. Chapman, 3 vols, Oxford, 1952.

The Lives of the Poets, ed. G. B. Hill, 3 vols, Oxford, 1905 (reprinted New York, 1967).

Johnson's Lives of the Poets: A Selection, ed. J. P. Hardy, Oxford, 1971.

Samuel Johnson: Life of Savage, ed. Clarence Tracy, Oxford, 1971.
The Poems of Samuel Johnson, ed. D. Nichol Smith and E. L. McAdam, Jr, Oxford, 1941 (reissued, 1951); 2nd rev. edn, ed. J. D. Fleeman, 1974.
Samuel Johnson: The Complete English Poems, ed. J. D. Fleeman, London, 1971.
Samuel Johnson: Selected Poetry and Prose, ed. Frank Brady and W. K. Wimsatt, Los Angeles and London, 1977.
Selected Prose and Poetry, ed. B. H. Bronson (Rinehart), New York, 1952; *Rasselas, Poems, and Selected Prose*, enlarged edn, New York, 1971.
Prose and Poetry, ed. Mona Wilson, London, 1950 (reissued, 1957).
The Political Writings of Dr. Johnson: A Selection, ed. J. P. Hardy, London, 1968.
Samuel Johnson's Prefaces and Dedications, ed. A. T. Hazen, New Haven, 1937.
The History of Rasselas, Prince of Abissinia, ed. J. P. Hardy, Oxford, 1968.
'Rasselas' and Essays, ed. Charles Peake, London, 1967.
Johnson on Shakespeare, ed. Walter Raleigh, London, 1908 (frequently reprinted).
Samuel Johnson on Shakespeare, ed. W. K. Wimsatt, Jr, New York, 1960; republished as *Dr Johnson on Shakespeare*, London, 1969.

Biographical Sources and Studies

Boswell's Life of Johnson, ed. G. B. Hill, rev. L. F. Powell, Oxford, 1934–50; 2nd rev. edn of vols v–vi, 1964.
Johnsonian Miscellanies, ed. G. B. Hill, Oxford, 1897.
Thraliana, ed. K. C. Balderston, Oxford, 1951 (2nd edn).
Bate, W. J., *Samuel Johnson*, London, 1978.
Clifford, J. L., *Young Sam Johnson*, New York, 1955; *Young Samuel Johnson*, London, 1955.
Hodgart, M. J. C., *Samuel Johnson and his Times*, London, 1962.
Krutch, J. W., *Samuel Johnson*, New York, 1944; London, 1948.
Wain, John, *Samuel Johnson*, London, 1974.

Critical and Other Studies

Bate, W. J., *The Achievement of Samuel Johnson*, New York, 1955.
Bloom, E. A., *Samuel Johnson in Grub Street*, Providence, 1957.
Bronson, B. H., *Johnson and Boswell: Three Essays*, Berkeley and Los Angeles, 1944; *Johnson Agonistes and Other Essays*, Cambridge, 1946.
Chapin, C. F., *The Religious Thought of Samuel Johnson*, Ann Arbor, 1968.
Fussell, Paul, *Samuel Johnson and the Life of Writing*, New York, 1971.
Greene, D. J., *The Politics of Samuel Johnson*, New Haven, 1960.
Greene, D. J. (ed.), *Samuel Johnson: A Collection of Critical Essays*, Englewood Cliffs, 1965.
Greene, D. J., *Samuel Johnson*, New York, 1970.

Hagstrum, J. H., *Samuel Johnson's Literary Criticism*, Minneapolis, 1952; rev. edn, Chicago, 1967.
Hardy, J. P., *'Dictionary' Johnson*, Armidale, 1967.
Hilles, F. W. (ed.), *New Light on Dr. Johnson*, New Haven, 1959.
Hoover, B. B., *Samuel Johnson's Parliamentary Reporting: Debates in the Senate of Lilliput*, Berkeley and Los Angeles, 1953.
Lascelles, M. M., Clifford, J. L., Fleeman, J. D., Hardy, J. P. (eds), *Johnson, Boswell and their Circle: Essays Presented to Lawrence Fitzroy Powell*, Oxford, 1965.
McIntosh, Carey, *The Choice of Life: Samuel Johnson and the World of Fiction*, New Haven, 1973.
Quinlan, M. J., *Samuel Johnson: A Layman's Religion*, Madison, 1964.
Raleigh, Walter, *Six Essays on Johnson*, Oxford, 1910.
Sachs, Arieh, *Passionate Intelligence: Imagination and Reason in the Work of Samuel Johnson*, Baltimore, 1967.
Sledd, J. H. and Kolb, G. J., *Dr. Johnson's Dictionary: Essays in the Biography of a Book*, Chicago, 1955.
Voitle, Robert, *Samuel Johnson the Moralist*, Cambridge, Mass., 1961.
Wahba, Magdi (ed.), *Johnsonian Studies*, Cairo, 1962.
Wain, John, *Johnson on Johnson*, London, 1976.
Wimsatt, W. K., Jr, *The Prose Style of Samuel Johnson*, New Haven, 1941.
Wimsatt, W. K., Jr, *Philosophic Words: A Study of Style and Meaning in the 'Rambler' and 'Dictionary' of Samuel Johnson*, New Haven, 1948.

Bibliographies and Catalogues

W. P. Courtney, *A Bibliography of Samuel Johnson*, rev. D. N. Smith (*Oxford Historical and Literary Studies*, vol. iv), Oxford, 1915 (reprinted with facsimiles, 1925, 1968).
R. W. Chapman and A. T. Hazen, 'Johnsonian Bibliography: A Supplement to Courtney', *Proceedings of the Oxford Bibliographical Society*, v (1939), 119–66.
J. D. Fleeman, *A Preliminary Handlist of Documents & Manuscripts of Samuel Johnson, Oxford Bibliographical Society Occasional Publications no. 2*, 1967.
J. D. Fleeman, *The Sale Catalogue of Samuel Johnson's Library, a Facsimile Edition* (*ELS Monograph Series No. 2*), University of Victoria, 1975.
J. L. Clifford and D. J. Greene, *Samuel Johnson: A Survey and Bibliography of Critical Studies*, Minneapolis, 1970 (important editions, books and articles are marked with an asterisk, and this work incorporates the material of the two earlier bibliographies, *Johnsonian Studies 1887–1950*, 1951, and 'A Bibliography of Johnsonian Studies, 1959–60' in *Johnsonian Studies*, ed. Wahba, 1962, and extends it both backwards to Johnson's lifetime, and forwards to 1968).

Index